ACKNOWLEDGEMENTS

Picture this book as a tree—not the actual one that it was before being felled for printing purposes—but a massive oak with a near iron-plated trunk. Let's say there were a hundred people with a hundred axes, each taking a turn to chop it down. Now say I was the hundredth of these editorial lumberjacks, and thanks to all the ax strokes of all those who went before me, I was able to finally send it plummeting. If you've been able to follow this, then it's safe to say you understand my being able to write this now is the result of good fortune and more importantly, an incredibly talented and dedicated team of individuals who did their best to make this book a reality. I'm indebted to say the least.

First and foremost, this book could not have seen any bookshelf if not for the participation and efforts of our partner schools. They worked tirelessly with us to make this guide the definitive testament to New York City private and selective public high schools.

Also, a very special thanks to Suzanne Podhurst, editor extraordinaire, who first put this project in my hands and helped me every bit of the way. Our author, Alex Altman deserves praise for his insightful and entertaining introduction, as do Chaitra Ramanathan and Jen Adams for their help in rustling up some of the more hard-to-find data.

Appreciation also goes to the eagle eyes of our production team, Christine LaRubio and Scott Harris, who put a brilliant polish on everything we put to paper, and to our publisher, Robert Franek, whose stalwart support and unending dedication make my job an easier one.

Finally, thanks to our friends at Random House, Tom Russell and Jeanne Krier, and to John Katzman, for making this guide and The Princeton Review even possible.

Adam O. Davis
Editor
May 2007

So many people participated in the genesis and publication of this book that it would take pages to list them all. Apologies to anyone I neglect. First off, to the staff of The Princeton Review: Thanks for recognizing the value in this project, and for all you have done to help realize it. In particular, thanks to Rob Franek, whose dedication to the cause is unsurpassed and whose eloquence in speaking to it is a source of inspiration. You are the best, Rob. Additionally, in his capacity as editor, Adam Davis displayed patience, professionalism, and performance beyond the call of duty on a project fraught with challenges. Adam, you've spoiled me for all future editors.

On a more personal note, I would like to thank both my parents, Alan Altman and Irene Larsen. Dad, thanks for impressing upon me the value of education and for encouraging me to pursue not just success but significance; what I've learned from you has helped shape me and will last a lifetime. Mom, you've devoted yourself to making sure that, regardless of what I do, I make happiness and self-fulfillment my main goals. Thank you for your unconditional love.

Finally, to Lisa Marie Rovito, soon to be Lisa Marie Altman: None of this would have been possible without you. Your love keeps me going!

Alex Altman
2007

D0878468

TABLE OF CONTENTS

INTRODUCTION

New Yorkers considering sending their children to private secondary school today face a fleet of difficult questions that range from the academic to the emotional to the financial, but all have one thing in common: What is the best school for my child? Ultimately this is the most important question a parent can ask. A good match results in a happier, more productive student, and can mean the difference between success after graduation or an imposing question mark. You may also ask yourself: Does my child have the talent and personality to excel in a competitive academic environment? Is a private education in New York truly superior to its public counterpart? Where will my child's talents be best developed? How do we choose a school of prestigious reputation that will also be a good personal fit? And then of course there are the more practical questions: What is it going to take to get in? How can I help my child get admitted to schools that often have more rigorous admissions standards than universities? Is the investment—in some cases thirty thousand dollars a year—worth it? And don't forget about New York City's selective public schools, which offer every educational benefit of their private counterparts at no cost to the student's family—provided your child aces the entrance exams.

Unfortunately most parents have to go this road alone, without the help of guides or other resources, because unlike college, there is a substantial lack of sources, information, and support for those families seeking high-level secondary education for their children. And as such, the process of discovering schools and applying to them often comes with an "enter at own risk" sign. Luckily we're here to take that sign down—or at least put the quotation in parentheses.

The choice of a child's secondary school has become increasingly important as students and parents seek every advantage in the race to college. Because of this, students are pushing themselves further, learning more at younger ages, and achieving more than previously expected so they can get the jump on university-level studies and hit the proverbial ground running. But the right school isn't all about academics. High school is a time when young adults find themselves and begin to discover who they'll eventually become. When considering secondary schools, one of the most important things you can ask yourself is "Will my child be happy here?" The right school can mean the difference in many things—a solid education, an institution of prestige and reputation, entrance to the first college of your choice—but more than anything, this institution will be the location and influence on some of the students' most formative years. Will the school provide them with the academic means to excel? Will it support their personal and emotional growth?

The hallmark of the hit-or-miss high school search process tends to be misinformation (or a lack of), rumor, and celebrity, with families attaching themselves to big names without considering student-school compatibility. In other instances, families underrate selective public high schools or assume that private education is out of reach. In the words of Douglas Adams, the best advice we can offer to families embroiled in the down and dirty world of high school admissions is, "Don't panic." Private school. Selective school. These are just words and yet somehow, are more than the sum of their parts. The most important thing to remember is the journey that will take your child from prospective applicant to enrolled high school student is a deeply personal one. Only through clear communication with your child can you find the school that will best suit any current and future academic needs. When dealing with a city as multifaceted as New York, the odds of finding a perfect match are, in reality, highly stacked in your favor. Sit back. Put the kettle on. Take out a highlighter. Let's get started.

PART I—CONSIDERING PRIVATE & SELECTIVE PUBLIC HIGH SCHOOLS

WHY PRIVATE SCHOOL?

Simply put, private school attendance is booming, and not just in the city. Over the past decade, private day school attendance in the United States has risen 15 percent. By stark contrast, attendance at boarding schools is up less than 3 percent for the same time period. Why are more and more families considering the private day school option? Primarily because it offers the perfect compromise between the academic rigor and educational opportunities of a boarding school, with the supervision, nurturing, and close relationships that can only be found within the family home. When you factor in the lower cost (even in New York, private day schools often cost little more than half the tuition of their boarding counterparts) and the peace of mind that comes with having your child home each night, the private day school argument becomes exceedingly compelling.

But regardless of the choice in private school, it all comes down to chemistry. When properly matched, the relationship between school and student can yield more than just good grades and future success—it can influence, to a large degree, how the child grows and develops. An enviable advantage private schools have over their public counterparts is increased (and in some cases unlimited) funds and smaller populations. Thanks to healthy endowments and tuition costs, private secondary schools simply have more resources to invest in each student, which translates directly into a breadth of personalized academic and extracurricular opportunities.

Examples of these opportunities abound, but some of the most notable include the following:

- A more rigorous educational environment. A Department of Education Study found that students at private schools do more homework than their public school counterparts. They also watch less television, participate in more afternoon activities (athletic and otherwise), and plan to graduate from college with greater frequency.

- Customized education with personal attention. With more money to spend per student, private schools can afford to personalize a child's academic experience, while lower student-teacher ratios mean more individualized attention in the classroom. Students at private schools have a greater breadth of options and choices when it comes to their curricula. Private schools also generally have a higher number of teachers with advanced degrees than at public schools.

- An unparalleled wealth of extracurricular opportunities. Interestingly, one of the biggest advantages to a private education comes outside the classroom—private schools may have as many as fifty different sport activities, and many also boast student-run newspapers and impressive theater, art, and music departments.

- Small class sizes. With such low student-teacher ratios, prep schools can afford to devote plenty of personalized attention to each student. Fewer students in each class mean that your child will be able to learn at their own pace, whether he or she leads the class or needs a little extra assistance.

- Superior college placement. Most private schools have a full-time, dedicated staff of college counselors to see students through the entire college admissions process.

- Access to a diverse peer group. New York is a diverse town and no one would argue that a public education in a New York City school would be any different in its demographics. However, private schools are going to increasingly greater lengths to admit students from an array of ethnicities, cultures, and economic backgrounds. This outreach includes hosting exchange students from around the world, creating a diverse group of peers who impart a worldly perspective.

- An environment where academic excellence is encouraged. At private schools, successful students rarely feel embarrassed about excelling academically. Disruptive students and the desire to fit in can be major obstacles for a fourteen-year-old to overcome, but private schools are quick to emphasize—not to mention more readily equipped to enforce—the notion that the classroom is a place for learning and achieving.

- Preparation for the college experience. Private school students tackle difficult (often college-level) subject matter on their own, have significant choice in their curricula, are exposed to a diverse peer group, and pursue a wide array of interests. Thanks to this exposure to advanced studies, students report that they reach college with a superior level of preparation, and in particular find their freshman year both academically and socially easier.

Add to this list the less-tangible but equally important benefits of networking opportunities, heightened emotional growth, a greater sense of independence and maturity, increased confidence and feelings of self-worth, and you have a fairly persuasive argument for considering private school as an option.

SELECTIVE PUBLIC SCHOOLS: ALL THE BENEFITS WITHOUT THE COST

As great as it is, living in New York City certainly has its disadvantages, cost of living and high taxes both among them. But New Yorkers also possess certain privileges unheard of in other American cities. Imagine this: Your child could go to a school in New York City with all the benefits of a top-notch private school—world-class facilities, small class sizes, some of the best teachers in the city, major prestige and a magnetic pull with colleges—all without tuition!

Welcome to the world of New York selective public schools, known collectively as the Specialized High Schools of New York City. In the beginning, there were three—Bronx High School of Science, Stuyvesant High School, and Brooklyn Technical High School (commonly known as "Brooklyn Tech"). At current count, there are nine of these schools (ten if you count Harvey Milk High School—created specifically for LGTB students), and these public, tuition-free institutions lure the city's best students, while rivaling the city's elite private schools for quality of education and college placement.

In short, for those who can gain admittance (admission is extremely competitive and largely based upon the student's performance on the New York City Specialized Science High Schools Admissions Test (SSHSAT)), selective public schools provide their students with nearly all the benefits of private schools, including a superior educational environment, smaller classes with more qualified teachers than in traditional public schools, a greater variety of extracurricular opportunities, and better college placement as well as more thorough college-preparatory program. In addition, selective public schools also offer some truly unique and surprising benefits:

- Specialized curricula and particular areas of expertise at each school. The city's selective public schools are specialized—that is, each school emphasizes a particular area of excellence (though the overall education is also excellent). These specialties range from the classics to science to performing arts, meaning that a talented child has the opportunity to develop and explore his or her particular talents and interests in great depth.

- Access to a peer group with specialized talents and common interests. Another advantage to these specialty schools (also called magnet schools) is that they draw the best students in their particular areas of expertise. For example, if your child goes to Bronx High School of Science, her peers will be students who share a math and science interest and aptitude, and this goes a long way to enhance classroom learning and encourage academic excellence.

- Access to teachers with expertise in specific fields and specialized facilities for those fields. A further benefit of these schools is the access to superior teachers and facilities within a school's sphere of expertise. Students will be exposed to the best teachers in these fields and delve more deeply into their preferred subjects. They will have the ability to develop their academic interests to a greater extent and will be challenged to the limits of their abilities much more than they would be at a regular public school.

- Zero tuition. No explanation needed here. All costs for attending selective public schools are covered by the city, just as at any other public school, so your child can receive a million dollar education without you having to write a million dollar check.

POPULAR PRIVATE SCHOOL MISCONCEPTIONS DEBUNKED

From their portrayals in books and film to urban legends and word of mouth, misconceptions about private schools are widespread and difficult to verify. As is often the case, any institution or experience that is seen as exclusive is often the target of rumor or speculation. A majority of blame falls upon the lack of readily available information about private school life and the ensuing air of secrecy that enshrouds it, leading to speculation and in some cases, disdain. This is to be expected, to a degree, is even understandable. But when misconceptions deter students who would thrive at private school from even applying, this realm of myth and hearsay must be confronted and debunked.

1. **Attending private school guarantees admission into an Ivy League university.**

Four years at an elite private preparatory school and the doors to the hallowed halls of the Ivy League "open sesame". If only it were this easy! Like many of the misconceptions that follow, this bit of lore was probably truer in decades past than it is today. And even though it may have contained a grain or two of truth back in the day, this idea was never especially accurate in the first place. But let it be said—this is the worst possible reason to attend private school, and is completely counter to what an educational experience should be about. If the decision to invest your family's time, money, and energy in a private educational experience is made merely on the basis of ensuring your child's collegiate career at Harvard or Yale, you should rethink private school. There are no guarantees when it comes to private schools and the Ivy Leagues, and it's best to focus on your child's current educational experience rather than their future one.

Private schools can provide life-changing advantages for the right student, but it's unwise to think of them as an expressway to the Ivies. The main reason being that Ivy League colleges are under significant pressure to ensure their student bodies reflect the most talented students from all regions, religions, countries, and backgrounds. Taking 100 students each from Collegiate, Dalton, Horace Mann, and Trevor Day, not to mention the hundred each from Andover, Exeter, and Deerfield each year, would do very little to achieve these diversity goals. Instead, only top applicants from each of these schools are accepted, along with the top applicants from public and private schools all over the country and world.

At a competitive New York City private school, students have the additional disadvantage of competing against the city's brightest students in the most rigorous of academic environments. An academic resume that would put a student at the top of his public school class might leave him or her in the middle of the pack at a top private school. So if Ivy League admission is his only goal, she'd be better off attending a school where she could really stand out and catch admissions officers' notice.

2. **Private schools are only for the rich.**

This misconception is particularly damaging because it discourages many promising students from applying to schools at which they have every chance of being admitted, and in all likelihood, would be able to afford. The truth is that at many New York City private schools, more than one in three students receive some type of financial aid. Since the schools have a number of tools at their disposal to help meet families' financial needs, a financial aid package can often be devised to help students who might otherwise not be able to attend.

Private schools want the most talented students, regardless of their socioeconomic backgrounds. To attract these students, schools do the best they can to accommodate families in spite of their incomes. However, keep in mind that although financial aid may be offered, it is still a much rarer occurrence than it is in college. For families who cannot afford private tuition even with aid, there is the excellent option of attending a selective public school that rivals the private school education at a pittance of the cost.

3. Private schools do not welcome students of color.

This falsehood shares a large sum of responsibility for keeping many qualified students from applying to private schools. And like the previous misconception, this myth is not only off the mark but completely opposed to the private schools' objectives. Fostering an atmosphere of diversity is one of the primary missions of every private school, and exposure to a diverse peer group is one of the major advantages of a private school education. To achieve this end, most schools encourage applicants from all backgrounds and work diligently to ensure that as many cultures, religions, socioeconomic backgrounds, and parts of the world are represented in the student body.

One of the main reasons for this skyrocketing interest in promoting diversity in New York City private schools is largely due to the stance Ivy League colleges have taken in regards to talented minority students. Simply put, private schools are taking their cues from the Ivies when it comes to forming their student bodies. After all, if a private school's prestige is based largely on the number of students who are admitted to Ivy League universities, and these universities want talented underrepresented individuals, having a diverse population of talented students is likely to help both sides of this educational equation.

Today in New York City private schools, it is quite common to see one out of every five students as a student of color, and some schools are even more diverse. While this may not quite match the United Nations' standard, it is a far and refreshing cry from the image of private schools as a playground reserved exclusively for privileged, white students.

4. Private day school students are students that didn't get admitted to boarding schools.

As private day schools gain in popularity across the country (often at the expense of boarding school enrollments), retaliatory rumors have abounded, painting the private day student as a second-class citizen when compared to the boarding student. While it is true that boarding school students do more homework on average, watch less television, and do have a slightly higher batting average with respect to Ivy League admission, these factors have relatively little to do with the quality of education to be had at either type of institution. Education at boarding schools, as at day schools, is decidedly mixed, with rather ordinary educations being offered alongside quite exemplary ones.

The truth is that top day schools are quite competitive with their boarding brethren, and that academic potential isn't a major factor on the list of considerations when deciding whether to board or not to board. More than anything, the growing success of day schools indicates a desire to keep families together and children close to home.

5. You've seen one private school, you've seen them all.

Private schools in New York City are every bit as varied as New Yorkers themselves. There is a school for every type of student with every type of unique interest, talent, or special need. As you will see from the school profiles in this book, experiences vary greatly from school to school, both inside the classroom and out. We've done our best to capture the unique spirit of each school. This should enable you to make a short list of potential best fits based upon your child's interests and talents. After that bit of research, it's time to schedule visits to the schools on the short list and fill out applications. It will soon become apparent just how varied the atmosphere is on each campus—even among schools that might seem similar based upon their profiles. Ultimately, it's up to your child to find the place that feels right.

Is Private School Right for Your Child?

For many parents, the decision to consider sending their child to private school is relatively easy; in fact, if you are reading this book, it's likely that your child exhibits many of the characteristics that mark a good candidate. Children who are socially and intellectually precocious, who seek out new experiences and opportunities, who function well independently, and who enjoy managing their own academic affairs, are obvious choices likely to benefit from a private school education. Other parents are confronted with more nebulous decisions. For example, perhaps a child is academically gifted, but lacks the social maturity or independence to interact with a peer group. Or maybe a child has a tremendous natural facility with languages or a musical instrument, but has yet to learn how to budget her time without substantial parental intervention.

The important thing to realize is that, no matter what your child's academic and personality profile, there is a school out there that is a perfect match. It may not, however, be the school you think it is. The key to finding a school at which your child will flourish intellectually and emotionally is honest appraisal and thorough research. The good news is that you've already taken the first step by buying this guide!

Next, talk with teachers, coaches, and camp counselors—basically everyone who has had a chance to interact with your child outside the home. Seek out as much information as possible about your child's strengths and areas of improvement. Would more challenging schoolwork be a welcome change, or an overwhelming one? Will your child better flourish in a more rigorous environment or a nurturing one? Consulting with these people will augment your knowledge of your child's abilities and give you a broader scope when making decisions.

It is also possible to hire professional guidance counselors who can help you answer these questions. These experts have years of experience working with prep-bound students. They analyze report cards, standardized test scores, and other academic records, and get to know your prospective private school student. They can help assess what type of a school matches your child's academic and personality profile, and provide valuable assistance during the application process.

Most importantly, talk to your child. At thirteen years old, it is already a time of uncertainty for many children. This can make going to an unfamiliar place away from current friends to meet unknown challenges even more of a daunting prospect. One of the best ways to determine if your child is ready is simple and honest conversation. Let them know that their opinions matter and that they will be an integral part of the process. Make certain they know that they will not be sent anywhere without their consent and, no matter what happens, you are committed to finding the school at which they will have the most rewarding and enjoyable experience. With these assurances, most children feel comfortable offering their candid—and often surprising—opinions.

Is Private School Not Right for Your Child?

With small classes, attentive teachers, and personalized attention for each student, private school might seem like a panacea for any number of behavioral and academic troubles. The truth is that while there are many special schools geared toward children with unique needs, most of these children would not fare as well in the traditional, college-preparatory private school environment.

Students who are not known to take academic initiative and are uncomfortable seeking out new experiences, who require frequent academic guidance from parents, and those who don't fare well when placed in new social situations may find private school disconcerting, especially at the tender age of fourteen. The prep school environment can be overwhelming to a child who is removed from his comfortable, peer-group support system. Children who don't take easily to independence or have difficulty budgeting time may also have difficulty managing the academic rigors of a private education.

This is not to say that your child should abandon the idea of private school if they have yet to exhibit a great deal of independence since developing maturity and independent thought is an attribute of receiving a private school education. The most important thing is that a student has the capacity to learn these characteristics in an environment that suits them. Because there are a wide variety of different school types available, each student can be placed accord to his or her needs.

What Are Our Chances?

Is it all about who you know and what you can pay? Do "real" families even have a chance at admission to a top-tier private school in New York City? If you've read the section on private school misconceptions, you know by now that your chances are better than you might have originally thought. Percentages of legacy students admitted to private schools are shrinking, while percentages of minority students, international students, and students from less privileged backgrounds are on the rise. Admission to private school is less dependent on where you're coming from than where you could potentially go. In the end, the best way to get a school's attention is by highlighting your child's unique talents while communicating to admissions officers your child's potential to excel and grow in a challenging and exciting educational environment.

PART II—THE SEARCH

There is no such thing as the perfect all-purpose private school. Private schools come in all sizes with all sorts of specialties. The breadth and variety of choices can be daunting, but you should also find this reassuring, as there is most certainly a school out there that will provide your child with the perfect experience. The trick is to find a school with a program that matches your child's interests, personality, and academic and extracurricular needs. You are looking for a place with a nurturing environment that encourages independence and self-reliance, one that challenges without overwhelming, and an education that extends beyond the classroom.

In this chapter, you will assemble a picture of your child as a potential private school student. You will start by considering your child's unique strengths and individual characteristics, and identifying any areas in which your child may need special help. This is the time to sit down together and discuss your individual hopes and goals for the prep school experience. At this point, you will be able to apply these considerations and a smattering of other criteria to assemble a preliminary list of schools that may suit your child. When you have finished assessing the first batch of schools, you will have a list of possible matches, and with those you will be ready to enter into the application process.

Identifying Your Child's Unique Strengths and Needs

The first and most critical step in the school search process is to gain an in-depth understanding of your child's academic and personal profile. This step will require some research as well as some open and honest dialogue, but the results will be tangible: For the first time, you will have a true sense of your child's strengths and special needs as a student, an athlete, and a member of a community. These will be invaluable tools when assessing which schools may be a good match.

You may think you already know your child. You've read their report cards and helped with homework. You've attended their recitals and football games. But choosing to enroll a child in a private high school—where the environment is academically rigorous and independence is expected—requires a deeper understanding of who your child is, both academically and personally.

The first step is to talk to your child to get a sense of how they assess themselves. This conversation doesn't have to be a monumental, three-hour marathon, but you'll want to get as much information as possible. Over the course of these discussions, you'll want to delve into the following topics:

- What does your child see as their strengths and weaknesses?

- Which subjects come naturally and which are more of a struggle?

- Does she enjoy working alone, or require assistance with homework?

- Are reading and writing enjoyable pastimes?

- Where is there room for improvement?

- Is she being challenged at school?

- Would a greater academic challenge be welcomed or overwhelming?

- Are there special subjects or areas of interest she'd like to explore that aren't offered at her current school?

Now these may not be easy—or comfortable—questions to ask and answer, so make sure to keep the mood relaxed and nonjudgmental to encourage your child to be as honest as possible.

Consulting with teachers can be a fantastic way of building upon what you've learned from your child. This is especially true if a student's abilities are tough to pinpoint or yet undiscovered. A good teacher will have an attuned sense of your child's abilities and be able to locate their areas of distinction and difficulty. They will also be able to tell you more about your child's characteristics as a student. Does your child participate enthusiastically in class? Does she write well? Would she benefit from a more rigorous academic environment? Are there certain areas in which she needs to improve? It is also important to consult coaches and other instructors in this fact-finding mission. Does your child have special extracurricular gifts (e.g., athletics, music, art) that should be considered when selecting potential schools?

Once this research is done you'll have a much better sense of your child's strengths and weaknesses. Take notes. Assemble a profile of your child as an applicant. If you feel that you need extra help, you can hire a private secondary-school consultant to help you perform a more detailed assessment to complete the picture. Consultants have honed their experience working with many students, and they can prove to be quite helpful in the search process. That said, if you and your child put in the necessary time and effort, there is no reason you can't succeed without professional help.

DISCUSSING GOALS—A COLLABORATIVE EFFORT

Having created your child's private school profile, it's now time discuss goals. What do each of you hope will come of the private school experience? What is it about private school that seems like the right fit for your child? What about private school seems most exciting? What about it seems scary? What are some of the characteristics of an ideal private school?

It is extremely important to keep this discussion collaborative—your child's perspective here is equally important (possibly even more) as your own. His answers will not only give you helpful clues about where he should apply, but they will also offer a much better sense about whether private school is the right choice for him. Gauge your child's enthusiasm carefully—is he genuinely excited by the prospect of private school or just telling you what you want to hear? Does the idea of new challenges and experiences seem appealing? Would he be as quick to suggest going to XYZ school if his buddies weren't also planning to apply? Go over his motivation for being interested in a private high school with the most finely-toothed comb—then do the same with your own.

Lastly, getting into a good college should not be the sole reason for either of you to consider a private high school. While attending an Ivy League school is certainly a noble goal, it isn't worth spending four critical and formative years at a place where your child doesn't want to be. (Plenty of students who excel in public high schools are accepted at Ivy League colleges, too.) Once you have a few clearly defined goals, think about what would make for a perfect private school experience and jot some notes. Below are some criteria you may want to consider.

CRITERIA FOR CONSIDERATION

Big-Name School vs. Lesser Known School

Many parents have been led astray by the glamour and history of an especially prestigious private school, only to have their child suffer through some or all of their high school years simply because the institution was not the right fit. This outcome also happens to children looking to please their parents, but who aren't thinking of themselves. Wherever you and your child finally decide on is important; your child will be spending a critical amount of time at his or her school. Not only are these the years leading up to college, but also the first explorations of adulthood—nothing less than a stable base will do. If your child gets a bad feeling about a specific institution, weigh that feeling very seriously. The bottom line is that the name and reputation of a school are of slight concern when compared to the experience the child receives there. And while the Collegiates and Horace Manns of the world certainly provide a world-class education, there are many other schools your child might be happier at. In fact, the best school out there may be the one you've yet to discover.

Large School vs. Small School

Private schools vary wildly in size and while classes are generally small and personalized attention available, the size of a school community can have major social and academic impact. True, all private schools are concerned with fostering important and meaningful relationships between students and faculty. However, a schools with 100 students will achieve this in a very different way than a school with 1,200. Equally important is the interaction within the student community. Smaller schools create environments in which everyone knows one another. Generally, while all private schools are small enough to have a "personal" feel (they are usually smaller than even the smallest liberal arts colleges), a community of a couple hundred students will feel worlds away from a community of 1,000. While some students prefer an intensely personal, familial feeling for their high school community, others find it stifling. The trick is to find a school that is cozy enough without risk of smothering, but large enough to offer your child plenty of opportunities to branch out and take risks.

It is also important to consider the effects of school size upon academic and extracurricular competition. Even very selective smaller schools will be less competitive academically, if only for the fact that there is a smaller pool of students with which to compete. Athletic teams will also be less competitive at a smaller school, and as such, less talented athletes may prefer this opportunity to play varsity sports, albeit on a less competitive scale. On the other hand, elite athletes may need the challenge and excitement that comes at larger, more competitive athletic programs.

Single Sex vs. Coeducational

Private school administrators recognize the relative immaturity of their charges, as well as the potential for trouble between the sexes. This being the case, teachers at coeducational schools are always on the lookout for inappropriate situations. Though coeducation has, for the most part, become the norm in New York City, it does provide some issues that need be addressed. Would a coeducational environment be too distracting for your child, or is socializing and learning with members of the opposite sex a valuable tool for emotional growth? Again, this decision is intensely personal. Take a look at your child's current group of friends for clues on what kind of school might be the best choice.

Distance from Home

Ultimately, the location of a school is less important than many other factors, but there are some distance-from-home issues to address. To some students, there is something psychologically comforting about knowing a parent is never far from school. For others, getting out of their neighborhood can be a liberating experience with startlingly positive results. A new group of peers in a brand-new setting offers a chance for your child to reinvent herself as she sees fit—a new beginning without the burden of having played in the sandbox with half the kids in her class.

How she will get to school (mass transit, car service, driven by you) will also play into the convenience—and therefore enjoyment—of your child's experience. Same story for how long it takes her to get there. An hour each way, for example, can make for a long school day and calls into question if that time may be better spent on homework, extracurricular activities, and spending time with family and friends.

Athletics and Other Special Programs

Athletics can be a tricky issue for parents and private school-bound athletes, especially if these athletes have excelled in local competition but have yet to encounter a true challenge. Honest appraisal of your child's talent and open discussion of athletic goals are critical here. It may be tempting to think of your son or daughter as a top-notch athlete, but bear in mind that New York's schools are filled with students whose parents feel the same way. Talk to your child's coaches to get a sense of where your child fits into the broader scheme of things athletically. If your child would prefer simply to have a chance to play four years of varsity-level athletics in their chosen sport, a smaller, less competitive athletic program is probably a better choice. However, if your child hopes to continue on to Division I athletics in college, he may benefit from the challenge and development opportunities that a larger, more competitive school and athletic program would provide. Be warned, though: Not all of these students will be talented enough to excel at the city's most competitive programs. Be honest about your child's ability and goals, and choose accordingly.

ASSEMBLING YOUR LIST OF SCHOOLS

Hopefully, the information above has encouraged productive discussions with your child. By now you have learned about his aptitudes and challenges, outlined goals and assembled the list of criteria that describes your ideal school.

Now is the time to reference the school profiles in the Part IV of the book. Starting with the schools you know is fine, but do your homework! Read about each school. Consider its location, size, cost, and other factors. Using its description, picture your child as a student there. Does it seem like a place where your child would be comfortable? Where his interests would be developed? Where he would grow intellectually and personally?

Using the list of schools, create a "short list" of potential schools that seem well suited to your child's personality. Don't forget to have a backup plan. You may not want to jinx yourself, but it's much worse being hung out to dry. To be safe, it's best to include a school or two that have slightly less competitive entrance requirements. This way, on the off-chance your dream school doesn't come calling, you'll have plan B to fall back on.

Once you've decided on your list, it's time to move on to the next step—gaining admission.

PART III - THE PROCESS

What Schools Are Really Looking For

You've decided that a private high school is right for your child, and with her help, you've assembled a list of schools that seem like a good match. Now all she has to do is get in! To that end, what factors are the most crucial in getting the admissions committee's attention? What factors are less important than you might think? Above all, how can you give your child the best chance at being admitted to the best school for him or her?

First, it is important to realize that the admissions process is an inherently random one; there is no magic formula for guaranteeing admission to a school. Your best bet at admission (and at a positive private high school experience) lies in choosing schools that are a good fit for your child; a good admissions officer can spot this almost immediately. Obviously, high test scores, grades, and personal achievements go a long way in convincing admissions officers of a candidate's promise. But equally important is the depth of thought, maturity, academic ambition, and other personality characteristics that emerge during the interview and application process. All of these factors contribute to the overall profile of an applicant—the profile that is then used to judge their potential to succeed at a specific school.

Many parents are understandably frustrated with the notion of legacies, and of securing a student's place through a sizable donation. It must be said that a little of this (a very little) does occur. Naturally, a higher percentage of legacy applicants are admitted than are standard applicants, and if your father donated three million dollars to build a new science building, it's unlikely you'll be turned away. However, the number of times that this goes on each year is staggeringly small. So don't worry. These cases aren't frequent enough to affect your child's chances of admission, nor should they affect a good night's sleep.

Concentrate on being organized, sticking to a timetable, choosing schools carefully, getting a very good look at them, and on helping your child present the best possible picture of himself on his application. The rest will take care of itself.

Timetables and Deadlines

Setting a timeline and application schedule and sticking to them are perhaps the most crucial steps toward a successful application process. Planning things out in advance makes certain nothing is forgotten in the last minute rush to complete things. It also gives the prospective student more of an opportunity to evaluate the schools she is considering. The worst thing you can possibly do for your child is to decide at the last minute that private school is a good idea, then rush through the application process, and send your child off to a school with fingers crossed that it will all work out.

But if you or your child develops an interest in private schools late in the process (according to the timeline detailed below), by all means go ahead with the process. Applying can't hurt! Just remember, your goal is for your child to find the school that is the right fit. If you are settling for a school that you aren't sure about just to say your child is attending X, Y, or Z school, think very carefully before you accept.

Dates vary by school, but generally, your application timeline should look something like this:

End of 7th Grade
MAY:

Before school ends and teachers are swallowed up by summer, arrange to meet with them to discuss your child. Inform them that you are considering private school, and talk about your child's strengths and weaknesses. Of course, now is also the time to begin discussing private school with your child, if you haven't already.

Early to Mid Summer
JUNE:

Early in the summer, before the weeks begin to slip away, is the time to contact schools to request catalogs and applications. This book should be a valuable resource. Use the school profiles we've created to help decide which schools interest you and the contact information to contact schools.

JULY:

When they arrive, review the school catalogs in conjunction with the profiles in this book. Using these sources, make a list of schools that interest you and, after making a round or two of eliminations, the ones you want to visit. It will also be important to note the admissions requirements for those schools that interest you. Many schools require applicants to take the same test (see the ERB test below), but it will vary by school so always ask. If you want to use a private counselor to help you with the application process, now is the time to contact one.

Schedule interviews with all the schools that interest you and your child, and create an interview schedule. It's important to visit all the schools that sound promising—but not so many that your child loses interest and all the schools blur into one. Make sure to assess his and your stamina before the process to determine a reasonable number of places to check out.

Late Summer
AUGUST:

At this point, you have a bit of breathing room. Use this time to discuss how you and your family will be paying for private school. Does your family have the ability to meet the costs, or will you need assistance? Consult with this book or with the schools directly.

Begin preparations for school visits.

Beginning of 8th Grade
SEPTEMBER:

Now is the time to start fulfilling admissions requirements. One of the first things this will include is the standardized test portion of your application. Private schools in New York City will require you to take either the ISEE or the SSAT (usually the ISEE), while the selective public schools have their own individual tests. Check with each school to determine their application requirements and then schedule the appropriate exam. Note: If applying to a parochial school, check with them to see which exam they require. The ISEE can be scheduled online at erbtest.org, or by calling 800-446-0320. The Secondary School Admission Test can be scheduled online at ssat.org, or by calling 609-683-4440. Both organizations will send practice materials for a small fee. For more information, see the section on standardized testing.

Toward the end of September, begin going school visits and admission interviews. Attending admission open houses is also a good way to pick up tips and have questions answered.

Keep in mind that the interview should be as much about the school getting to know your child, as it is you and your child learning about the school. Ask the school about what to expect from the interview and visit in advance so you can prepare your child and you both can walk into it more relaxed. Once you're there, ask the tough questions you need answered in order to help make that final decision.

OCTOBER:

Review the various admissions requirements at the schools that your child will apply to ensure you're on track. Typical elements to complete the application process include: an application form, recent report cards, past standardized testing results, and the interview. Some schools will ask for teacher references; if they don't, it isn't necessary to send them. Some schools will also want a statement from the parent, student samples of writing, artwork, or the like, and additional specialized testing.

Stay on top of deadlines, which will vary by school. If you are interested in professional test preparation for required tests, contact a tutor or service such as The Princeton Review.

NOVEMBER:

Now is the time to start filling out actual applications. If you aren't working online, photocopy the applications to practice on. It is fine, even encouraged, to help your child fill out the application, but allow him to write the first draft of his essay without your help.

DECEMBER:

Take the ISEE or other required test(s) around this time.

If you haven't yet completed the school applications, do so during this month. Winter vacation should give you extra time if they aren't yet done. Financial aid forms must also be completed (see the section on the Parents' Financial Statement).

Well before winter vacation, ask teachers for references and letters of recommendation if you need them for the application. Make sure to give them plenty of advanced notice—you'll find the earlier they know about the letter, the nicer they are about writing it (not to mention what they write in it!).

JANUARY:

The application deadline for some schools is January 15. Others may be as late as February 1. Deadlines vary from school to school, so make sure to check the due dates for all the schools to which you are applying. Make photocopies of anything you send in the mail, send everything certified mail, and allow plenty of time. The online application process simplifies most of this.

FEBRUARY:

All your work is done! Soon, schools will let you know the results. But for now, try not to think about it. Do something to let your child know you are proud of her for applying and making the effort.

This past year, members of the Independent Schools Admissions Association of Greater New York (ISAAGNY), which includes many of the city's top private schools, mailed notifications no earlier than February 16, and no later than February 22, for all 9th–11th grade applications completed before January 30.

MARCH:

This is the month when families must notify schools of their decisions. Last year, for member schools of the ISAAGNY, 9th-11th grade applicants needed to give their acceptance or rejection notification by March 15. Make certain to know the deadlines for each of the schools to which you were accepted! You don't want to miss out on your first choice because you failed to accept their offer in time.

Congratulations, the process is over—and welcome to private school!

MAKING YOUR APPLICATION STAND OUT

Generally, a private school application consist of: school records, standardized test scores, references, a student statement, a writing sample or essay, the child's medical history, and an application fee. But your child is only 13 years old. How do you use the application process to give a complete picture of him, and to demonstrate his potential to people who have never met him? The grades and test scores will speak for themselves; so the trick is to use the other pieces of the application to round out your child's image as an applicant. The essay and teacher recommendations portions of the application give you an excellent opportunity to do this; your child will be able to highlight his strengths and explain his shortcomings, perhaps even turning negatives into positives in the admissions officers' eyes.

General Points about Applications

Most schools have deadlines in January or February by which the applications must be turned in. In order to make certain you have plenty of time, you and your child should start filling out applications in November. You should not feel uncomfortable about applying to multiple schools. Casting a wide net will give you a better chance at finding the perfect match for your child.

These days, with nearly everything done on the Internet, it is very likely that you have the option to fill out your applications online. This is perfectly fine; using an online application system will not hurt your child's chances, and many people find it easier than dealing with a mass of paperwork. Also, online applications are much easier to edit if you discover a mistake once they have been filled out. One shortcoming of the online application is that it may be more difficult to spot mistakes on the computer screen than it is on the page. For this reason, create your essays in a word processing program such as Microsoft Word before posting them into you online application. It also helps to print the first draft of an essay out and edit it by hand. Make certain to review all the information you submit online before clicking that "Send" button. Catching that one last mistake will make all the reviewing worthwhile.

If you are filling out the more traditional paperwork applications, you'll want to practice filling out the application on a copy—do not go directly to the application and begin writing, unless you have plenty of correction fluid handy and you don't mind a mess! Once your application is completed make sure you photocopy it before you send it in. This way, you will have a backup if it becomes lost in the mail. Make sure to send it certified mail with tracking so you will have a paper trail and know when it reaches its destination.

A quick note on the Common Application: Traditionally used for mass college applications, some independent boarding and day schools have begun to consider such a form as an alternative to their own unique school application. While this will certainly make many potential students' lives easier, it should be noted that this approach has only recently been suggested, meaning that while the majority of institutions out there do not yet accept the Common Application, they may consider doing so in the near future. This application can be found at schools.com/forms/applicationform.pdf, and in theory (dependent on whether the schools applied to accept it) allows you to fill out one application and then submit it to multiple schools. If more than one school to which you are applying accepts the Common Application, it's probably worthwhile to use it to apply to those schools. In all cases, check with the schools beforehand—as potentially helpful as this application is, it won't do much for your child's chances for admission if it's not even accepted.

References and Recommendations

Teacher recommendations can be very important pieces of the admissions puzzle. They enable respected figures that have dealt with your child in an academic setting to speak about his potential. Admissions officers look carefully at these statements. When choosing a reference, it's important to take several things into account. First, choose a teacher who knows your child's personality and academics well. It can also help to choose the teacher of a subject in which your child excels. Teachers who have had a long career have perhaps done this before, and often speak with more authority in their recommendations. Their references also tend to carry more weight. Finally, make sure you give your choices plenty of time to complete their recommendations. No one likes to have work piled on them at the last minute, so give them time to do the best job they can.

Essays

Essays and student statements are another important component of the application. It is here, for the first time, that an applicant has the opportunity to speak candidly about herself, and to demonstrate maturity of thought and writing ability. The best essays are personal—they describe the applicant through events or issues that are important to her. A laundry list of achievements or awards will do little to win over admissions officers. Instead, an applicant should use this chance to introduce herself, to explain who she is, to demonstrate why she thinks private school is right for her, and why she thinks this particular school is a good fit. Be personal. Be honest. Be enthusiastic.

One further note: The applicant, not the parent, should write essays. Editing a final draft with your child is fine, as is talking with your child beforehand about a plan and outline for the essay, but your involvement should end there. It may seem like a good idea to add a more adult level of writing to the essay, but admissions officers are quite shrewd at picking this up, and it will be clearly apparent in the interview. Help your child plan and execute his or her best work, but refrain from doing the work yourself.

VISITING

Reading about schools in catalogs and watching their videos is certainly helpful, but ultimately, the only way your child is going to get the sense of a private school is to visit. It is critical that you and your child visit all the schools that you are considering. For a question as important as where to spend four years of one's life, answering blindly after reading a catalog simply won't do, particularly when your school is only a train ride away! There's another benefit to school visits: You would be astounded at the number of times a child tours a school and says to their parents, "This just feels right." And that instinct is usually spot-on.

Your tour will likely cover the grounds, athletic facilities if applicable, some of the more impressive academic buildings, the library, the cafeteria. Along the way, feel free to ask your tour guide questions; the guide will likely be a student and eager to provide answers. At the end of the tour, you might want to ask your guide what he or she is happiest with at the school, and what could stand to be improved. Other questions to consider and pose to admissions officers are how the school supports those students with academic difficulties, and what encourages students to excel and how they are nourished intellectually. What kind of support, both personal and financial, does the school expect of parents? And how big a role do arts, music, drama and sports play in student life?

Along the way, take note of the other students you pass on campus. Do they seem happy, energetic? Are they enjoying themselves? Are you comfortable with the level of formality of the student body? How does the school look, feel, and sound? Are you comfortable with the school's demographic mix? Keep your eyes and ears open during the visit, and trust your own impressions about the school. It is surprisingly easy to get the feel of a place by visiting and to sense whether or not a specific school is the right one. Don't miss out on the chance to see for yourself.

Successful Interviews

The interview provides a second chance for an applicant to give a personal impression, and for admissions officers to see if the applicant has the maturity, inquisitiveness, and enthusiasm to succeed at their school. First of all, there is nothing to be nervous about. Admissions officers are a friendly, chatty bunch and are very good at putting interviewees at ease. If your child is nervous before an interview, it helps to remind him of two things: First, he will not be making any speeches be quizzed on anything he had to study; he is simply going to meet someone who is friendly and wants to learn more about him. Encourage your child to speak naturally and honestly about himself—once he starts talking, he will have a much easier time. The second thing to remember is that your child is interviewing the school just as much as the school is interviewing your child. He can use the interview to ask any questions at all about the school— the more the better. Your child needs to interview them! Realizing that he is taking an active role in evaluating the school and not just being evaluated can be very empowering for your child.

Admissions officers love to see an applicant who is enthusiastic about private school in general—and their school in particular. Learning a little about the school before the interview is a good way to generate questions and demonstrate interest. It is a good idea to ask questions in a way that highlights your child's strengths and interests, and that shows a clean connection with the school he or she is visiting. Examples of these questions are: "I play tennis seriously at home. I love it and would love to play high school tennis. How is your school's tennis team?" or: "I love writing and want to be a journalist when I grow up. I read that your school's paper is one of the oldest in the country. What is it like to work on the paper?" Specific questions like these show real enthusiasm and personal interest.

Finally, a note about what to wear: Some schools may make suggestions about what to wear to the interview, but it's safe to say that your child can't go wrong by dressing too nicely. Wearing a coat and tie or a nice dress demonstrates his or her respect for the school s/he is visiting and for the process. Remember, it's better to appear more interested than less in these types of situations, and points are never taken off for being too dressed up.

Standardized Testing

A great many New York City private and selective public schools require the Educational Records Bureau's Independent School Entrance Exam (ISEE). For prospective students this eliminates the necessity of having to test at each school that interests them. Register your child for the test by calling the New York City testing center to make an appointment. The test—which may only be taken once within a six-month period and which does not offer practice tests—covers quantitative and verbal skills. Sections include verbal reasoning, quantitative reasoning, reading comprehension, mathematics achievement, and an essay portion that, while not given a score, is sent to the schools to which you are applying along with your child's results. The New York City testing center, located at 220 East 42nd Street, can be reached at 212-672-9800 and further information is available at erbtest.org. School records and a personal interview also factor heavily into a school's decision-making process, so avoid panicking over this standardized test.

Instead of the ISEE, some schools may ask for the SSAT. The Secondary School Admission Test is a multiple-choice test that takes over two hours and covers both math and verbal skills in separate sections. There are sites in which to take the SSAT in every state, with over 600 sites across the country. The test is generally offered on Saturdays from November through June. The Secondary School Admission Test can be scheduled online at SSAT.org, or by calling 609-683-4440.

Many selective public schools may require students to take the SSHSAT (Specialized Science High School Admissions Test) or SHSAT (Specialized High School Admissions Test). On the day of the exam, students must state in order of preference to which of three selective public high schools they wish to apply. Students are then admitted to these schools depending on how well they score and how quickly the school fills up; needless to say, the higher the score, the better the chance of getting in. These exams are offered to all 8th and 9th grade students who live within New York City's five boroughs. Note: Certain creative talent–oriented schools, such as Fiorello H. LaGuardia High School of Music & Art and Performing Arts, require an audition in place of a formal exam. For further information, check out the NYC Department of Education's website at http://schools.nyc.gov.

If applying to a parochial school, keep in mind they may have their own admission tests. Some New York City Jewish schools require applicants to take the Jewish Entrance Exam which is offered by the Jewish Board of Education. Please visit their website at bjeny.org for more information. The majority of Catholic schools in New York City require applicants to take the TACHS (Test for Admission into Catholic High Schools). This test, usually offered in November, lasts approximately two hours and deals with four key areas: reading, language, mathematics, and ability. During the exam, students list their three top schools—the test results (along with academic records) are then sent to these three schools for review. For more information, please visit the TACHS website at tachsinfo.com or contact them by phone at 866-618-2247.

All of these tests enable private schools to help evaluate their candidates against the entire pool of applicants. Whereas some schools may be more difficult than others, standardized tests are carefully crafted to provide no advantages, so they can be taken as a fair and unbiased representation of a student's ability. That said, there are plenty of factors that can drastically affect a student's performance on the day of the test. The following tips should help your child do their best on their exams (also check out Part V of this book, which features tips, info, and practice drills, and also Part VII, which has an upper level ISEE practice test!).

TEST-TAKING TIPS

Get plenty of rest on the day before the test. You want to be well rested so that you can focus on answering questions quickly and efficiently. It's also a good idea to eat a balanced meal before the test to make sure you don't run out of energy midway through. When you register for the SSAT, you are sent a test packet with explanations of the different sections and a sample test. If you are taking the ISEE, you may order What to Expect on the ISEE for $15.00. This book provides half-length practice tests for middle and upper levels and an extensive number of practice questions for all three levels. It is available only at the ISEE Operations Office at 800-446-0320. Reviewing all the materials well in advance of test day should help to familiarize you with the different types of questions, and will save you time. Take a practice test—test day will be much easier if you've already had the experience before. Tutor services and preparation books can also give you an edge on test day. Also, The Princeton Review offers a number of test prep courses in the New York City area. And not to toot our own horn here, but *Cracking the SAT & ISEE* is an extremely helpful resource to have in your months and days leading up to the exam.

On your way to the test site, don't forget to bring your registration ticket and several sharpened pencils. Wear layered clothing so that you can add or remove layers depending on room temperature. Plan to arrive at the test site early—you don't want to miss your test because of traffic or mass transit delays, and last minute arrivals can be stressful and hurt your performance.

On the test itself, remember that the sections are timed, so you need to keep moving. If you hit a difficult question, don't dwell on it—skip forward and then return to it when you have finished the section. Above all, relax. You'll do just fine.

Paying for Prep School

The PFS and Needs-Based Aid

Private school has a reputation as being affordable only to the rich, but as we saw in the misconceptions section, this is far from the mark. Schools want the best students, not the wealthiest students, and there are plenty of resources available to help families pay for school. Many private schools offer need-based financial aid. Schools evaluate a family's finances and charge only what that family has ability to pay. A full 20 percent of students in NAIS schools received this type of aid.

The School and Student Service for Financial Aid (SSS) is a service used by thousands of schools to evaluate each family's ability to pay school costs. The Educational Testing Service (ETS), the same organization that manages the ISEE, also manages the SSS program and provides support and services to families and schools. The SSS fosters objectivity and consistency in financial aid procedures among schools, and is dedicated to the idea that parents should finance their child's education only to the extent they are able.

The SSS works by having each family fill out a questionnaire called the Parents' Financial Statement (PFS). This is the tool private schools use to evaluate family need. It takes into account family size, income, expenses, assets, other children in private school or college, as well as other factors. Using the PFS and other info, such as a family's tax return, schools estimate what a family is able to contribute toward their child's education. It is important to note that the SSS only gathers this information and distributes it to schools. The schools themselves make the decisions about a family's financial need. The Parent Financial Statement can be completed online. It currently costs $22 for the first school you choose to send your PFS to, followed by $12.50 for each additional school. A family report can also be created for $12.50. If you cannot afford this fee, the schools to which you apply can provide a fee waiver.

The online Parents' Financial Statement can be found at https://sss.ets.org/.

Ultimately, each school's total tuition, endowment, and approach to financial aid will affect the dollar amount a family will receive in aid and the amount of out-of-pocket money they will be responsible for. Two schools may look at the same PFS and offer a drastically different aid amount. It is possible for families to "shop around" for the best deal. Financial aid announcements are generally made within or soon after the admission notification period.

Merit-Based Aid

While the PFS and need-based financial aid is often critical for a family's ability to pay for private school, it isn't the only aid available to prospective students. Merit-based aid provides additional resources for students with exceptional academic qualifications, or with exceptional talent in athletics, a musical instrument, the performing arts, sciences, or other areas. Financial aid of this type comprises only 5 percent of all available aid, a small but still potentially important component of a financial aid package. Merit-based aid varies from school to school. It is also important to note that community organizations, cultural or religious groups, philanthropic organizations, and private companies all offer financial aid grants to private school bound students. The Internet can be a great resource for finding further information about these grants and scholarships.

Tuition Payment Plans

Once you know the total amount you'll owe your child's school, you can enroll in a tuition payment plan, which spreads tuition payments over eight to ten months. Two examples of payments plans, with their contact information and details, are offered below. These are not the only two available—contact your school to find out which organizations that they work with.

Key Education Resources
745 Atlantic Avenue, Suite 300
Boston, MA 02111-2735
800-KEY-LEND (800-539-5363)
Fax: 617-451-8990
www.keybank.com

Monthly Payment Plan: School must be a participant; nonrefundable annual application fee; no interest; flexible terms and customized plans: school chooses start date and number of payments, Key disburses money to school monthly; full online and electronic capabilities; family has choice of direct debit, check, money order, or credit card; deadlines and late charges determined by the school.

Sallie Mae
463 Swansea Mall Drive
Swansea, MA 02777
800-556-6684
Fax: 508-235-2970
www.TuitionPayEnroll.com

The TuitionPay Monthly Plan lets families break tuition bills into more manageable, interest-free installments. Reduces the need to borrow and saves on interest charges. Low annual enrollment fee includes life insurance coverage. Payments can be made by check, money order, automatic debit from a checking or savings account, or by credit card through the mail, over the phone, or online. Families and schools have 24/7 access to real-time account information attuitionpay.com. Free budget counseling helps families establish the right monthly payment; interactive websites and budgeting tools offer convenient online enrollment/renewal. Plan can be seamlessly integrated with the Sallie Mae K-12 Family Education Loan. Sallie Mae has served more than five million families since 1970.

Tuition Loan Programs

If you need further help, there are many organizations that offer loans to help cover costs. For the most part, the terms of these loans are much more favorable than regular loans, and don't need to be repaid until after your child graduates. A few examples are listed below. Contact your school for a list of loan providers that work with them.

Citibank / The Student Loan Corporation
750 Washington Boulevard
Stamford, CT 06901-3722
800-967-2400
www.StudentLoan.com

CitiAssist K-12 loan: May borrow up to $15,000 per year; 10-year repayment period; cosigner optional; no application, origination, or repayment fees; interest rate set to prime + 1.5 percent; minimum annual income of $18,000; online application available.

Key Education Resources
745 Atlantic Avenue
Suite 300
Boston, MA 02111-2735
800-KEY-LEND (800-539-5363)
Fax: 617-451-8990
www.KeyBank.com

Achiever Loan: Reserve funds for up to four years of education with one application; apply online or by fax, phone, or mail; pre-qualify in as little as 24 hours; repaid over 20 years; no prepayment penalty; interest varies quarterly set to LIBOR + 3.5 percent; funds paid to school on due dates; 2 percent origination fee added to loan amount; can borrow up to cost of education less financial aid received.

Sallie Mae
463 Swansea Mall Drive
Swansea, MA 02777
888-2-SALLIE
Fax: 508-235-2970
www.SallieMae.com/k12loan

The Sallie Mae K-12 Family Education loan helps parents afford the private education of their choice for their children. Borrow from $1,000 up to the total cost of your child's education. You can also apply for 60 percent of the tuition amount (not to exceed $6,000) for education-related expenses. The interest rate can be as low as prime + 1 and fees as low as 2 percent. You can take up to twenty years to repay the loan, which can keep your payments low and affordable. Apply online or by fax. Loans can be seamlessly integrated with the TuitionPay Monthly Payment Plan.

HOW TO USE THIS BOOK

The first part of this book is a primer on all the ins and outs of private and selective public schools in New York City. From testing info to interview tips to tuition payment options, it's a veritable night school to prepare you to apply to college preparatory schools.

The second part is more personal, a chance to explore the schools on a more detailed basis. The following pages present an alphabetical listing of New York City's finest private and selective public high schools, complete with profiles, important data, and in most cases, a few words from the students, parents, and alumni connected to these schools, detailing what made their educational experience such a special one. In all instances, the data provided usually reflects the figures for the academic year prior to publication. Since school offerings and demographics vary greatly from one institution to another, and some schools report data more thoroughly than others, some entries will not include all of the individual data described below.

Please know that we take our data collection process with the utmost seriousness. We reached out to schools numerous times throughout this endeavor to ensure we can provide you with the most accurate, up-to-date, and informative figures and facts. Each profile in this book goes through a series of checkpoints to ensure accuracy of the information. Even so, from the moment a book circumnavigates the printing press, it is dated. If a school changes its policies, procedures, or requirements once our book is bound and on shelves, it's too late for us to change it. So be sure to double-check with any schools that you plan to apply to—make sure you are able to get them everything they need in order to meet any deadlines and ensure your child gets in to the school of their dreams.

DECODING THE PROFILES

THE TEXT

There are ten sections of text in each profile.

About the School

This section describes the school in question, using historical and academic information to give you an idea of its character and educational stance.

Mission Statement

In its own words, the school discloses its vision of academic and personal achievement.

The Ideal Applicant

The school describes what kind of student it is looking for come admissions time.

Where Students Come From

This section details where the school's students live and commute from in relation to the campus.

Orientation for New Students

A chance for prospective students and their parents to see things (hopefully) to come—how the school will introduce the student to the school, as well as how the school will introduce itself to the family.

Colleges that Recent Grads Are Attending

A comprehensive listing of colleges and universities that recent graduates have attended.

Students Say

Current students sound off on what they like best about their school.

Parents Say

Parents of current students explain the reasons why they chose their child's school and how rewarding the experience has been.

Alumni Say

Alumni of the school recall their fondest memories of their alma mater and what they gained from their years there.

THE DATA

Not all of the data categories will be listed for every school. If a school fails to report their numbers for a certain category, that category is not included in their profile.

The Heading

First things first: the school's name, address, phone number, website, and the names of the head of the school and admissions. Use this information to contact them and familiarize yourself better with the institution of your interest.

General

Type of School

This lets you know whether the school is private or public.

Religious Affiliation

This lets you know any religious order with which the school is affiliated.

Coeducational

Whether the school accepts students of both sexes, and if not, that which is encouraged to enroll.

Boarding

This lets you know whether the school boards students.

Day School

This lets you know whether the school operates as a day school.

Dress Code

This details whether a dress code is enforced or not.

Founded

Gives you the year when the school was founded.

Students

Enrollment

Number of student enrolled in grades 9 through 12.

% Male/Female

The percentage of male and female students at the school.

% African American*

The percentage of African American students at the school.

% Hispanic/Latino*

The percentage of Hispanic/Latino students at the school.

% Asian*

The percentage of Asian students at the school.

% Caucasian*

The percentage of Caucasian students at the school.

% Other*

The percentage of any students who are not Caucasian and whose ethnicities were not explicitly detailed by the school.

% International Students

The percentage of international students at the school.

% Out-of-State Students

The percentage of out-of-state students at the school.

Countries Represented

The number of countries represented at the school.

States Represented

The number of states represented at the school.

* Unless given to us directly by the school, the data for this section was garnered from the following sources: PrivateSchoolReview.com, SchoolTree.org, InsideSchools.org, and NewYorkMetro.com.

ADMISSIONS SELECTIVITY

Applications Received

The number of applications the school received.

Applicants Accepted

Out of the applications received, the number of applicants the school accepted.

Accepted Applicants Who Enrolled

Out of the students accepted, the number of applicants who enrolled.

Requires Standardized Test Scores

This tells you whether the school requires standardized test scores (namely any tests required to be taken in order to apply) for applicants.

Application Essay

This lets you know whether the school requires applicants to submit an application essay.

SAT Scores

This tells you whether the school requires SAT scores from applicants.

Comparable Schools

Lists any comparable schools with regards to formal partnerships, admission, religious affiliation, students, or boarding criteria.

Academics

Required Classes

This lists which classes students are required to take in order to graduate.

Additional Requirements

This lists any additional requirements outside of electives.

Student/Faculty Ratio

This gives you the student/faculty ratio at the school in question.

Extracurricular

Most Popular Interscholastic Sports

Lists the school's most popular sports and whether they allow both sexes to play or not.

% Students Who Play Interscholastic Sports

This gives you the percentage of students at the school who play interscholastic sports.

Financial

Annual Tuition

The cost of tuition for an academic year.

Boarding Tuition

The total annual tuition for boarding students.

% Students Receiving Financial Aid

This lets you know the percentage of students who receive financial aid.

Average Financial Aid/Scholarship

The average dollar amount of financial aid or scholarship money a student receives.

Below Financial you'll notice either one or two asterisks. One asterisk denotes a school partnered with us to provide the most comprehensive and up-to-date info on their institution. Two astrisks appear when a school declined to partner with us; as such all info on them has been taken from the public domain or, if stated, their website. In all cases, be sure to contact any school you are interested in for clarification or further information as the narrative and statistics are subject to change.

PART IV—THE SCHOOLS

THE ABRAHAM JOSHUA HESCHEL HIGH SCHOOL

20 West End Avenue, New York, NY 10023

Phone Number: 212-246-7717 • **Website:** www.heschel.org

Head of School: Ahuva Halberstam • **Director of Admissions:** Rabbi Dov Lerea

General

Type of School	Private
Religious Affiliation	Jewish
Coeducational	Yes
Boarding	No
Day School	Yes
Dress Code	No
Founded	1983

Students

Enrollment (Grades 9–12)	143
% African American	1
% Caucasian	99

Admissions Selectivity

Requires Standardized Test Scores	Yes
Application Essay	None

COMPARABLE SCHOOLS

Ramaz—The Rabbi Joseph F. Lookstein Upper School; Solomon Schechter High School of New York; Yeshiva of Flatbush

ABOUT THE ABRAHAM JOSHUA HESCHEL HIGH SCHOOL

Founded in 1983, The Abraham Joshua Heschel School has grown exponentially from its original twenty-eight students and fulfilled its goal of becoming a new model of Jewish day school education (the high school itself being a recent addition to its ranks), with a dual curriculum that places an emphasis on curiosity fulfilled and excellence achieved along with an immersion in Jewish history, belief, and culture. By employing a creative learning style, the body of committed teachers and administrators actively engage students in their studies, encouraging and cultivating their interests, talents, and potential while developing a vibrant Jewish community both locally and globally.

Completed in 2002, the high school building is the most recent addition to the ever-expanding Heschel School. It has adopted state-of-the-art tools to help teach students—namely the laptops used by both teachers and students in the classroom—effectively honoring educational goals through the implementation of technology. Along with core subjects, students attend Tefilla; study Hebrew, Torah, and Talmud; and participate in a multitude of Jewish events during retreats, holidays, celebrations, and field trips. As its website states, the school's educational ideals are drawn from "the strands of the Jewish, Western, and world traditions to which we belong. They are reflected in our deep concern for the whole child and the balance in each child's academic, aesthetic, emotional, intellectual, physical and spiritual growth."

Mission Statement

According to the school's website, The Abraham Joshua Heschel High School is dedicated to broadening the academic potential of each student by "incorporating teaching strategies that engage a broad range of learning styles." The school involves students personally in the learning process by providing stimuli and activities "to promote critical thinking and a love of learning." In this, the school is dedicated to the values and principles that characterized Rabbi Heschel's life: integrity, intellectual exploration, traditional Jewish study, justice, righteousness, human dignity, and holiness. It views the texts of the Jewish tradition and the history of the Jewish people "as fundamental resources for developing ideas, beliefs, behaviors, and values to shape and inspire the lives of individuals."

The Ideal Applicant

The school looks for students who seek, question, and think for themselves—in other words, passionate learners. Heschel students are "creative, articulate, socially conscious critical thinkers, and they are prepared to contribute to the larger community."

Where Students Come From

Abraham Joshua Heschel High School students come from all over New York City, as well as from Westchester and Riverdale counties.

Academics
Curriculum
A rigorous and balanced curriculum that involves religious studies along with traditional subjects

Additional Requirements
Community service

Student/Faculty Ratio   10:1

Extracurricular
Most Popular
Interscholastic Sports
Male
Basketball, cross-country, soccer, tennis, track & field
Female
Basketball, cross-country, soccer, tennis, volleyball, floor hockey, track & field

---

Financial
Annual Tuition $20,000
Endowment $5 million
**

Special Ed.

AICHHORN SCHOOL

23 West 106th Street, New York, NY 10025

Phone Number: 212-316-9353 • **Website:** www.aichhorn.org

Head of School: David Washburn • **Program Director:** Clarence Leach

General

Type of School	Private
Religious Affiliation	None
Coeducational	Yes
Boarding	Yes
Day School	Yes
Dress Code	No
Founded	1991

Students

Enrollment (Grades 9–12)	32
% African American	39
% Hispanic/Latino	48
% Caucasian	13

Academics

Student/Faculty Ratio	4:1

**

ABOUT THE AICHHORN SCHOOL

Located at the August Aichhorn Residential Treatment Facility (RTF), the Aichhorn School is a secondary special education school chartered by the New York State Board of Regents that serves the thirty-two residents of the Aichhorn RTF. The school offers approved New York State curriculum for grades 7 through 11 in language arts, social studies, science, math, art, and physical and health education.

All children at the Aichhorn School are certified as special education students in need of educational and emotional services, with the primary diagnostic category for students being emotional disability. In addition to this, many students also have learning disabilities. Student age ranges from twelve to eighteen years old and the average stay at Aichhorn is two and a half years.

In conjunction with formal classes, the school has incorporated an afterschool program of trips and workshops during afternoons and weekends broaden the borders of children's experiences at Aichhorn.

Education is viewed as a key component in a student's progress at the school, which also includes ongoing psychiatric treatment, daily conduct reports and monthly progress reports, all of which assist each student's development. This is bolstered by the personal approach that teachers at Aichhorn take by participating actively in each student's treatment planning meetings as well as their academic and clinical plans. In addition, many teachers orchestrate and conduct workshops in which they can share their particular talents and interests with the children.

MISSION STATEMENT

The school's mission is to supply students with the necessary "academic, social, and vocational skills" so that they can successfully "return to their communities as self-sufficient adults."

THE BARD HIGH SCHOOL EARLY COLLEGE

525 East Houston Street, New York, NY 10002

Phone Number: 212-995-8479 • **Website:** www.bard.edu/bhsec

Head of School: Raymond Peterson • **Director of Admissions:** Monica Hidalgo

ABOUT THE BARD HIGH SCHOOL EARLY COLLEGE

As a partnership of the New York City Department of Education and Bard College, Bard High School Early College (BHSEC) has thrived since 2001 in offering high school–age students the chance to excel at college classes—for college credit! Thanks to BHSEC's enterprising program, the school can offer not only a Regents high school diploma but also an Associate in Arts degree to students upon graduation. The first two years at BHSEC (9th and 10th grades) are devoted to completing Regents exams and most of the high school academic requirements, while the subsequent two years involve college classes in a liberal arts curriculum (though certain classes must be taken in accordance with the school's core requirements). By the end of their four years at BHSEC, students are eligible to transfer with up to two years of college credit, to four-year colleges and universities. Note that admission to this program is also highly selective and applicants must submit grades, exam scores, and attendance records. They also have to take the required writing and math assessment exams. Viable candidates will be invited to an interview.

MISSION STATEMENT

"This unique institution is based on Bard's recognition that many bright, highly motivated young people are ready to begin serious college work after Grade 10. Since the mid-1960s, Simon's Rock College of Bard, the nation's only four-year college specifically designed for younger scholars, has provided such students the opportunity to prove

General:	
Type of School	Public
Religious Affiliation	None
Coeducational	Yes
Boarding	No
Day School	Yes
Dress Code	No
Founded	2001

Students	
Enrollment (Grades 9–12)	530
% Male/Female	30/70
% African American	18
% Hispanic/Latino	18
% Asian	11
% Caucasian	37
% Other	16
% International Students	2
% Out-of-State Students	0
# States Represented	1

Admissions Selectivity	
Applications Received	>2,000
# Applicants Accepted	270
# Accepted Applicants Who Enrolled	150
Requires Standardized Test Scores	Yes; BHSEC assessment exam
Application Essay	None
Median SAT	Reading: 600; Math: 570; Writing: 600

COMPARABLE SCHOOLS
Simon's Rock of Bard

themselves in a rigorous and supportive learning environment. Bard College, with the support of the New York City Department of Education, has adapted this model to the urban public school setting."

THE IDEAL APPLICANT

Ideal applicants will demonstrate intellectual aptitude and curiosity. They will welcome the opportunity to learn in a diverse environment that fosters the exchange of ideas through academic discourse.

WHERE STUDENTS COME FROM

Students come from all five boroughs of New York City.

ORIENTATION PROCESS FOR NEW STUDENTS

During the summer preceding 9th grade, students are invited to participate in the BHSEC Bridge Program, a one-week orientation designed to introduce incoming students to the social and academic expectations of our school.

COLLEGES THAT RECENT GRADS ARE ATTENDING

American University in Paris, Boston University, Harvard University, International University of Bremen (Germany), New York University, Pennsylvania State University, Princeton University, Spellman College, Stanford University, State University of New York—Binghamton, Syracuse University, Temple University, Trinity College (Dublin), University of Chicago, Wesleyan University (For a complete list please visit the website at Bard.edu/bhsec.)

Students Say

Students appreciate the "incredible diversity" of "ethnicity, religion, and ideas" at BHSEC, noting that "students . . . respect each other's ideas yet thrive" thanks to "engaging debates and dialogue." One student mentions "the close interaction between the professors and students" as forming a "special" part of the school's supportive community. This relaxed and academically challenging environment is enhanced by a complete lack of "competitive atmosphere." In the words of one student, "the only thing we are in competition with are our previous grades and performances." Ultimately, one of the school's true joys is being "surrounded by intellectually curious and interesting teenagers who also love to have a good time."

Parents Say

Parents chose to send their children to BHSEC because of the "multifaceted" entry criteria that are "designed to look at the whole child" to ensure a right match and complete understanding of the student's talents and abilities. Also mentioned is the school's celebration of "intellectual exploration, depth and quality of thinking, and genuine liberal education," all of which enforce BHSEC's central mission of "love of learning for its own sake." The "exemplary" teaching staff and "challenging and rigorous" classes, combined with a "commitment to reflect the racial, ethnic, and economic diversity" of New York City, result in the "exciting, culturally rich, and socially aware community" that exists at Bard.

Alumni Say

Alumni resoundingly agree that "community is the defining characteristic of a BHSEC education." Rather than allow students to keep to themselves "on their own personal track of study," Bard encourages "an atmosphere in which all aspects of school life overlap," thereby affirming that success doesn't happen singularly, but for all students. Many former students recall the events of 9/11 coinciding with BHSEC's first days of school. And while the memory certainly isn't a happy one, students took comfort "in the sense of unity that flooded the building," as they faced their future together with the "intellectual zeal, curiosity, and cultural diversity" the school provided.

THE BEEKMAN SCHOOL & THE TUTORING SCHOOL

220 East Fiftieth Street, New York, NY 10022

Phone Number: 212-755-6666 • **Website:** www.beekmanschool.org

Head of School and Director of Admissions: George Higgins

General

Type of School	Private
Religious Affiliation	None
Coeducational	Yes
Boarding	No
Day School	Yes
Dress Code	No
Founded	1925

Students

Enrollment (Grades 9–12)	100
% Male/Female	60/40
% African American	9
% Hispanic/Latino	8
% Asian	8
% Caucasian	75
% International Students	15
% Out-of-State Students	7
# Countries Represented	8
# States Represented	3

Admissions Selectivity

Applications Received	18
# Applicants Accepted	17
# Accepted Applicants Who Enrolled	16
Requires Standardized Test Scores	No
Application Essay	No
Median SAT	1067

COMPARABLE SCHOOLS

The school's academic standards are on par with other private secondary schools; however, the structure and approach to education at The Beekman School is unique.

ABOUT THE BEEKMAN SCHOOL & THE TUTORING SCHOOL

Founded in 1925, The Beekman School & The Tutoring School is a private high school for grades 9 through 12 that combines a college preparatory school curriculum with a commitment to highly individualized instruction. Teaching at this school is designed to meet the specific needs of the students. To facilitate this philosophy, the school limits class size to ten students in The Beekman School and three students in The Tutoring School. Students are provided with as many classes as is appropriate based on their individual learning needs. Afterschool tutors or private classes are also available.

MISSION STATEMENT

"The Beekman School & The Tutoring School offers a traditional, competitive preparatory education in a unique, supportive environment. The faculty encourages students to become actively involved in their education and develop a sense of academic commitment and responsibility. The school is dedicated to providing each student with the personalized support s/he needs to succeed."

The Ideal Applicant

The ideal applicant is college-bound and intellectually curious, with a commitment to learning and making a difference in the world.

Where Students Come From

Although the majority of students come from Manhattan, many students commute daily from New Jersey, Connecticut, Westchester, and Long Island.

Orientation Process for New Students

Since the school has a rolling admission policy, students may enter at any time throughout the year. Students are placed in classes according to ability, not necessarily age or grade level. The school's flexibility allows teachers and administrators to meet with new students after their initial placement to determine whether or not they have been appropriately situated. If not, they will be reassigned to a class better suited to their individual abilities and strengths. All students must complete The Beekman School's requirements and pass five Regent Exams to graduate.

Academics	
Required Classes	
4 years	English, history
3 years	Science, math
2 years	Foreign language
1 year	Art/music
1 semester	Computer science, health
Student/Faculty Ratio	6:1
Financial	
Annual Tuition	$24,000
*	

Colleges that Recent Grads are Attending

Arizona State University, Bryn Mawr University, Goucher College, Harvard University, Hofstra University, Marymount Manhattan College, New York University, Sarah Lawrence University, the School of Visual Arts

Students Say

Students are quick to say that "Beekman is the best place ever" thanks to "small class sizes" and teachers who "talk to you on a mature level." Combine this with the school's "family setting" and "friendly faces," it's no wonder that students agree that "you really get the personal attention needed to succeed."

Parents Say

Earning high marks is the "compassionate and caring staff of teachers" whose work in this "unique, small, hands-on environment" not only "mitigates damage" that students incurred at prior schools due to learning difficulties, but also gives children the opportunity to "like school" and "love learning." Also, many parents single out "the incredible headmaster George Higgins" for praise, noting the "integrity, warmth, and intellectual enthusiasm" that help him "craft individual curriculum and classes for each and every student." "Small class sizes" lend themselves to "instruction at the highest intellectual level" and "a great sense of friendship and support among the students for one another." Not surprisingly, the consensus among parents is that Beekman is "education at its most excellent."

Alumni Say

Alumni cite The Beekman School's "individualized attention" as a defining characteristic in not only their education but their lives. In the words of one graduate, "teachers pushed us when we wanted it and supported us when we needed it." Such positive development is due to "a deep sense of respect between the teachers and students," and the comfort of "coming into school every morning and knowing everyone's name."

Upper School Chris

THE BERKELEY CARROLL SCHOOL

181 Lincoln Place, Brooklyn, NY 11217

Phone Number: 718-789-6060 • **Website:** www.berkeleycarroll.org

Head of School: Jodie Corngold • **Director of Admissions:** Chris Weeks

ABOUT THE BERKELEY CARROLL SCHOOL

Having just celebrated its 120th birthday, The Berkeley Carroll School's college-preparatory academic program continues to emphasize the importance of education and its place in a fulfilled life. With a strong emphasis placed on developing writing skills for research, analytical, and creative expression, and under the guidance of dynamic teachers, students are challenged to reach beyond their perceived limits to discover their true creative and intellectual talents. Teachers demand an active approach to the learning process and support their students in an atmosphere of respect, personal attention, and care.

Academic opportunities abound for students interested in advanced foreign languages, history, literature, mathematics, and science work. In addition, the school hosts a foreign exchange program, creative arts electives, independent study, internships, and community service programs. School officials are proud to note on their website that "100 percent of graduates attend colleges and universities throughout the country."

General	
Type of School	Private
Religious Affiliation	None
Coeducational	Yes
Boarding	Yes
Day School	Yes
Dress Code	No
Founded	1886

Students	
Enrollment (Grades 9–12)	480
% Caucasian	70

Admissions Selectivity	
Requires Standardized Test Scores	Yes
Application Essay	Yes

MISSION STATEMENT

According to the school's website, Berkeley Carroll fulfills its goal of being a diverse academic institution that makes students feel comfortable enough to take a hands-on approach to their own education. Participation here is key, and this is fostered by a caring group of administrators, teachers, and students who believe in respect, integrity, understanding, and kindness. In this, Berkeley Carroll is deeply committed to "the highest standards of ethical behavior." The school maintains a "strong relationship" with parents, whose involvement is "actively sought and appreciated." In line with this stance on around-the-board participation, the school endeavors to solidify existing relationships and forge new ones with local and citywide cultural and civic institutions in order to "strengthen the larger community." Students are expected to "balance individual achievement with social responsibility" and graduate from the school with "a

Academics

REQUIRED CLASSES

English, history, math, science, foreign languages, electives

ADDITIONAL REQUIREMENTS

Community service

Student/Faculty Ratio   7:1

Extracurricular

MOST POPULAR

INTERSCHOLASTIC SPORTS

MALE

Baseball, basketball, cross-country, soccer, swimming, tennis, track, volleyball

FEMALE

Basketball, cross-country, soccer, softball, swimming, tennis, track, volleyball

Financial

Annual Tuition $20,250

**

commitment to a life of learning, service, and growth."

WHERE STUDENTS COME FROM

The school's website states that 60 percent of Berkeley Carroll's students come from Brooklyn, with the rest from the other boroughs of New York City, Long Island, Westchester, and New Jersey.

ORIENTATION PROCESS FOR NEW STUDENTS

New students and their parents attend an orientation meeting prior to the beginning of the school year.

COLLEGES THAT RECENT GRADS ARE ATTENDING

Allegheny College, Bard College, Barnard College, Boston College, Boston University, Brown University, Carnegie Mellon University, City University of New York—Baruch College, Claremont McKenna College, College of William & Mary, Cornell University, Eckerd College, George Washington University, Gettysburg College, Hampshire College, Johns Hopkins University, Mount Holyoke College, Muhlenberg College, New School University, New York University, Northwestern University, Pomona College, Rensselaer Polytechnic University, Sarah Lawrence College, Stanford University, Swarthmore College, Syracuse University, Temple University, Tulane University, Universidad de Buenos Aires, University of California—Santa Cruz, University of Miami, University of Vermont, University of Virginia, University of Wisconsin—Madison, Vassar College, Yale University

THE BIRCH WATHEN LENOX SCHOOL

210 East Seventy-seventh Street, New York, NY 10021

Phone Number: 212-861-0404 • **Website:** www.bwl.org

Head of School: Frank J. Carnabuci • **Director of Admissions:** Julianne Kaplan

ABOUT THE BIRCH WATHEN LENOX SCHOOL

Located on the Upper East Side of New York City, the Birch Wathen Lenox School is "a traditional, coeducational independent school that offers a rigorous college preparatory curriculum within the context of a nurturing environment." Both within the classroom and after school, BWL's goal is to help students fulfill their various potentials through academic achievement, athletic competition, and extracurricular activities by offering both tremendous challenges and exceptional support to all members of the student community. Students also increasingly see their responsibilities extend beyond their academic work, and as such they have received a great deal of recognition for the community service work they have completed. Faculty members are "devoted and trained professionals with the common goal of teaching their students to surpass their expectations." In turn, students are "inquisitive, articulate, disciplined, motivated, compassionate, and strong," paving the way for exceptional achievement at the School, as well as for students' future academic and personal success.

MISSION STATEMENT

"The Birch Wathen Lenox School provides a rigorous, yet nurturing academic environment which enables students to fulfill their greatest potential. The School atmosphere is intimate and friendly, with an emphasis placed on small class sizes. We are able to give our students individualized attention, and our faculty takes the initiative to recognize and support many different learning styles. At BWL, the goal for our students is to develop the whole person—mind, body, and heart."

THE IDEAL APPLICANT

With a student body comprising both boys and girls who have many diverse interests, the ideal applicant is one "who is enthusiastic about learning and shares the common goal of striv-

General

Type of School	Private
Religious Affiliation	None
Coeducational	Yes
Boarding	No
Day School	Yes
Dress Code	Yes
Founded	1916

Students

Enrollment (Grades 9–12)	170
% Male/Female	50/50
% International Students	20

Admissions Selectivity

Applications Received	120
# Applicants Accepted	20
# Accepted Applicants Who Enrolled	15
Requires Standardized Test Scores	Yes
Application Essay	None

COMPARABLE SCHOOLS

Allen-Stevenson; Browning; Riverdale; Trinity Hewitt

ing to do their best in a rigorous yet nurturing academic environment."

WHERE STUDENTS COME FROM

"Our students come from all areas of New York, the United States, and about 70 percent from abroad."

ORIENTATION PROCESS FOR NEW STUDENTS

The orientation process for new students involves an ongoing support system of peer buddies, attentive faculty, and open communication with student and parents.

COLLEGES THAT RECENT GRADS ARE ATTENDING

Brown University, Colgate University, Columbia University, Dartmouth College, Davidson College, Harvard University, Johns Hopkins University, Kenyon College, New York University, Northwestern University, Princeton University, Rhode Island School of Design, Sarah Lawrence College, University of Pennsylvania, and Washington University

STUDENTS SAY

Students note that The Birch Wathen Lenox School "stands out" from the crowd, going to great lengths to guide each student "academically and as a person." As one student points out, the school "expects much from its students, but in return [it] offers unusual encouragement and care."

PARENTS SAY

For parents, the key to their children's success "is a balanced approach to education," and Birch Wathen Lenox delivers this with "the challenge of excellence and power of compassion" in a "warm and supportive environment." These "fundamentals of a college preparatory education" are a "great relief" to parents, who can sleep well at night knowing their children's futures are constantly "nurtured, supported, and encouraged."

ALUMNI SAY

According to alumni, "any student who enjoys being challenged academically and learns best in an atmosphere of encouragement and cooperation will thrive at Birch Wathen Lenox."

Math F/T
Scie P/T

THE BREARLEY SCHOOL

610 East Eighty-third Street, New York, NY 10028

Phone Number: 212-570-8600 • **Website:** www.brearley.org

Head of School: Stephanie J. Hull • **Director of Admissions:** Joan Kaplan

ABOUT THE BREARLEY SCHOOL

Since 1884, The Brearley School has dedicated itself to providing a quality college-preparatory education for young women, while at the same time readying these students for progressive and successful places in the world of tomorrow. With a long-standing reputation as one of the most academically challenging schools in the nation, Brearley employs time-honored as well as creative teaching methods that take into account students' individual needs and potential. This personalized approach to education is further bolstered by an enviable array of extracurricular activities such as athletics, community service, and the performing and visual arts. The school prides itself on its rigorous curriculum and nurturing environment, as well as the committed team of teachers who contribute to the deep-rooted sense of community and confidence that Brearley instills in students. In the end though, the mark of a great college preparatory school is how well students do after graduation.

General	
Type of School	Private
Religious Affiliation	None
Coeducational	No
Boarding	No
Day School	Yes
Dress Code	Yes
Founded	1884

Students	
Enrollment (Grades 9–12)	200
% Male/Female	0/100
% Caucasian	76
% Other	24

MISSION STATEMENT

According to the school's website, a Brearley education "encourages students to solve problems and to take risks" in a setting that both encourages and challenges. Their caring and supportive teachers are "attentive to the interests and abilities" of each student, while also instilling a feeling of "collective responsibility" in the classroom. Thanks to a diverse student body, everyone at Brearley comes to cherish the many opinions and points of view that each person holds, thereby fostering a sense of reverence and respect not only for their peers but for education. Students here are taught to evaluate what they "hear, read, or see," while developing a strong sense of discipline and integrity. Ultimately, the proof is in the pudding, and Brearley's graduating students prove themselves testimony to their secondary school experience through their postsecondary school accomplishments.

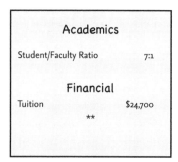

Academics	
Student/Faculty Ratio	7:1

Financial	
Tuition	$24,700
**	

WHERE STUDENTS COME FROM

The Brearley School students come from throughout the New York metropolitan area.

COLLEGES THAT RECENT GRADS ARE ATTENDING

American University, Amherst College, Bard College, Barnard College, Bates College, Boston College, Bowdoin College, Brandeis University, Brown University, Bryn Mawr College, Carleton College, Case Western Reserve, City University of New York, Clark University, Colby College, Colgate University, College of William & Mary, Colorado College, Columbia University, Connecticut College, Cornell University, Dartmouth College, Davidson College, Drew University, Duke University, Eckerd College, Emory University, Eugene Lang College, George Washington University, Georgetown University, Hamilton College, Hampton University, Harvard College, Harvard College, Johns Hopkins University, Macalester College, Middlebury College, New York University, Oberlin College, Oxford University, Pomona College, Pratt Institute, Princeton University, Rice University, Sarah Lawrence College, Stanford University, State University of New York at Binghamton, State University of New York—Oneonta, Swarthmore College, Trinity College, Tufts University, Tulane University, United States Military Academy, University of Chicago, University of Pennsylvania, University of St. Andrews, University of Southern California, Vanderbilt University, Vassar College, Washington University, Wellesley College, Wesleyan University, Yale University

THE BRONX HIGH SCHOOL OF SCIENCE

75 West 205th Street, Bronx, NY 10468

Phone Number: 718-817-7700 • **Website:** www.bxscience.edu

Head of School: Valerie J. Reidy • **Director of Admissions:** Rosemary VonOhlen

ABOUT THE BRONX HIGH SCHOOL OF SCIENCE

Founded in 1938, The Bronx High School of Science describes itself as "a place where students and faculty alike experience the excitement of the motivated mind and the Samaritan heart." The school prides itself on being not just an educational institution, but a close-knit community that encourages both personal and societal growth. The curriculum favors ambition and curiosity, giving students an impressive range of honors and Advanced Placement college level courses such as ARISTA National Honor Society, the Intel Research Program, a Holocaust Studies Center and Museum, instruction in nine foreign languages, distance learning, drama courses, a DNA Research Lab, and computer technology certification.

Admission to the program involves taking a comprehensive exam in both math and verbal reasoning. The minimum score required for admission fluctuates from year to year depending upon availability.

MISSION STATEMENT

The school aims to give its gifted and talented students every educational and social opportunity "so as to prepare them for meaningful and useful roles in science and society."

General	
Type of School	Public
Religious Affiliation	None
Coeducational	Yes
Boarding	No
Day School	Yes
Dress Code	No
Founded	1938

Students	
Enrollment (Grades 9–12)	2,437
% Male/Female	50/50
% African American	6
% Hispanic/Latino	8
% Asian	54
% Caucasian	33

Admissions Selectivity	
Applications Received	26,000
# Applicants Accepted	800
# Accepted Applicants Who Enrolled	700
Requires Standardized Test Scores	Yes
Application Essay	None

COMPARABLE SCHOOLS

Brooklyn Latin School; Brooklyn Technical High School; High School of American Studies at Lehman College; High School for Mathematics, Science and Engineering at City College; Queens High School for the Sciences at York College; Staten Island Technical High School; Stuyvesant High School

Academics

REQUIRED CLASSES

4 years: English, social studies, science, physical education

3 years: Math, foreign language

1 year: Technical drawing

1 semester : Heath education, music, art

Student/Faculty Ratio   20:1

Extracurricular

MOST POPULAR
INTERSCHOLASTIC SPORTS
MALE

Baseball, basketball, bowling, crew, cross-country, fencing, golf, gymnastics, handball, soccer, swimming, tennis, track, volleyball

FEMALE

Basketball, bowling, crew, cross-country, fencing, golf, gymnastics, handball, track, soccer, softball, swimming, tennis, track, volleyball

Financial

Annual Tuition   None

**

THE IDEAL APPLICANT

Students at Bronx High School of Science represent the cream of the crop academically—meaning that they get good grades; participate in extracurricular activities; and have exemplary attendance records, a zeal for education in and out of the classroom (along with equally committed parents!), and a respectful attitude.

WHERE STUDENTS COME FROM

Students are from all five boroughs of New York City.

Middle/Upper Theater

BROOKLYN FRIENDS SCHOOL

375 Pearl Street, Brooklyn, NY 11201

Phone Number: 718-852-1029 • **Website:** www.brooklynfriends.org

Head of School: Michael Nill, PhD • **Director of Admissions:** Jennifer Knies

ABOUT BROOKLYN FRIENDS SCHOOL

Founded in 1867 by The Brooklyn Meeting of the Religious Society of Friends, Brooklyn Friends School is an independent, college preparatory Quaker school guided by the ideals of "acceptance, compassion, equality and non-violence." Located in downtown Brooklyn, the school boasts spacious classrooms, four science labs, two libraries, a ceramics studio, two dance studios, two gymnasiums, a media center, a 300-seat theater/meeting house, a woodshop, a cafeteria, and a rooftop playground.

BFS charges itself with sparking students' "natural curiosity" and "passion for learning" through a comprehensive curriculum that involves traditional and hands-on learning experiences designed to "expand intellectual abilities" and encourage "personal growth, self-motivation and responsibility." The school also offers a wide breadth of extracurricular activities and resources such as athletics, clubs, workshops, community service, and internships. All of this, in the words of an administrator, helps students to "explore new and undiscovered talents" while becoming "critical thinkers who question assumptions about the world around them."

MISSION STATEMENT

"Brooklyn Friends School is committed to educating each student intellectually, aesthetically, physically, and spiritually in a culturally diverse community. Guided by the Quaker principles of truth, simplicity, and peaceful resolution of conflict, Brooklyn Friends School offers each student a challenging education that develops intellectual abilities and ethical and social values to support a productive life of leadership and service."

General

Type of School	Private
Religious Affiliation	Quaker
Coeducational	Yes
Boarding	No
Day School	Yes
Dress Code	Yes
Founded	1867

Students:

Enrollment (Grades 9–12)	160
% Male/Female	40/60
% African American	35
% Hispanic/Latino	2
% Asian	2
% Caucasian	61
% Out-of-State Students	1
# Countries Represented	1
# States Represented	2

Admissions Selectivity

Requires Standardized Test Scores: No
Application Essay: Yes; student supplement

Academics:

REQUIRED CLASSES

4 years: English, math, phys ed
3 years: History, science, foreign language, visual & performing arts
1 year: Study skills
1 semester: Religion, Quakerism, technology, health

ADDITIONAL REQUIREMENTS

100 hours of community service, senior internship program

Student/Faculty Ratio	7:1

THE IDEAL APPLICANT

Brooklyn Friends School is interested in "enthusiastic learners and motivated students who show strong potential for future academic success and whose background and experience demonstrate an ability and willingness to make a positive contribution to the school community and who will actively support the school's values."

WHERE STUDENTS COME FROM

"The majority of our students come mainly from New York State."

ORIENTATION PROCESS FOR NEW STUDENTS

Enrolled students are first invited to visit the school in spring and then a full day orientation program is held prior to beginning of fall classes.

COLLEGES THAT RECENT GRADS ARE ATTENDING

Amherst College, Brooklyn College, Bryn Mawr College, Carleton, Denison University, Dickinson College, Drew University, Drexel University, Eckerd College, Emory University, Fordham University, Rhode Island School of Design, Oberlin College, Haverford College, Towson University, John Jay College of Criminal Justice, George Washington University, Roger Williams College, University of Vermont, University of San Francisco, Savannah College of Art and Design, Pitzer College, Temple University, Syracuse University, Wheaton College, Alfred University, Lincoln University, University of North Carolina—Chapel Hill, Colgate, Boston College, Hofstra University, Skidmore College, Goucher College, Emerson College, Guilford College, Rochester Institute of Technology, Bard College, SUNY Buffalo, Sacred Heart University, Arcadia University, Manhattanville College, Marlboro College, Columbia University, Monmouth University, Ithaca College, Sarah Lawrence University, Vassar College, Maryland Institute College of Art.

BROOKLYN LATIN SCHOOL

325 Bushwick Avenue, Brooklyn, NY 11206

Phone Number: 718-935-3199 • **Website:** None

Head of School: Jason Griffiths

ABOUT BROOKLYN LATIN SCHOOL

Established in 2006 by John Elwell, Brooklyn Latin School is the newest addition to New York City's selective public high schools. Starting in fall 2006, students have entered the hallowed halls of this East Williamsburg establishment whose curriculum and philosophy is based wholly on the Boston Latin School (of which Benjamin Franklin was a graduate). The school's goal is to provide a challenging program of study in the classical tradition (including Greek and Latin) with a strong focus on the humanities. According to the school's principal, this education will provide "the groundwork for an understanding of the foundations of our society, while developing the leadership capacity of our students so that they may serve as leaders in their community."

The school also believes that education isn't just relegated to students. Every Wednesday afternoon, classes end early and teachers gather for professional development instruction, working together to better their technique and delivery to ensure that students are challenged in understandable and advantageous ways.

A sense of formality and pride in education guides a student's experience here, from the Latin terms for all things academic to the Phoenician purple dress code, everything is given special consideration. And though new, Brooklyn Latin is on the move. The class of 2010 will be the Brooklyn Latin's first graduating class, and by that point enrollment for all four grades is expected to be at its maximum of 800 students.

General

Type of School	Public
Religious Affiliation	None
Coeducational	Yes
Boarding	No
Day School	Yes
Dress Code	Yes
Founded	2006

Students:

Enrollment (Grades 9–12)	50

Admissions Selectivity

Requires Standardized Test Scores	Yes
Application Essay	None

COMPARABLE SCHOOLS

Bronx High School of Science, High School for Mathematics, Science and Engineering at City College, High School of American Studies at Lehman College, Queens High School for the Sciences at York College, Staten Island Tech. High School, Stuyvesant High School

Extracurricular
MOST POPULAR
INTERSCHOLASTIC SPORTS
MALE

Basketball, baseball, Greco-Roman wrestling, movement, speed walking/running, yoga

FEMALE

Basketball, movement, softball, speed walking/running, yoga

Academics:

REQUIRED CLASSES

4 years: Latin, foreign language, math
2 years: Science
Student/Faculty Ratio   10:1

Financial:

Annual Tuition   None

THE IDEAL APPLICANT

Brooklyn Latin attracts a diverse crowd who is bonded by one commonality—good grades (an A-average and at least a 3 on state reading and math tests). High performance on the SHSAT is a must, and a flair for ancient languages wouldn't hurt.

WHERE STUDENTS COME FROM

Students come to the school from all five boroughs of New York City.

BROOKLYN TECHNICAL HIGH SCHOOL

29 Fort Green Place, Brooklyn, NY 11217

Phone Number: 718-804-6400 • **Website:** www.bths.edu

Head of School: Randy Asher

ABOUT BROOKLYN TECHNICAL HIGH SCHOOL

Founded in 1922 by Dr. Albert L. Colston, Brooklyn Technical High School was instituted by a New York State legislative mandate and is open by competitive examination to all students of the City of New York. It describes its mission as a commitment "to inspire and challenge potentially high achievers to maximize their talents for the benefit of society."

Brooklyn Tech offers a core program in Regents-level courses and engineering. In addition, Advanced Placement courses in American history, biology, chemistry, calculus, computer science, economics, English, and physics are offered.

Brooklyn Tech prides itself on its many graduates who went on to become Nobel Prize laureates, corporate executives, city and state elected officials, university recognized scientists, engineers, architects and educators, as well as noted leaders in business, finance, industry, publishing, and the arts.

General

Type of School	Public
Religious Affiliation	None
Coeducational	Yes
Boarding	No
Day School	Yes
Dress Code	No
Founded	1922

Students

Enrollment (Grades 9–12)	4,700
% Male/Female	55/45
% African American	33
% Hispanic/Latino	17
% Asian	32
% Caucasian	18

Admissions Selectivity

Requires Standardized Test Scores	Yes
Application Essay	None

COMPARABLE SCHOOLS

Bronx High School of Science; Brooklyn Latin School; High School of American Studies at Lehman College; High School for Mathematics, Science and Engineering at City College; Queens High School for the Sciences at York College; Staten Island Technical High School; Stuyvesant High School

MISSION STATEMENT

Brooklyn Tech seeks to provide its students with the necessary tools and environment for educational, social and emotional growth while those with "superior scholastic aptitudes can develop their intellectual gifts and become committed to an examination of ethical approaches to solve world problems." Academic excellence is a key to success, and Brooklyn Tech endeavors to promote education as a means to "leadership and professional roles" not just in college but in life.

WHERE STUDENTS COME FROM

Students come from all five boroughs of New York City.

THE BROWNING SCHOOL

52 East Sixty-second Street, New York, NY 10021

Phone Number: 212-838-6280 • **Website:** www.browning.edu

Head of School: Stephen M. Clement III

About the Browning School

Founded in 1888, The Browning School still operates on the principles laid down by the distinguished scholar and teacher, John A. Browning, whose goal was to create a varied and comprehensive education for boys that instilled a feeling of self-reliance and a passion for learning. As one of his first students, John D. Rockefeller Jr., said of Mr. Browning: "[He] helped me to study and to concentrate.... I owe a great deal to him, more than to any other teacher I ever had." It is The Browning School's mission to continue this history of excellence.

Under the guidance of the school's fifth headmaster, Stephen M. Clement, III, Browning has continued to expand (its student body now more than double its size from fifty years ago), while also developing its vision of continued academic excellence and integrity for young men. The schools maintains its focus on small classes and close personal attention and has recently completed work on a new library, three new science laboratories, and additional classrooms. In addition, thanks to its membership in the Interschool consortium (consisting of Brearley, Chapin, Nightingale-Bamford, Dalton, Trinity, Spence, and Collegiate) as well as its affiliation with The Hewitt School and The Marymount School, Browning's students have been able to benefit from shared opportunities for academics, the arts, and social activities.

General	
Type of School	Private
Religious Affiliation	None
Coeducational	No
Boarding	No
Day School	Yes
Dress Code	Yes
Founded	1888

Students	
Enrollment (Grades 9–12)	360
% Male/Female	100/0

Academics

REQUIRED CLASSES

English, history, foreign languages, mathematics, science, visual arts, music, computer, health, physical education

Extracurricular

MOST POPULAR
INTERSCHOLASTIC SPORTS

Baseball, basketball, cross-country, soccer, tennis, track

Financial

Annual Tuition $29,496

**

MISSION STATEMENT

According to the school's website, The Browning School follows the goals of its founder, John A. Browning, namely in the "pursuit of academic excellence and a lifelong love of learning," the ideal of each person's individual dignity, the fostering of personal integrity in every student, and a sense of responsibility to communities both near and far. These values are instilled from a student's very first day at Browning, leading him to become "a good citizen" and caring, respectful individual of intelligent ideas and motives.

Subs

THE CALHOUN SCHOOL

443 West End Avenue, New York, NY 10024

Phone Number: 212-497-6500 • **Website:** www.calhoun.org

Head of School: Steve Nelson • **Director of Admissions:** Nancy Sherman

ABOUT THE CALHOUN SCHOOL

Founded in 1896, The Calhoun School seeks to develop in each student "a love of learning, the intellectual means to achieve learning, a high level of skill mastery, a belief in his or her self, respect for differences in people, and a commitment to the process of democracy." This commitment to progressive education finds expression in a broad appreciation of each student's unique development, learning style, and way of being in the world. The school community celebrates and nurtures each student's physical abilities, creativity, compassion, strength of character, good humor, and sense of social and economic justice. Such a challenging and supportive environment encourages students to take academic risks and value differences and strengths in others.

Students at Calhoun encounter a project-oriented, multicultural, and interdisciplinary curriculum that conveys a solid body of knowledge and values while allowing for teacher-developed materials on timely themes and age-appropriate subjects. Small classes (12-15) are discussion-based rather than teacher-dominated, and the flexible classrooms create a dynamic environment that supports collaborative learning and community among students and faculty. The fundamental tools for learning—the ability to read, research, analyze, compute, write, speak, and study—are firmly established and reinforced at every grade level. Students are encouraged to discover and pursue their passions through a breadth of co-curricular activities, independent study, honors courses, and study abroad opportunities. The school is equally committed to an environment where both mind and body are nurtured, as evidenced by the lunch program that has attracted international attention by developing good habits and sophisticated palates. The Green Roof Learning Center, recognized as a national role model for schools and public institutions, provides multiple ecological benefits while serving as an educational resource for botanical and environmental projects. Also, every student has a faculty advisor who plays the role of listener, advocate, and academic counselor. Easy access to the faculty and administration and open communication between family and school keep parents well apprised of their child's progress, and form the basis for the spirit of cooperation for which Calhoun is renowned.

General	
Type of School	Private
Religious Affiliation	None
Coeducational	Yes
Boarding	No
Day School	Yes
Dress Code	No
Founded	1896

Students	
Enrollment (Grades 2–12)	500
% Male/Female	50/50
% African American	6.6
% Hispanic/Latino	9
% Asian	7.4
% Caucasian	77

Academics

REQUIRED CLASSES

4 years: English, social studies, physical
education

3 years: Math, foreign language, science, fine arts

1 semester: Health education

ADDITIONAL REQUIREMENTS

60 hours of Community Service

Student/Faculty Ratio   7:1

Extracurricular

MOST POPULAR

INTERSCHOLASTIC SPORTS

MALE

Baseball, basketball, cross-country,
football, golf, soccer, tennis, track,
volleyball

FEMALE

Basketball, cross-country, golf, soccer,
softball, tennis, track, volleyball

Financial

Annual Tuition $29,900
% Students Receiving
  Financial Aid   20

*

MISSION STATEMENT

"Calhoun seeks to inspire a passion for learning in each child through a progressive approach to education that values intellectual pursuit, creativity, diversity, and community involvement."

THE IDEAL APPLICANT

The Calhoun School selects students who have "the potential to be focused and self-motivated, who have the aptitude and desire necessary to meet the demands of a challenging program, and who will be responsive to the values of the school community. The school seeks students who will bring a diversity of talents, backgrounds, and experiences."

WHERE STUDENTS COME FROM

The majority of students come from "the five boroughs and New Jersey; and a minority of students come from other states as well as countries outside of the Unites States."

ORIENTATION PROCESS FOR NEW STUDENTS

All incoming 9th graders and new 10th–12th grade students attend an orientation meeting prior to the official starting day of school. The orientation familiarizes students with all facets of the program as well as the building layout. Senior peer leaders also help faculty to guide the activities of the morning. Within the first few days of classes, 9th graders go on a camping trip, and 10th and 11th grade students take trips based on their curriculum. These excursions help students to get to know one another and form a cohesive and mutually-supportive class. Finally, throughout the school year, 9th graders participate in a seminar run by peer leaders called "Life Skills," which covers a wide range of topics from homework to areas of social and emotional concerns, all of interest to teenagers and new upper-school students.

Colleges that Recent Grads Are Attending

Amherst College, Bard College, Bates College, Beloit College, Boston University, Brandeis University, Brown University, Bryant College, Bryn Mawr College, Bucknell University, Centre College, Clark University, Connecticut College, Eckerd College, Emory University, Emerson College, Fordham University, Goucher College, Grinnell College, Harvard College, Hobart & William Smith College, Kenyon College, Mount Holyoke College, New York University, Northwestern University, Oberlin College, Rensselaer Polytechnic Institute, Sarah Lawrence College, Skidmore College, Smith College, Stanford University, State University of New York at Albany, Tufts University, University of Chicago, University of Michigan, Ursinus College, Utica College, Vassar College, Wesleyan University, Wheaton College

Alumni Say

In the words one alumnus, "Calhoun is an active place." Whether it's within or outside of the classroom, students are involved in "anything and everything" the school has to offer since "groups here are student run" and "fun." The "small classes" contribute to this atmosphere of "participation" with teachers "encouraging teamwork" and "fostering creative ways of thinking" in individual students. Simply put, at Calhoun "school is not a chore—it's an active learning experience."

CARDINAL HAYES HIGH SCHOOL

650 Grand Concourse, Bronx, NY 10451

Phone Number: 718-292-6100 • **Website:** www.cardinalhayes.org

Head of School: Br. Christopher J. Keogan • **Director of Admissions:** Olvin Caba

General

Type of School	Private
Religious Affiliation	Catholic
Coeducational	No
Boarding	No
Day School	Yes
Dress Code	Yes
Founded	1941

Students

Enrollment (Grades 9–12)	1,126
% Male/Female	100/0
% African American	34
% Hispanic/Latino	64
% Asian	1
% Caucasian	1

Admissions Selectivity

Requires Standardized Test Scores	Yes; TACHS
Application Essay	No

COMPARABLE SCHOOLS

Fordham; Loyola; Monsignor Scanlan; Regis; Rice; St. Agnes Boys; Xavier

ABOUT CARDINAL HAYES HIGH SCHOOL

Since its founding in 1941, the goal of Cardinal Hayes High School has been "to engender a life-long intellectual curiosity, awakening within the student the need for self-discipline, the value of personal integrity and the responsibility of engaged citizenship—all emerging from the tenets and principles of a faith-filled Catholic education." The school has the lowest annual tuition of any New York City Catholic high school ($4,900) and welcomes approximately 1,100 students every year. On average, 99 percent of students graduate and of those, 96 percent attend college or university. The school is also a member of the Middle States Association.

MISSION STATEMENT

Cardinal Hayes High School looks to academically challenge young Catholic men by nurturing individual talents and supporting self-development. Cardinal Hayes High School seeks to "inspire students to strive for personal excellence and responsible citizenship rooted within a Catholic framework and traditional Gospel values." They succeed in this through a "rigorous program of academics, extracurricular activities, discipline, and spiritual growth."

The Ideal Applicant

According to the school's website, Cardinal Hayes High School looks for students "interested in a Catholic education," with an emphasis on "spiritual formation, educational development, and recreational opportunities."

Orientation Process for New Students

An orientation meeting for freshman is held before the beginning of the school year.

Colleges that Recent Grads Are Attending

Boston College, Cornell University, Fordham University, Harvard University, Holy Cross College, Iona College, Manhattan College, New York University, Syracuse University, St. John's University

Academics

Required Classes

4 years: Religion, math, English, social studies
3 years: Foreign language, science
1 year: Art, music, health education

Student/Faculty Ratio   18:1

Extracurricular

Most Popular Interscholastic Sports

Baseball, basketball, bowling, cross-country, football, golf, soccer, track & field

Financial

Annual Tuition $4,900
% Students Receiving
    Financial Aid   33
             **

CATHEDRAL HIGH SCHOOL

350 East Fifty-sixth Street, New York, NY 10022

Phone Number: 212-688-1545 • **Website:** www.cathedralhs.org

Head of School: Sister Elizabeth Graham OP • **Director of Admissions:** Vincent Marino

General	
Type of School	Private
Religious Affiliation	Catholic
Coeducational	No
Day School	Yes
Dress Code	Yes
Founded	1905

Students	
Enrollment (Grades 9–12)	825
% Male/Female	0/100

ABOUT CATHEDRAL HIGH SCHOOL

Founded in 1905, Cathedral High School is an Archdiocesan Catholic college preparatory school that was created with the goal of providing young woman of all faiths future success through education. The school offers students "an excellent education at a very reasonable cost with tuition at only $5,675 per year." With a 17:1 student-faculty ratio and fifteen full-tuition scholarships, Cathedral is dedicated to providing young women an affordable and comprehensive education. The school is particularly proud of its "Gateways to Health" program, in which junior year students are given the opportunity to explore medical careers first as interns at medical facilities, and then they work "one-on-one" with professional mentors to help them in long-range career planning. Cathedral's faculty is highly accomplished, and possess among them "over fifty master's degrees, five of which have double master's, and one a PhD."

MISSION STATEMENT

"Cathedral High School, a Catholic college preparatory school of the Archdiocese of New York located in the heart of Manhattan, welcomes young women of all faiths and cultures. We are a community of students, teachers, staff, and parents committed to excellence in education, as well as the continued growth of our students in religious maturity, moral integrity, and a sense of social justice."

THE IDEAL APPLICANT

Cathedral High School seeks "young women with professional goals who have a desire to achieve academically and wish to grow spiritually and socially."

WHERE STUDENTS COME FROM

Students come to the school from "all five boroughs of New York City."

Orientation Process for New Students

Incoming students are invited to an open house and tour the school prior to the beginning of classes. Then, once school has started, students attend an orientation meeting and are assigned a student mentor.

Colleges that Recent Grads Are Attending

Adelphi University, Albertus Magnus College, Albright College, Alfred University, American International College, Arcadia University, Berkeley College, Boston College, Boston University, Brandeis University, Bryant College, Canisius College, City University of New York—Baruch College, City University of New York—Brooklyn College, City University of New York—Hunter College, City University of New York—John Jay College, City University of New York—Queens College, City University of New York—York College, Clark Atlanta University, College of Mount St. Vincent, College of New Rochelle, College of Notre Dame—Maryland, College of St. Rose, College of Westchester, Columbia University, Concordia College, Cornell University, Harvard University, New York University, Rochester Institute of Technology, Rutgers University, Sacred Heart University, Saint Leo University, Salem State College, Seton Hall University, Siena College, Simmons College, St. Francis College, St. John's University, St. Joseph College, St. Peter's College, St. Thomas Aquinas College, St. Thomas University, State University of New York at Albany, State University of New York at Binghamton, State University of New York—University at Buffalo, State University of New York—New Paltz, State University of New York—Oswego, State University of New York-Stony Brook University, Suffolk University, Swarthmore College, Syracuse University, Temple University, University of Bridgeport, University of Hartford, Yale University

Academics

Required Classes

4 years: Religion, English, social studies, physical education

3 years: Math, science

1 year: Foreign language, music/art

1 semester: Health education

Student/Faculty Ratio   17:1

Extracurricular

Most Popular Interscholastic Sports

Basketball, soccer, softball, tennis, volleyball

Financial

Annual Tuition $5,675

*

Students Say

One student notes, "We are like family." This environment is nurtured by faculty who teach students about "trust, friendships, and how not to get frustrated when learning something new." The end result being self-belief and a can-do attitude toward academics and life, and a school dedicated to "camaraderie" through a "sense of belonging."

Parents Say

Parents agree that "being in the right school at the right time" makes all the difference—a difference they and their children found at Cathedral with its "good quality education, solid Christian values, and financial assistance."

Alumni Say

Alumni remember Cathedral High School as "a place where the ideas and thoughts of young women were accepted and discussed—where our voices mattered and were heard." The "dedicated" faculty fostered "a sense of self-worth and assurance in all students," drawing the school's inspiration and uniqueness from a diverse group of young women whose "limits were imposed by intellect and not by prejudice or society." This "family-like atmosphere" brought all in the community together to "achieve, dream, and give back." The school itself is a perfect example of this belief as it "not only educated young women, but was educated by them."

No Positions

THE CHAPIN SCHOOL

100 East End Avenue, New York, NY 10028

Phone Number: 212-744-2335 • **Website:** www.chapin.edu
Head of School: Dr. Patricia T. Hayot • **Director of Admissions:** Tina Herman

ABOUT THE CHAPIN SCHOOL

Founded in 1901 by Maria Bowen Chapin, The Chapin School is an independent day school dedicated to "the intellectual and personal growth" of young women. With an alumni roster that ranges from Jackie O. to Ivanka Trump, students here find themselves fulfilling their academic and personal potential through a rigorous liberal arts program and illustrious school history. Enthusiasm, curiosity, integrity, and creativity are encouraged through a dedicated community of administrators, teachers, parents, alumni, and students, allowing the school and its students to thrive. In this respect, Chapin is committed to fostering diversity in its culture and program, and the school actively seeks families, faculty, and staff who bring a range of experiences to the school, as openness and respect for others is a hallmark of their educational process.

General	
Type of School	Private
Religious Affiliation	None
Coeducational	No
Boarding	No
Day School	Yes
Dress Code	Yes
Founded	1901

Students	
% Male/Female	0/100
% Caucasian	78
% Other	22

Students have a nearly endless supply of extracurricular activities to choose from, all of which play a major role in the development of strong, intelligent, and confident young women. The school also boasts forty-nine classrooms, a two-story library with a multimedia room and video editing room, six science laboratories, four art studios (including a photography darkroom and ceramics studio), two music studios, a black box theater, a dance studio, two computer laboratories, four gymnasiums, and a greenhouse.

MISSION STATEMENT

According to its website, The Chapin School is dedicated to offering young women the best education possible to ensure their success in any postsecondary-school endeavor they undertake. After graduation, Chapin students are ready to become leaders through their pursuit of "academic excellence, personal integrity, and community responsibility."

THE IDEAL APPLICANT

According to its website, The Chapin School seeks students with strong academic talent and a commitment to schoolwork. The school believes that "an equitable, inclusive community provides the strongest environment for learning," and that its diverse and welcoming student body fulfills this ideal.

Academics

REQUIRED CLASSES

English, foreign language, history, mathematics, science, computer science, physical education, arts (drama, dance, music, visual arts)

ADDITIONAL REQUIREMENTS

Public Speaking

Extracurricular

MOST POPULAR

INTERSCHOLASTIC SPORTS

Badminton, basketball, fencing, lacrosse, soccer, softball, squash, swimming, tennis, track, volleyball

Financial

Annual Tuition	$27,300
% Students Receiving Financial Aid	16

**

COLLEGES THAT RECENT GRADS ARE ATTENDING

American University, Amherst College, Bates College, Barnard College, Bennington College, Boston College, Bowdoin College, Brandeis University, Brown University, Bucknell University, Carleton College, Catholic University, Claremont McKenna College, Colby College, Colgate University, Colorado College, Columbia University, Connecticut College, Cornell University, Dartmouth College, Davidson College, Duke University, Emory University, Fairfield University, Georgetown University, Grinnell College, Hamilton College, Harvard University, Johns Hopkins University, Kenyon College, Lehigh University, Middlebury College, New York University, Northwestern University, Oberlin College, Ohio Wesleyan University, Pennsylvania State University, Pitzer College, Pomona College, Pratt Institute, Princeton University, Sarah Lawrence College, Skidmore College, Southern Methodist University, St. Lawrence University, Stanford University, Swarthmore College, Trinity College, Tufts University, Tulane University, University of Chicago, University of California—Los Angeles, University of California—Santa Cruz, University of Colorado—Boulder, University of Edinburgh, University of Michigan, University of North Carolina—Chapel Hill, University of Pennsylvania, University of Southern California, University of St. Andrews, University of Virginia, University of Wisconsin, Vanderbilt University, Washington University in St. Louis, Wesleyan University, Wheaton College, Williams College, Yale University

Special Ed.

THE CHILD SCHOOL LEGACY HIGH SCHOOL

587 Main Street, Roosevelt Island, NY 10044

Phone Number: 212-223-5055 • **Website:** www.thechildschool.org

Head of School: Maari de Souza • **Director of Admissions:** Sheila Steiner

ABOUT THE CHILD SCHOOL LEGACY HIGH SCHOOL

The Child School Legacy High School is "an academically rigorous yet supportive community serving children with special needs. We focus on awakening students to the fact that learning is a wondrous, enjoyable activity, and that the unfamiliar presents an exciting frontier. A core part of the school's curriculum is helping the bright student realize their potential while offering remediation to fill in conceptual gaps for those who need it. Students' personality and interests are addressed. Within the classroom, psychologists, a speech therapist, and an occupational therapist partner with the teacher on lessons that develop each child's special talents academic and otherwise and work together to enhance problem-solving skills and to develop a code of ethics and values to guide each student through life."

MISSION STATEMENT

"We offer a unique academic/therapeutic community where children with learning disabilities can achieve their maximum intellectual and emotional potential. We embrace the total child, in the belief that their self-image, motivation, and ability to interact are critical to their ultimate success. Our students have disorders in thinking, listening, speaking, reading, spelling, and/or perception. We develop each child's self-concept, not only an understanding of the disability, but a heightened self-awareness through social interaction. In a highly structured, family-like atmosphere we encourage three principles: learning, compassion, and respect. We provide children and their families hope; a vision of a bright future. The school fulfills a vital function by serving children whose special needs cannot be met elsewhere."

General	
Type of School	Private
Religious Affiliation	None
Coeducational	Yes
Boarding	No
Day School	Yes
Dress Code	Yes
Founded	1973

Students	
Enrollment (Grades K–12)	275
% Male/Female	75/25
% African American	22
% Hispanic/Latino	26
% Asian	2
% Caucasian	46
% Other	4

Admissions Selectivity	
Applications Received	500
# Applicants Accepted	50
# Accepted Applicants Who Enrolled	50
Requires Standardized Test Scores	No
Application Essay	Yes

COMPARABLE SCHOOLS

Winston Churchill Prep, Summit

Academics

REQUIRED CLASSES

The Child School Legacy High School follows the NY State Board of Regents guidelines for graduation and students take either the Regents or RCT exams. Classes include literature, social studies, history, math, science, Spanish, art, phys and health ed, computers, and electives. AP courses are available off campus.

Student/Faculty Ratio 12:2

Extracurricular

MOST POPULAR
INTERSCHOLASTIC SPORTS
MALE
Basketball, soccer, softball, track
FEMALE
Basketball, soccer, softball, track
% Students Who Play Interscholastic Sports 39

Financial

Annual Tuition $27,050
% Students Receiving
  Financial Aid 98
  *

THE IDEAL APPLICANT

"Our students have IEP classifications of learning disabled, speech and language impaired, or emotionally fragile and have either average or above-average intelligence."

WHERE STUDENTS COME FROM

"Our students come from all five boroughs of New York City, as well as from Nassau and Westchester Counties."

COLLEGES THAT RECENT GRADS ARE ATTENDING

City University of New York, City University of New York—Borough of Manhattan Community College, Claflin University, Culinary Institute of America, Marymount College, Mercy College, New York University, Pratt Institute, Rochester Institute of Technology, School of Visual Arts, Seton Hall University, St. Francis College, St. John's University, State University of New York, State University of New York—Fashion Institute of Technology

STUDENTS SAY

Students looking to escape "the swarming chaos of New York City" love The Child School, where "everyone knows everyone." The "wonderful, sweet, and helpful" teachers go "all the way to help you" with their "unique way of teaching" that makes "learning fun" while "preparing students for the real world." By guiding with "compassion, respect, and patience," the faculty provides children with positive examples of "how to be a leader and not a follower," and the headmaster, Maari de Souza, is a favorite with "the nice trips she plans to Costa Rica and Panama" and the "June Play."

Parents Say

One of the main factors in parents' decisions to send their children to The Child School is "the nurturing yet academically rich environment" that gives "individualized attention to each student's needs." This belief that "each student can succeed" is bolstered by a program that utilizes "creative methods of working with the student to address not only their weaknesses but also their strengths" in a "caring, positive environment." Parents also appreciate the "June Play" and "spring trips" that combine "social and academic skills outside of the classroom." As one parent notes, "the spring trip offered a very unique and well structured opportunity to improve our son's social skills while developing independence." Ultimately, "the decision to enroll is easy" thanks to "the staff and administration's outlook, philosophy, and flexible approach to education" in developing "academically enriched programs in which each student can thrive."

Alumni Say

As a former student says, "The defining characteristic of The Child School is its extraordinary teachers and teaching methods," not to mention the "extremely fun and interesting" chance to "experience a different culture" during a trip to Morocco, and "being part of the June Play."

Special Ed.

THE CHURCHILL SCHOOL

301 East Twenty-ninth Street, New York, NY 10016

Phone Number: 212-722-0610 • **Website:** www.churchillschool.com

Head of School: Kristine Baxter • **Director of Admissions:** Wendy Federico

General

Type of School	Private
Religious Affiliation	None
Coeducational	Yes
Boarding	No
Day School	Yes
Dress Code	Yes
Founded	1972

Students

Enrollment (Grades 9–12)	144
% Male/Female	60/40

Admissions Selectivity

COMPARABLE SCHOOLS

The Gateway School, The Windward School, The Stephen Gaynor School

ABOUT THE CHURCHILL SCHOOL

The Churchill School was founded in 1972 as an elementary school for children with specific learning disabilities. The school proved to be such a success that a middle school was added and then in 2000, The Churchill High School was opened. The school's students are children of "average to above-average intelligence who have specific learning disabilities," and whose progress in a traditional institution may have been hindered by language or reading disabilities, attention difficulties, or perceptual/motor weaknesses. As such, they most often benefit from the "smaller, more individualized and therapeutic learning environment" that Churchill offers in order to help them best achieve their academic potential. Classes are limited to twelve students and staffed with a head teacher and an assistant teacher, so that any student needs can be efficiently addressed. The school boasts a multitude of state-of-the-art facilities, including a multimedia library, two computer labs, a regulation-size gymnasium and large auditorium, three science labs, three art studios, occupational therapy rooms, and a sky-top playground. Churchill is chartered by the New York State Department of Education, and accredited by NYSAIS, as an independent, nonprofit, coeducational day school, offering a comprehensive education at the elementary, middle, and high school levels. In 2004, the board of Regents granted full registration status to The Churchill High School. Churchill is also on the State Education List of approved, nonpublic schools.

Mission Statement

"At Churchill, our goal is to educate every student with a program emphasizing academic and social growth. Churchill's programs are constructed to capitalize on each child's strengths, aptitudes, and affinities while at the same time encouraging growth specific areas of weakness. Full attention is paid to the learning differences that distinguish each child. Our students become aware of their many strengths, work hard on their learning problems, and develop strategies to help them become self-confident and successful members of the community."

Where Students Come From

The Churchill School's students come from "all five boroughs of New York City, as well as from Westchester, Long Island, and New Jersey."

Academics

REQUIRED CLASSES

4 years: English, history
3 years: Math, science, Career
    Development
2 years: Physical education
1 year: Art, health education

Student/Faculty Ratio   6:1

Extracurricular

MOST POPULAR
INTERSCHOLASTIC SPORTS
MALE

Basketball, cross-country, soccer, softball, track

FEMALE

Basketball, cross-country, soccer, softball, track

Financial

Annual Tuition $32,500

*

Science?

COLLEGIATE SCHOOL

206 West Seventy-eighth Street, New York, NY 10024

Phone Number: 212-815-8500 • **Website:** www.collegiateschool.org

Head of School: John W. Beall • **Director of Admissions:** Kathleen J. Sullivan

General	
Type of School	Private
Religious Affiliation	None
Coeducational	No
Boarding	No
Day School	Yes
Dress Code	Yes
Founded	1628

Students	
% Male/Female	100/0
% Caucasian	70
% Other	30

ABOUT THE COLLEGIATE SCHOOL

Founded in 1628 by the Reformed Protestant Dutch Church, the Collegiate School is the oldest independent school in the United States. Located next to the West End Collegiate Church on the Upper West Side of Manhattan, the school is nondenominational though it maintains its historic ties with this church and shares its facilities.

The school prides itself on developing students' independence and confidence by impressing upon them that the responsibility for their academic and lifelong success belongs to themselves alone. They are guided in this process by a dedicated team of advisors, teachers, administrators, and parents, ensuring their passage from young men of promise to adults of distinction.

MISSION STATEMENT

According to the school's website, the Collegiate School strives to help students reach their "highest level of intellectual, ethical, artistic, and physical development." By offering a rigorous academic program that encourages boys to develop their talents and interests "in a climate of collaboration and respect," Collegiate fulfills its historic tradition of nurturing a diverse student body and, come graduation, introducing "independent adults and responsible citizens" to the world.

WHERE STUDENTS COME FROM

Collegiate School's students come from all five boroughs of New York City, as well as from Westchester, Long Island, and New Jersey.

Colleges that Recent Grads Are Attending

Amherst College, Bard College, Bates College, Boston College, Boston University, Bowdoin College, Brandeis University, Brown University, Carleton University, Carnegie Mellon University, Case Western Reserve, Colby College, Colgate University, Columbia University, Connecticut College, Cornell University, Dartmouth University, Davidson College, Duke University, Embry Riddle Aeronautical University, Emerson College, Emory University, Georgetown University, George Washington University, Gettysburg College, Hamilton College, Harvard University, Haverford College, Johns Hopkins University, Kenyon College, Lehigh University, Macalester College, Massachusetts Institute of Technology, McGill University, Middlebury College, Morehouse College, Muhlenberg College, New York University, Northwestern University, Oberlin College, Oxford University, Pennsylvania State University, Pomona College, Princeton University, Sarah Lawrence University, Skidmore College, Stanford University, Swarthmore College, Tufts University, Tulane University, Union College, United States Naval Academy, University of Arizona, University of Pennsylvania, University of St. Andrews, University of Virginia, Vanderbilt University, Vassar College, Wesleyan University, Williams College, Yale University

Extracurricular

MOST POPULAR INTERSCHOLASTIC SPORTS

Baseball, basketball, lacrosse, soccer track, tennis, wrestling

Financial

Annual Tuition	$27,100

**

COLUMBIA GRAMMAR AND PREPARATORY SCHOOL

Five West Ninety-third Street, New York, NY 10025

Phone Number: 212-749-6200 • **Website:** www.cgps.org

Head of School: Dr. Richard J. Soghoian • **Director of Admissions:** Simone Hristidis

General

Type of School	Private
Religious Affiliation	None
Coeducational	Yes
Boarding	No
Day School	Yes
Dress Code	No
Founded	1764

Students

Enrollment (Grades 9–12)	541
% Male/Female	50/50
% African American	4
% Hispanic/Latino	5
% Asian	4
% Caucasian	87

Admissions Selectivity

Requires Standardized Test Scores	Yes

ABOUT COLUMBIA GRAMMAR AND PREPARATORY SCHOOL

Founded in 1764, Columbia Grammar School was originally established as a boys' preparatory school for Kings College (now Columbia University) and became a coed institution in 1956. As a school, they are firmly committed to coeducation, believing that "boys and girls learn more effectively and successfully together—not separately."

The school has one of the lowest student/faculty ratios of any school in New York City, creating an atmosphere of small classes and personal attention to each child's needs. In the words of its headmaster, "the quality of our teachers and academic program are the keys to our success as a school." Over the past decade, they have developed an impressive core of teachers whose "energy, enthusiasm, and love of learning" are reflected in every aspect of school life.

In the last decade, Columbia has expanded, opening two new buildings with a variety of facilities, from a state-of-the-art theater to computer and science labs, five art studios (including filmmaking and photography), a third library, and a host of other academic areas. These new facilities have allowed the school an opportunity "to create an enriched and exciting curriculum." While their requirements and expectations in the traditional areas of English, history, math, science, and foreign languages are demanding, their offerings in art, music, and theater, along with an extensive physical education and athletic program, allow students to develop all aspects of their interests and talents.

Mission Statement

Columbia Grammar and Preparatory School is committed to providing students, families, and the larger world with "well-educated, responsible, caring, and productive" individuals. This goal is achieved through a rigorous curriculum that places a emphasis on art, music, drama, and the development of "good character, standards of conduct, and sense of social responsibility within the school community." As the school's website states, "Cultivating our students' minds, supplying them with a substantial fund of knowledge and providing them with the basis for making sound ethical judgments remain the foundations of the school's philosophy and mission."

The Ideal Applicant

Students are chosen for their maturity, ability to work under a challenging academic program, and "potential for growth in a social environment devoted to creating an appreciation and concern for others."

Where Students Come From

Students come from all five boroughs of New York City as well as Long Island, Westchester County, and New Jersey.

Academics	
Required Classes	
4 years	English, history, math
3 years	Science, foreign language
1 year	Art/music/theater history
Student/Faculty Ratio	7:1

Extracurricular

Most Popular

Interscholastic Sports

Male

Baseball, basketball, cross-country, golf, ice hockey, soccer, tennis, track

Female

Basketball, cross-country, golf, soccer, softball, swimming, tennis, track, volleyball

% Students Who Play Interscholastic Sports	63

Financial

Annual Tuition	$29,000
Endowment	$16 million
**	

Colleges that Recent Grads Are Attending

Arizona State University, Art Institute of Chicago, Bard College, Bates College, Boston University, Brown University, Clark University, Colgate University, Columbia University, Connecticut College, Cornell University, Emerson University, Emory University, Fordham University, George Washington University, Gettysburg College, Goucher College, Indiana University, Johns Hopkins University, Lafayette College, Lehigh University, Muhlenberg, New York University, Northeastern University, Northwestern University, Oberlin College, Parsons School of Design, Princeton University, Rochester Institute of Technology, Rollins College, Skidmore College, Syracuse University, Tulane University, University of Arizona, University of Iowa, University of Michigan, University of Pennsylvania, University of Rochester, University of Southern California, University of Vermont, University of Wisconsin, Vanderbilt University, Vassar College, Washington University in St. Louis, Wesleyan University, Wheaton College

CONVENT OF THE SACRED HEART

One East Ninety-first Street, New York, NY 10128

Phone Number: 212-722-4745 • **Website:** www.cshnyc.org

Head of School: Patricia C. Hult • **Director of Admissions:** Barbara S. Root

General	
Type of School	Private
Religious Affiliation	Catholic
Coeducational	No
Boarding	No
Day School	Yes
Dress Code	Yes
Founded	1881

Students	
Enrollment (Grades 9–12)	650
% Male/Female	0/100

ABOUT CONVENT OF THE SACRED HEART

The Convent of the Sacred Heart is New York City's oldest independent school for girls, established in 1881 by the Society of the Sacred Heart. It is part of a worldwide network of over 150 schools committed to the mission of Sacred Heart education. From its inception, Convent of the Sacred Heart was governed by a strong commitment to the education of the whole child, addressing her intellectual, spiritual, social, and emotional development.

Enrollment currently stands at 650 young women from the prekindergarten through grade 12. The curriculum is recognized for its rigor and depth, and the academic program is accredited by both the National Association of Independent Schools and the New York Association of Independent Schools. The school recently completed an ambitious, multiyear construction and renovation project that provides students with state-of-the-art facilities in science, technology, and the arts.

The school has proven its excellence in interscholastic sports, with teams ranking at the top of the Athletic Association of Independent Schools by combining solid instruction with an emphasis on team play and good sportsmanship.

Mission Statement

The educational policies at Covent of the Sacred Heart are governed by the "Goals and Criteria": the set of principles that express the values, intentions, and hopes of the Sacred Heart tradition. The school commits itself to "a personal and active faith in God, a deep respect for intellectual values, a social awareness which impels to action, the building of community as a Christian value, and encouraging personal growth in an atmosphere of wise freedom."

Colleges that Recent Grads Are Attending

Barnard College, Brown University, Cornell University, Georgetown University, Harvard University, Johns Hopkins University, Princeton University, Wesleyan University, Yale University

Academics

REQUIRED CLASSES

4 years: Religion, English, physical education

3 years: Math, social studies, science, foreign language

1 year: Performing arts/visual arts/technology

ADDITIONAL REQUIREMENTS

Community Service

Extracurricular

MOST POPULAR

INTERSCHOLASTIC SPORTS

Basketball, cross-country, lacrosse, soccer, softball, swimming, tennis, track & field, volleyball

Financial

Annual Tuition $13,860–$25,545

*

THE DALTON SCHOOL

108 East Eighty-ninth Street, New York, NY 10128

Phone Number: 212-423-5462 • **Website:** www.dalton.org

Head of School: Ellen Stein • **Director of Admissions:** Elizabeth Krents

General	
Type of School	Private
Religious Affiliation	None
Coeducational	Yes
Boarding	No
Day School	Yes
Dress Code	Yes
Founded	1919

Students	
% Male/Female	50/50

ABOUT THE DALTON SCHOOL

Founded in 1919 by the renowned progressive educator Helen Parkhurst, The Dalton School is an independent, coeducational day school, located on Manhattan's Upper East Side. "The Dalton Plan" remains the keystone of the school's progressive educational philosophy and is now the model for over two hundred Dalton schools in other parts of the world.

Dalton is recognized for its rigorous, innovative educational curriculum and offers its students a breadth of stimulating and challenging programs taught by a dedicated faculty. Their high academic standards are complemented by a vibrant fine arts program and impressive number of athletic and extracurricular activities.

The Dalton School is committed to providing an unparalleled education that promotes each student's individual talents while supporting a diverse and caring environment. It is the school's goal to challenge each student to develop intellectual independence, creativity, curiosity, and a sense of responsibility toward others both within the institution and the community at large. Guided by the Dalton Plan, the school well prepares students to, in the words of its motto, "go forth unafraid."

Mission Statement

According to the school's website, The Dalton School seeks to offer to students and instill in them a commitment to education and excellence in line with their particular interests, talents, needs, and abilities. In this, the school guides students academically and emotionally through "a common curricular framework" that promotes the understanding and appreciation of diversity both locally, nationally, and globally. Dalton's goal is "to challenge each student to develop intellectual independence, creativity, and curiosity," along with a demonstrated belief in caring for the community that surrounds them.

The Ideal Applicant

The school's website states that while there is no "Dalton type" of child, its students share in common strong academic performance, inquisitive minds, and the ability to work well in an environment that will challenge them and encourage them to think for themselves. Students are expected to actively engage themselves in "the learning process and acquire knowledge through direct experience and primary sources."

Colleges that Recent Grads Are Attending

Amherst College, Bard College, Barnard College, Bates College, Boston University, Bowdoin College, Brown University, Carnegie Mellon University, Colby College, Colgate University, Columbia University, Connecticut College, The Cooper Union for the Advancement of Science and Art, Cornell University, Dartmouth University, Duke University, Emory University, Fordham University, George Washington University, Harvard University, Hamilton College, Johns Hopkins University, Kenyon College, Lehigh University, Northwestern University, Oberlin College, Princeton University, Skidmore College, Smith College, Stanford University, Swarthmore College, Syracuse University, Trinity College, Tufts University, University of Chicago, University of Michigan, University of Pennsylvania, University of Rochester, University of Virginia, University of Wisconsin, Washington University in St. Louis, Wellesley College, Wesleyan University, Williams College, Vassar College, Yale University

Academics
Required Classes
4 years: English, physical education
3 years: History, foreign language, math
2 years: Art
1 year: Health education

Additional Requirements
Community Service

Extracurricular
Most Popular
Interscholastic Sports
Male
Basketball, cross-country, football, lacrosse, tennis, soccer, swimming, track & field
Female
Basketball, cross-country, lacrosse, tennis, softball, soccer, swimming, track & field, volleyball

Financial
Annual Tuition	$29,250
% Students Receiving Financial Aid	20
**	

DAYTOP PREPARATORY SCHOOL

54 West Fortieth Street, New York, NY 10018

Phone Number: 212-354-6000 • **Website:** www.daytop.org

Head of School: Michael Shulman

General

Type of School	Private
Religious Affiliation	None
Coeducational	Yes
Boarding	Yes
Day School	Yes
Dress Code	No
Founded	1919

Students

Enrollment (Grades 9–12)	147
% African American	35
% Hispanic/Latino	28
% Asian	1
% Caucasian	36

Academics

Student/Faculty Ratio	7:1

**

ABOUT DAYTOP PREPARATORY SCHOOL

Daytop Preparatory School is a registered nonpublic school in New York State for adolescents who are in of treatment for problems related to alcohol and substance abuse. The school has a dual function in rehabilitation and education, giving students the opportunity to work toward a high school diploma, take the Regents and other standardized tests, and eventually transfer credits to the student's home school district.

Daytop has a high success rate in its admirable goal as 92 percent of students who participate in Regent Exams pass and proceed to their next grade level. As school officials explain, "Our students typically have not experienced success in school prior to coming into Daytop. Our small classes and individual instruction make school a positive experience as they target personal goals specific to each student's academic plan."

MISSION STATEMENT

Daytop Preparatory School is committed to "addressing the substance abuse and life problems of adolescents and adults." Daytop insists that individuals take responsibility for their actions and behavior, yet understand that such endeavors cannot be completed alone. Through a positive support network, involving peer interaction in a highly structured familial environment known as a "Therapeutic Community," the school offers a multidisciplinary program of education and treatment. Daytop is determined to return students to society as productive, responsible, and drug-free citizens with designs on further education.

THE IDEAL APPLICANT

Adolescents who enter the Daytop program often have many types of behavioral issues with regards to family, social, or educational environments, some of which were exacerbated by substance abuse.

DOMINICAN ACADEMY

44 East Sixty-eighth Street, New York, NY 10021

Phone Number: 212-744-0195 • **Website:** www.dominicanacademy.org

Head of School: Sister Joan Franks

ABOUT THE DOMINICAN ACADEMY

Founded in 1897 by the Dominican Sisters of Saint Mary of the Springs, the Dominican Academy still carries on its mission to deliver to young women "quality education, social development, and personal growth through the integration of Christian values."

The school is accredited by the New York Board of Regents, the Middle States Association for Secondary Schools, and in 1996 was awarded a Blue Ribbon School of Excellence by the United States Department of Education, placing the academy as "one of the best secondary schools in the entire United States." Among its twenty-nine faculty members, all twenty-nine have masters degrees and one has a PhD.

MISSION STATEMENT

According to the school's website, the mission of Dominican Academy is "to educate young women through their spiritual, intellectual, aesthetic, moral, physical and social development in a diverse society." As a Catholic college preparatory school in the tradition of Saint Dominic, the Academy combines a challenging curriculum with the teachings of the Catholic faith so as to best inform and enlighten their students in the process of nurturing "responsible, self-respecting citizens and truth seekers, who are aware of their own needs and gifts and responsive to the needs of others."

WHERE STUDENTS COME FROM

Dominican Academy students come from all five boroughs of New York City, as well as New Jersey, Westchester County, and Long Island.

General

Type of School	Private
Religious Affiliation	Catholic
Coeducational	No
Boarding	No
Day School	Yes
Dress Code	Yes
Founded	1897

Students

Enrollment (Grades 9–12)	260
% Male/Female	0/100
% African American	5
% Hispanic/Latino	26
% Asian	11
% Caucasian	59

Academics

REQUIRED CLASSES

4 years: Religion, English, social studies, physical education/dance

3 years: Math, foreign language (including Latin), science

1 year: Music/drama

1 semester: Health education

Student/Faculty Ratio	9:1

Extracurricular

MOST POPULAR INTERSCHOLASTIC SPORTS

Basketball, cross-country, soccer, softball, swimming, tennis, track & field, volleyball

Financial

Annual Tuition	$8,500
**	

THE DWIGHT SCHOOL

291 Central Park West, New York, NY 10024

Phone Number: 212-724-6360 • **Website:** www.dwight.edu

Head of School: Stephen H. Spahn • **Director of Admissions:** Marina Bernstein

General

Type of School	Private
Religious Affiliation	None
Coeducational	Yes
Boarding	No
Day School	Yes
Dress Code	Yes
Founded	1872

Students

Enrollment (Grades 9–12)	250
% Male/Female	54/46
% African American	5
% Hispanic/Latino	5
% Asian	3
% Caucasian	87
% International Students	25
# Countries Represented	40

Admissions Selectivity

Applications Received	300
# Applicants Accepted	80
# Accepted Applicants Who Enrolled	50
Requires Standardized Test Scores	Yes
Application Essay	Yes
Median SAT	1205

About the Dwight School

Founded in 1872, The Dwight School is a private international school located on Manhattan's Upper West Side. Dwight's rigorous IB program and world-class faculty prepare a future generation of "well-educated and ethical global leaders who will seek to create an environment of equality and respect for all human beings." The school believes and expects that its students will one day use "their unique 'spark of genius' to build a better world." Dwight also became the first school in North America to offer the full International Baccalaureate (IB) program from kindergarten through the 12th grade, and it is in this pioneering spirit that Dwight continues to serve as a trailblazer in international education.

In addition, Dwight has a sister school in London, The Woodside Park International School, that also offers all three International Baccalaureate programs. Families are assured places who move between London and New York. This formal exchange program has gone on between the schools for more than thirty years.

Mission Statement

"Through the International Baccalaureate Program, Dwight's goal is to educate globally-minded individuals who are curious, caring, principled leaders. Dwight students and faculty strive to live that credo daily."

The Ideal Applicant

The ideal Dwight School student is "an open-minded young person with a sincere interest in learning, and a spark of interest that can be fanned to illuminate the student's full array of talents."

Where Students Come From

Students come to The Dwight School from "forty different countries and study twelve foreign languages."

Orientation Process for New Students

Incoming students have the opportunity to start their Dwight experience during the summer vacation by building houses for the indigenous population in Lima, Peru or by constructing local schools in Kenya. In early September, all new 9th graders spend a day on a ropes course and later that week, grades 9 through 12 spend a day immersed in "outward bound" adventures. This provides a way for faculty and students to develop deeper bonds before formal classes start.

Colleges that Recent Grads Are Attending

Barnard College, Brown University, Carnegie Mellon University, Columbia University, Cornell University, Dartmouth University, Fordham University, Harvard University, Hebrew University, Julliard School, Massachusetts Institute of Technology, McGill University, New York University, Princeton University, Ohio Wesleyan University, Oxford University, Tokyo University, University of Brussels, University of Chicago, University of Edinburgh, University of London, University of Pennsylvania, University of Rome, Yale University

Academics

Required Classes
International Baccalaureate
Course Study Program

Additional Requirements
Community service, a two-year theory-of-knowledge philosophy course, a 4,000-word research essay, and a personal project for all 10th graders

Student/Faculty Ratio	6:1

Extracurricular

Most Popular Interscholastic Sports

Male
Baseball, basketball, cross-country, soccer, tennis, track & field

Female
Basketball, cross-country, soccer, tennis, track & field, volleyball

% Students Who Play Interscholastic Sports	50

Financial

Annual Tuition	$26,250 (Grades 9–10)
	$26,850 (Grades 11–12)
Endowment	$6 million
% Students Receiving Financial Aid	15
*	

Students Say

Students note that Dwight is "a home away from home" because they always feel "comfortable" and "welcomed by students, teachers, and administrators alike." This "supportive community" motivates students to excel academically, leaving them "encouraged to take risks" thanks to the "helpful" faculty who "want their students to succeed." It's this "personal approach toward learning" that inspires and entertains students, who knew they had picked the right school "the minute [they] arrived."

Parents Say

Parents of Dwight students appreciate the large amount of extracurricular activities and events, such as the "entertaining" auction that gives everyone the chance "to get to know each other better." And it's this combination of the educational and entertaining that make Dwight such a success in parents' eyes. In the words of one parent, "no other school in this country . . . can offer such a variety of educational opportunities to its students."

Alumni Say

Alumni credit Dwight with teaching them "a lot beyond the classroom," making them "kinder, stronger, and wiser" individuals as a result. Former students miss the "family feeling" they experienced while there, and remain "proud to be a part of a class that was so creative, giving, daring, enthusiastic, passionate, and unique." The lessons learned in this "sharing and caring" atmosphere remain as true today as they were when taught. As an alumnus explains, "I love Dwight because it gave me the chance to try things I had never done before."

THE FIELDSTON SCHOOL

Fieldston Road, Bronx, NY 10471

Phone Number: 212-329-7300 • **Website:** www.ecfs.org

Head of School: Dr. Joseph P. Healey • **Director of Admissions:** Taisha Thompson

ABOUT THE FIELDSTON SCHOOL

Founded in 1878 by Felix Adler, creator of the New York Society for Ethical Culture, The Fieldston School was opened—and has since operated—with the belief that a personalized and hands-on education elicits the most profound results from students. This program implements a varied curriculum that includes geography, history, nature study, fine arts, creative writing, arts and crafts, woodworking, and field trips.

A firm believer in education for all, regardless of class, gender, or race, Felix Adler dedicated fifty-five years of his life to building an institution that would promote academic excellence, creativity, and comprehension. This commitment to diversity in the composition of the community and curriculum remains central to the mission of the school. Students come to the campuses from a wide range of cultural, racial, religious, and socioeconomic backgrounds. To help ensure its founder's vision remains intact, the school supports a strong financial aid program—one of the largest of any independent coed day school in the country. A diverse group of students, faculty, staff, parents, and alumni participates actively in the school.

General

Type of School	Private
Religious Affiliation	None
Coeducational	Yes
Boarding	No
Day School	Yes
Dress Code	Yes
Founded	1878

Students

Enrollment (Grades 9–12)	519
% African American	8
% Hispanic/Latino	8
% Asian	8
% Caucasian	76

Admissions Selectivity

Requires Standardized Test Scores	Yes
Application Essay	None

COMPARABLE SCHOOLS

Horace Mann, Riverdale Country

MISSION STATEMENT

In the words of The Fieldston School's founder, the philosopher and humanist, Felix Adler, "The ideal of the school is to develop individuals who will be competent to change their environment to greater conformity with moral ideals."

Academics

REQUIRED CLASSES

4 years	English, physical education
3 years	Math, foreign language
2 years	Art, history, science
1 semester	Health education

ADDITIONAL REQUIREMENTS

Ethics and Community Service

Student/Faculty Ratio	9:1

Extracurricular

MOST POPULAR
INTERSCHOLASTIC SPORTS
MALE

Baseball, basketball, field hockey, football, lacrosse, soccer, swimming, tennis, track & field

FEMALE

Basketball, field hockey, lacrosse, soccer, softball, swimming, tennis, track & field, volleyball

Financial

Annual Tuition	$28,545
% Students Receiving Financial Aid	25
**	

ORIENTATION PROCESS FOR NEW STUDENTS

Orientation meetings and field trips are held for new students prior and after the start of classes.

COLLEGES THAT RECENT GRADS ARE ATTENDING

Antioch College, Bard College, Barnard College, Bates College, Bowdoin College, Brandeis University, Brown University, Bryn Mawr College, Carleton College, Colgate University, Columbia University, Cornell University, Dartmouth College, Drew University, Duke University, Emory University, Franklin & Marshall College, George Washington University, Gettysburg College, Harvard University, Haverford College, Hobart & William Smith College, Indiana University, Julliard School, Kenyon College, Macalester College, Marymount College, Middlebury College, Massachusetts Institute of Technology, McGill University, New York University, Northwestern University, Oberlin College, Pomona College, Reed College, Rutgers University, Sarah Lawrence College, Skidmore College, State University of New York—Binghamton, State University of New York—Stony Brook University, Swarthmore College, Syracuse University, Tufts University, Union College, University of Chicago, University of Maine, University of Michigan, University of Missouri, University of Pennsylvania, University of Redlands, University of Virginia, University of Wisconsin, Vanderbilt University, Vassar College, Washington University in St. Louis, Wellesley College, Wesleyan University, Williams College, Yale University

FIORELLO H. LAGUARDIA HIGH SCHOOL OF MUSIC & ART AND PERFORMING ARTS

100 Amsterdam Avenue, New York, NY 10023

Phone Number: 212-496-0700 • **Website:** www.laguardiahs.org

Head of School: Kim M. Bruno

ABOUT FIORELLO H. LAGUARDIA HIGH SCHOOL OF MUSIC & ART AND PERFORMING ARTS

Founded in 1936 by New York City Mayor Fiorello H. LaGuardia, the High School of Music & Art and Performing Arts was the first school in the nation to provide a free, publicly funded program for students with exceptional talent in the arts. Since its inception, the school has attracted students looking to pursue their passion in art, music, or performing arts, while at the same time fulfilling their academic requirements. As LaGuardia Arts is a specialized school in the arts, admission to the program relies heavily on auditions. Applying students must complete an audition in their particular area of interest in order to be considered for entrance.

Some of the school's special academic programs include pre-conservatory studios, an honors program, Advanced Placement courses in all academics, a peer tutoring program, internships in the arts, and a law studies and debate team.

General	
Type of School	Public
Religious Affiliation	None
Coeducational	Yes
Boarding	No
Day School	Yes
Dress Code	No
Founded	1936

Students	
Enrollment (Grades 9–12)	2,464
% African American	18
% Hispanic/Latino	20
% Asian	18
% Caucasian	46

Admissions Selectivity	
Requires Audition	Yes

COMPARABLE SCHOOLS

Professional Children's School

Academics
REQUIRED CLASSES
4 years: English, social studies, physical education
3 years: Math, science
1 year: Foreign language

Extracurricular
MOST POPULAR
INTERSCHOLASTIC SPORTS
MALE
Baseball, basketball, cross-country, fencing, gymnastics, soccer, tennis, track, volleyball
FEMALE
Basketball, bowling, cross-country, fencing, handball, gymnastics, soccer, softball, swimming, tennis, track, volleyball

Financial
Annual Tuition   None

**

MISSION STATEMENT

The school aims to provide each student with solid professional preparation in their chosen art along with an impressive college preparatory education. This fulfills the school's dual mission to educate and inspire gifted artists and talented students.

ORIENTATION PROCESS FOR NEW STUDENTS

Beginning in May, a series of orientation meetings are held for incoming students and their parents, during which issues involving the successful transition to high school, academics, college, career planning, and scheduling, are discussed. Each arts studio also presents an overview of its specific requirements during these meetings, and in order to answer any questions the parents might have, the Parents Association (PA) holds a special session to provide an insider's perspective to the school.

FORDHAM PREPARATORY SCHOOL

East Fordham Road, Bronx, NY 10458

Phone Number: 718-292-6100 • **Website:** www.fordhamprep.org

Head of School: Robert Gomprecht • **Director of Admissions:** Christopher Lauber

ABOUT FORDHAM PREPARATORY SCHOOL

Founded by the Society of Jesus in 1841, Fordham Preparatory School is a four-year, Catholic, college preparatory school located on Fordham University's campus. The school curriculum stresses "the development of excellence in the whole person: intellectual, religious, social, emotional and physical," which is supported by Fordham Prep's affiliation with Jesuit secondary schools worldwide. The school seeks to discover and encourage students' talents and abilities by fostering a sense of pride in learning. Students welcome academic challenges thanks to a dedicated team of teachers who are always available for extra help and consultation.

General

Type of School	Private
Religious Affiliation	Catholic
Coeducational	No
Boarding	No
Day School	Yes
Dress Code	Yes
Founded	1841

Students

Enrollment (Grades 9–12)	915
% Male/Female	100/0
% African American	10
% Hispanic/Latino	18
% Asian	5
% Caucasian	67

Admissions Selectivity

Median SAT	1204

COMPARABLE SCHOOLS

Cardinal Hayes; Loyola; Monsignor Scanlan; Regis; Rice; St. Agnes Boys; Xavier

Academics

REQUIRED CLASSES

4 years: English, foreign language, religion

3 years: Math, science, social studies

2 years: Physical education

1 semester: Heath education, computers, music

ADDITIONAL REQUIREMENTS

Community service

Student/Faculty Ratio   11:1

Extracurricular

MOST POPULAR INTERSCHOLASTIC SPORTS

Baseball, basketball, bowling, crew, cross-country, football, golf, ice hockey, lacrosse, soccer, swimming, tennis, track (indoor & outdoor), volleyball, wrestling

Financial

Annual Tuition $10,780

Endowment $10.5 million

**

MISSION STATEMENT

The school's website states, "At the heart of Jesuit education is the rigorous study of the humanities and the sciences," which mirrors Fordham's belief that the exploration of great ideas is "inextricably linked to the formation of character." Their academic program goes beyond simply gaining knowledge—it instills discipline and the pursuit of academic excellence in its students.

FRANK SINATRA SCHOOL
OF ARTS

30-20 Thompson Avenue, Long Island City, NY 11101

Phone Number: 718-361-9920

Head of School: Donna Finn

ABOUT THE FRANK SINATRA SCHOOL OF ARTS

Founded in 2001 by Exploring the Arts, a charitable program (created in part by Tony Bennett), the Frank Sinatra School of the Arts offers a challenging academic program along with professional training in acting, dancing, and music. FSSA prides itself on its friendly and family-like environment, thanks to small class sizes and a common passion shared by students and faculty alike for the arts. Teachers and administrators always make sure to make time for any student or parent needs. Even though it is a school primarily rooted in the arts, its academics don't suffer as evidenced by the many students who opt to take Advanced Regents diploma requirements. The school provides spectacular opportunities for its aspiring artists through its partnerships with the New York City Opera and Battery Dance Company, and also by offering studio courses taught by professional singers, artists, dancers, and actors. Entrance into this school is extremely competitive and based largely on performance during open auditions (check the school's website for exact audition dates as they can vary). Also worth mentioning is that the school's new building in Astoria—complete with an 800-seat auditorium, two dance studios, two recording studios, a gymnasium, two science labs, and a rooftop terrace—is slated for completion in 2008.

General

Type of School	Public
Religious Affiliation	None
Coeducational	Yes
Boarding	No
Day School	Yes
Dress Code	No
Founded	2001

Students

Enrollment (Grades 9–12)	546
% Male/Female	30/70
% African American	21
% Hispanic/Latino	25
% Asian	6
% Caucasian	49
% Out-of-State Students	0
# States Represented	1

Admissions Selectivity

COMPARABLE SCHOOLS

Fiorello H. LaGuardia High School of Music & Art and Performing Arts, Professional Children's School, Professional Performing Arts School

Academics

REQUIRED CLASSES

Students focus on developing their art while taking a range of classes that fulfill the New York City Regents diploma requirements.

Financial

Annual Tuition   None

**

WHERE STUDENTS COME FROM

Not surprisingly, the majority of students come from Queens, though there is a small contingent that travels from the surrounding boroughs.

COLLEGES THAT RECENT GRADS ARE ATTENDING

City University of New York, Columbia University, New York University, State University of New York, University of Connecticut, University of Delaware, Williams College

HACKLEY SCHOOL

293 Benedict Avenue, Tarrytown, NY 10591

Phone Number: 914-631-0128 • **Website:** www.hackleyschool.org

Head of School: Walter C. Johnson • **Director of Admissions:** Lawrence Crimmins

ABOUT THE HACKLEY SCHOOL

Founded in 1899 by Mrs. Caleb Brewster Hackley, the Hackley School is a nonsectarian co-educational, college-preparatory school enrolling day students in kindergarten through the grade 12, and five-day boarding for students in grades 9 through 12. The school believes in a diverse student body and assigns a significant percentage of its budget to scholarships. Hackley believes that "students will grow in character and responsibility by participating in structured activity that serves the needs of people outside the spheres of home and school." By committing their energy, time, and imagination to serving those needs, students experience the satisfaction of helping others and gain an appreciation of the larger community's complexity and concerns. As school officials note, "Hackley students are expected to be good citizens." The school shares an active commitment to character development as well as academic excellence with its parent community. Students are encouraged to act responsibly and have respect for themselves and others. Hackley strives to provide an overall environment that "supports the development of virtuous qualities and good personal habits, wherein students are expected to go beyond the mere observance of rules and strive to make the school a civilized community where courtesy, kindness, and forbearance reign, and incivility and intolerance are shunned."

General	
Type of School	Private
Religious Affiliation	None
Coeducational	Yes
Boarding	Yes (5-day)
Day School	Yes
Dress Code	Yes
Founded	1899

Students	
Enrollment (Grades 9–12)	393
% Male/Female	50/50
% African American	7
% Hispanic/Latino	7
% Asian	9
% Caucasian	75
% Other	2
% International Students	.5
% Out-of-State Students	6
# States Represented	3

Admissions Selectivity	
Requires Standardized Test Scores	Yes
Application Essay	Yes
Median SAT	1310–1470

MISSION STATEMENT

"Hackley challenges students to grow in character, scholarship, and accomplishment; to offer unreserved effort; and to learn from our community's varying perspectives and backgrounds."

THE IDEAL APPLICANT

Ideal applicants are "individuals who value an educational program that challenges students to strengthen their talents and find their passions, who want a diverse community reflective of the world in which they live, guided by an inclusive and democratic ethos, and families who want a community in purpose, values, and commitment to education."

WHERE STUDENTS COME FROM

The students mainly come from Westchester County, followed by Fairfield County, Connecticut, and various counties in New Jersey.

ORIENTATION PROCESS FOR NEW STUDENTS

It's a family affair for new students at the Hackley school. The Hackley Parents Associations welcomes new families to the school with a neighborhood get-together, and in turn, the school hosts these families at a beginning-of-the-year dinner. There is a special orientation for new students before the start of school that includes course selection, placement testing, and a book fair.

COLLEGES THAT RECENT GRADS ARE ATTENDING

Amherst College, Bard College, Boston College, Boston University, Bowdoin College, Brown University, Bucknell University, Colby College, Colgate University, Columbia University, Connecticut College, Cornell University, Dartmouth College, Davidson College, Duke University, Emory University, Fordham University, Franklin & Marshall College, George Washington University, Georgetown University, Hamilton College, Harvard University, Indiana University, Johns Hopkins University, Kenyon College, Lafayette College, Lehigh University, Massachusetts Institute of Technology, Middlebury College, Muhlenberg College, New York University, Northwestern University, Oberlin College, Pomona College, Princeton University, Rensselaer Polytechnic Institute, School of Visual Arts, Skidmore College, Smith College, Swarthmore College, Syracuse University, Trinity College, Tufts University, Tulane University, University of Chicago, University of Miami, University of Michigan, University of Pennsylvania, University of Rochester, University of Southern California, Vanderbilt University, Villanova University, Washington University in St. Louis, Wellesley College, Wesleyan University, Yale University

Students Say

Students resoundingly report that "community is my favorite aspect of Hackley," noting the relationship between teachers and students, who are "unified and supportive," all of which adds to "a sense of competition, not with one another but with oneself." Students here "think critically" and have "a great sense of work ethic and desire to succeed" thanks to the "high quality of intellectual discourse in the classroom" and the "diverse, inspirational, and rewarding" academic environment.

Parents Say

Parents appreciate the Hackley School's "commitment to excellence through the expertise and inspiration of its faculty, administration, and students," explaining that the "diverse community" and "right mix of academics, athletic opportunities and social awareness for our children" has left them with no doubt they made the right decision for their children. The "superior academic program" is enhanced by "high caliber" athletic and extracurricular activities, and the school itself acts as "a dynamic catalyst for growth" and "foundation for a lifelong pursuit of knowledge."

Alumni Say

Alumni credit a large part of their development into successful individuals to the Hackley School and its "motivating and supportive" teachers who brought out "the best in their students." As a "community of scholars and friends," the school builds confidence by "embracing students for who they are" and "allowing them to recognize their unique, natural talents." Former students recall "the lasting relationships between students and faculty" and the confidence this imbued, effectively teaching students to "embrace challenges and difficulties." Ultimately, as one alumnus notes, Hackley was "not only a school, but a home."

HARVEY MILK HIGH SCHOOL

2 Astor Place, New York, NY 10003

Phone Number: 212-477-1555 • **Website:** www.hmi.org

Head of School: William Salzman

General	
Type of School	Public
Religious Affiliation	None
Coeducational	Yes
Boarding	No
Day School	Yes
Dress Code	No
Founded	1984

Students	
Enrollment (Grades 9–12)	170
% African American	43
% Hispanic/Latino	44
% Asian	3
% Caucasian	12

Financial	
Annual Tuition	None
**	

ABOUT HARVEY MILK HIGH SCHOOL

Originally founded as a two-classroom public school in 1984, the Harvey Milk High School has grown into a fully-accredited voluntary public high school that addresses the educational needs of children who have reason to fear harassment or physical and emotional harm in a traditional educational environment. Its primary goal is to reach out to lesbian, gay, bisexual, transgender, questioning, at-risk, and other youth to offer them a place of refuge where they can fulfill their academic potential without fear of judgment or abuse.

HMHS functions as a transfer school for students in grades 9-12 who have not felt successful in at least one other high school prior to admission and who want to continue their education in an alternative, small school environment. As a testament to the school's success, 95 percent of Harvey Milk High School students graduate, and over 60 percent of students go onto advanced programs or college. In the school's own words, it seeks to "provide a rigorous academic program with all the necessary support systems to foster the development of an individual's character, self-respect, and ability to succeed in a diverse community."

MISSION STATEMENT

According to its website, the mission of Harvey Milk High School is to establish and promote a community of successful and independent students by creating a safe and challenging educational environment for all young people.

WHERE STUDENTS COME FROM

Students come to the school from all five boroughs of New York City.

THE HARVEY SCHOOL

260 Jay Street, Katonah, NY 10536

Phone Number: 914-232-3161 • **Website:** www.harveyschool.org

Head of School: Barry Fenstermacher • **Director of Admissions:** Ronald Romanowicz

ABOUT THE HARVEY SCHOOL

The Harvey School takes its role as a college preparatory institution seriously and challenges students to reach beyond their perceived levels of ability. The informal atmosphere puts students at ease and as such they are much more receptive to learning. The school stresses academic responsibility by encouraging students to learn and work independently. However, this independence is not exercised to the detriment of teamwork. Rather, the curriculum stresses the importance of investigating diverse and opposing points of view along with incorporating teamwork, which in turn nurtures respect, self-reliance, and confidence.

The Harvey School runs on the trimester system, with students expected to take a minimum of five courses each trimester. Faculty members are dedicated to their students' intellectual and emotional development and always make themselves available to help, often using study halls, free periods, and meal times for one-on-one or small-group help sessions. This kind of review before final exams is a regular feature of most classes and results in a group of students with a broader spectrum of abilities and interests. While the school does not offer special support for students with learning disabilities, it does report on its website that "those who are able to function in a closely monitored mainstream environment find success at Harvey."

General	
Type of School	Private
Religious Affiliation	None
Coeducational	Yes
Boarding	Yes
Day School	Yes
Dress Code	Yes

Students	
Enrollment (Grades 9–12)	220

Admissions Selectivity	
Requires Standardized Test Scores	No
Application Essay	None

MISSION STATEMENT

According to the school's website, Harvey invests in its students' "personal and academic growth" while preparing them for college by providing a supportive academic environment that challenges them "to reach beyond their perceived levels of ability."

THE IDEAL APPLICANT

The school's website states that Harvey seeks dedicated students of diverse backgrounds, abilities, and talents who are committed to succeeding in school and preparing for college.

Academics

REQUIRED CLASSES

4 years: English, math, science, history, foreign language
1 trimester: Health education

Student/Faculty Ratio   7:1

Extracurricular

MOST POPULAR
INTERSCHOLASTIC SPORTS
MALE

Baseball, basketball, cross-country, ice hockey, lacrosse, rugby, soccer, softball, tennis

FEMALE

Basketball, cross-country, lacrosse, soccer, softball, tennis

Financial

Annual Tuition	$25,400
Boarding Tuition	$32,400
**	

ORIENTATION PROCESS FOR NEW STUDENTS

New students and their parents are welcomed to Harvey with a orientation picnic prior to the start of classes.

COLLEGES THAT RECENT GRADS ARE ATTENDING

Bates College, Bentley College, Boston University, Brown University, Bucknell University, Cornell University, Drew University, Elon University, Fairfield University, Fordham University, Goucher College, Hamilton College, Hampshire College, Hobart & William Smith Colleges, Hofstra University, Indiana University, Iona College, Ithaca College, Johnson & Wales University, King's College, La Salle University, Lafayette College, Lehigh University, Lynn University, Marymount College, Mount Holyoke College, Mount Saint Mary's University, Nazareth College, Northeastern University, Oberlin College, Pace University, Pennsylvania State University, Providence College, Quinnipiac University, Rensselaer Polytechnic Institute, Rider University, Rochester Institute of Technology, Roger Williams University, San Jose State University, Sarah Lawrence College, Skidmore College, Smith College, St. Bonaventure University, St. Lawrence University, St. Thomas Aquinas College, State University of New York—New Paltz, State University of New York—Purchase College, State University of New York—University at Buffalo, Syracuse University, Temple University, Texas Christian University, Union College, University of Arizona, University of Delaware, University of Denver, University of Hartford, University of Michigan, University of Pennsylvania, University of Pittsburgh, University of Rhode Island, University of Richmond, Utica College, Villanova University, Wake Forest University, Wheaton College, Worcester Polytechnic Institute

THE HEWITT SCHOOL

45 East Seventy-fifth Street, New York, NY 10021

Phone Number: 212-288-1919 • **Website:** www.hewittschool.org

Head of School: Linda MacMurray Gibbs • **Director of Middle and Upper School Admissions:** Abby Katz

ABOUT THE HEWITT SCHOOL

Founded in 1920, The Hewitt School is committed to the education and development of the young women who will be the leaders of tomorrow. The school's motto, "By faith and courage," exemplifies the vision and direction that Hewitt was conceived and still thrives with an emphasis on "self-knowledge and confidence as well as courage to move forward with energy and enthusiasm." The academic standards are set high and every effort is taken to ensure that students can explore "personal interests, acquire new understandings, and become actively engaged in the learning process." Confidence is a key component of successful development at Hewitt, and teachers and administration go out of their way to nurture and encourage this by keeping classes small (with an average of fifteen students) and participation high. Also, every student is equipped with a laptop, allowing for enhanced learning opportunities. There is an overwhelming roster of AP and honors courses, electives, clubs, and extracurricular activities, as well as foreign exchange and travel programs.

General	
Type of School	Private
Religious Affiliation	None
Coeducational	No
Boarding	No
Day School	Yes
Dress Code	Yes
Founded	1920

Students	
Enrollment (Grades 9–12)	125
% Male/Female	0/100

Extracurricular
MOST POPULAR INTERSCHOLASTIC SPORTS

Basketball, cross-country, soccer, swimming, tennis, track & field, volleyball

MISSION STATEMENT

"The Hewitt School is an independent college preparatory school for girls in kindergarten through grade 12. Our mission is to provide a rigorous and stimulating program that encourages independent thinking and creativity. The school values each girl's individual talents and encourages respect for the diverse interests and backgrounds of others. Hewitt's small class size and supportive environment enable each student to reach her full potential and to become a responsible and socially aware leader. In keeping with its motto 'By faith and courage,' Hewitt seeks to instill in each girl lifelong faith in herself, personal integrity, and the courage to face challenges with confidence."

Financial

Annual Tuition	$29,100
Endowment	$9.4 million
% Students Receiving Financial Aid	18

*

THE IDEAL APPLICANT

The Hewitt School welcomes "outstanding girls who want to grow into extraordinary women."

COLLEGES THAT RECENT GRADS ARE ATTENDING

Barnard College, Boston University, Brown University, Dartmouth, Duke University, Cornell University, Georgetown University, George Washington University, Hamilton College, Harvard University, New York University, Princeton University, Stanford University, Syracuse University, Trinity College, Tufts University, University of Michigan University of Pennsylvania

HIGH SCHOOL FOR MATH, SCIENCE AND ENGINEERING AT CITY COLLEGE

138 Convent Avenue, New York, NY 10031

Phone Number: 212-281-6490 • **Website:** www.hsmse.org

Head of School: William Dugan

ABOUT HIGH SCHOOL FOR MATH, SCIENCE AND ENGINEERING AT CITY COLLEGE

A recent addition to the New York City public school system, the High School of Math, Science and Engineering at City College is located on the campus of City College (New York's flagship college in science, engineering and architecture), and offers a uniquely collaborative educational experience. Instructionally supported by the City University of New York, the school's academically rigorous learning environment focuses on math, science, and engineering while emphasizing social responsibility and the value of knowledge for its own sake. And thanks to this partnership, students can enroll in City University of New York courses, join in City College Collaborative Engineering/Architecture themes, and participate in many other university-level opportunities, thus fulfilling the school's goal of infusing the educational skills necessary to succeed as leaders in their field. Interested applicants must first take the New York City Specialized Science High Schools Admissions Test (SSHSAT), with places being offered in order of test ranking from highest to lowest.

General

Type of School	Public
Religious Affiliation	None
Coeducational	Yes
Boarding	No
Day School	Yes
Dress Code	No
Founded	2002

Students

Enrollment (Grades 9–12)	403
% African American	22
% Hispanic/Latino	28
% Asian	29
% Caucasian	22

Admissions Selectivity

Requires Standardized Test Scores	Yes
Application Essay	None

COMPARABLE SCHOOLS

Bronx High School of Science; Brooklyn Latin School; Brooklyn Technical High School; High School of American Studies at Lehman College; Queens High School for the Sciences at York College; Staten Island Technical High School; Stuyvesant High School

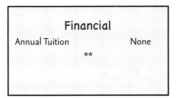

Financial	
Annual Tuition	None
**	

MISSION STATEMENT

According to its website, the school seeks to challenge students while expanding "their intellect and potential by developing the habits of inquiry, written and verbal expression, as well as critical thinking."

WHERE STUDENTS COME FROM

Students travel to the school from all five boroughs of New York City to the school.

HIGH SCHOOL OF AMERICAN STUDIES AT LEHMAN COLLEGE

2925 Goulden Avenue, Bronx, NY 10468

Phone Number: 718-329-2144 • **Website:** www.hsas-lehman.org

Head of School: Myra Luftman

ABOUT HIGH SCHOOL OF AMERICAN STUDIES AT LEHMAN COLLEGE

The High School of American Studies is a selective public high school operated by The New York City Department of Education, in collaboration with the City University of New York and the Gilder Lehrman Institute of American History. The school places a specialized emphasis on American Studies in conjunction with a rigorous college preparatory program. The relatively small size of the school allows it to give students individualized attention to students while offering a multitude of opportunities to take seminars, Advanced Placement courses, and regular Lehman College courses for college credit. The school also provides history enrichment courses that include field trips to historical sites, scholarships for summer study, guest lecturers, and many other interesting programs. In addition to this, and thanks to its partnership with Lehman College, students may use the Lehman College Library, Apex Gym, Art Gallery, Performing Arts Center, and other facilities. Admission to the school is based solely on a student's performance on the Specialized Science High Schools Admissions Test (SSHSAT), which is open to all 8th and 9th grade New York City students.

General

Type of School	Public
Religious Affiliation	None
Coeducational	Yes
Boarding	No
Day School	Yes
Dress Code	No
Founded	2002

Students

Enrollment (Grades 9–12)	320
% African American	23
% Hispanic/Latino	27
% Asian	21
% Caucasian	32

Extracurricular

MOST POPULAR INTERSCHOLASTIC SPORTS

MALE

Baseball, basketball, track, tennis

FEMALE

Basketball, track, tennis, softball

Admissions Selectivity

Requires Standardized Test Scores	Yes
Application Essay	None

MISSION STATEMENT

According to its website, the school's mission is to prepare students for higher education and "the challenges and responsibilities of citizens in a democratic, pluralistic society."

WHERE STUDENTS COME FROM

Students come to the school from all five boroughs of New York City.

HORACE MANN SCHOOL

231 West 246th Street, Riverdale, NY 10471

Phone Number: 718-432-4000 • **Website:** www.horacemann.org

Head of School: Dr. Tom Kelly • **Director of Admissions:** Dr. Barbara Tischler

ABOUT THE HORACE MANN SCHOOL

The Horace Mann School was founded in 1887 as a coeducational experimental and developmental unit of Teachers College at Columbia University. Despite the years since its inception, Horace Mann remains steadfastly dedicated to its five core values: "The life of the mind, mature behavior, mutual respect, a secure and healthful environment, and a balance between individual achievement and a caring community."

The upper division's academic programs and extracurricular activities seek to nurture, encourage, and challenge their students, thereby helping them to succeed not only within the academic program but also in their future studies, careers, and lives.

In addition to developing a strong background in each of the liberal arts disciplines, students have special opportunities to pursue individual interests through elective courses, independent study projects, and clubs. However, academic excellence at Horace Mann means more than good grades. As Dr. Barbara Tischler notes on the school's website, "Students should be able to follow through on commitments to others with attention to the final product as a whole and to its smallest details as well. We encourage students to define for themselves, and then to follow, a balanced path between self-interest and the greater good of community and society."

General	
Type of School	Private
Religious Affiliation	None
Coeducational	Yes
Boarding	Yes
Day School	Yes
Dress Code	No
Founded	1887

Students	
Enrollment (Grades 9–12)	710
% African American	8
% Hispanic/Latino	6
% Asian	11
% Caucasian	75
# States Represented	3

Admissions Selectivity	
Requires Standardized Test Scores	Yes
Application Essay	Yes

Academics

REQUIRED CLASSES

4 years: English, physical education
3 years: Math, foreign language
2 years: History, arts
1 year: Computers

ADDITIONAL REQUIREMENTS

Community service

Extracurricular

MOST POPULAR
INTERSCHOLASTIC SPORTS
MALE

Baseball, basketball, cross-country, football, fencing, golf, lacrosse, soccer, swimming, tennis, track, ultimate frisbee, water polo, wrestling

FEMALE

Basketball, cross-country, fencing, field hockey, golf, gymnastics, lacrosse, soccer, swimming, tennis, track, ultimate frisbee, water polo

Financial

Annual Tuition	$27,350
% Students Receiving Financial Aid	18
**	

MISSION STATEMENT

In the spirit of the school's namesake, Horace Mann, an emphasis is placed upon transforming students from learners to teachers so as to develop independent thinkers and leaders. In the school's own words, "The value and potential of each and every student remain at the core of our very existence in academic, artistic, or athletic pursuits."

COLLEGES THAT RECENT GRADS ARE ATTENDING

Amherst College, Barnard College, Brown University, Carnegie Mellon University, Colgate, University, Columbia University, Cornell University, Dartmouth University, Duke University, George Washington University, Georgetown University, Hamilton College, Harvard University, Johns Hopkins University, Northwestern University, Oberlin College, Princeton University, Skidmore College, Stanford University, Syracuse University, Tufts University, University of Chicago, University of Michigan, University of Pennsylvania, University of Wisconsin, Vassar College, Washington University in St. Louis, Wesleyan University, Yale University

HUNTER COLLEGE HIGH SCHOOL

71 East Ninety-fourth Street, New York, NY 10128

Phone Number: 212-860-1406 • **Website:** www.hchs.hunter.cuny.edu

Head of School: Dr. John Mucciolo • **Admissions Advisor:** Steve Ortega

ABOUT HUNTER COLLEGE HIGH SCHOOL

Originally established in 1869 as an all-female school, Hunter College High School today is a tuition-free, coeducational, laboratory high school and one of the oldest self-contained schools for intellectually gifted students in the nation. It is publicly funded, chartered by the Board of Trustees of the City University of New York, and administered by Hunter College in the City University of New York system.

Admission to the high school is allowed only at the 7th grade and only students who show "superior cognitive ability on standardized tests may sit for the Hunter College High School Entrance Examination while in the 6th grade." In order to be admitted to the school, students must live in New York City.

Hunter students pursue "an academically enriched six-year program of study," that features accelerated subjects so that high school studies "[begin] in the 8th grade and state educational requirements are completed in the 11th grade." During students' senior year they may take electives, internships, and attend courses at Hunter College and Columbia University for transferable credit. Nearly 99 percent of Hunter graduates go on to attend college, and of those, 25 percent attend Ivy League institutions.

General

Type of School	Public
Religious Affiliation	None
Coeducational	Yes
Boarding	No
Day School	Yes
Dress Code	No
Founded	1869

Students

Enrollment (Grades 7-12)	1,200

Admissions Selectivity

Applications Received	2,000
# Applicants Accepted	200
Requires Standardized Test Scores	Yes
Application Essay	Yes

COMPARABLE SCHOOLS

Bard High School Early College; High School of American Studies at Lehman College; High School for Math, Science & Engineering at City College; Townsend Harris High School; Queens High School for the Sciences at York College

MISSION STATEMENT

"Hunter College enters the twenty-first century faithful to its motto 'Mihi Cura Futuri' ('Mine is the care of the future'), with a continuing commitment to providing affordable, quality education to students, and to preparing them to meet the economic, political, social, and technological challenges of the new millennium."

Extracurricular

MOST POPULAR
INTERSCHOLASTIC SPORTS

MALE

Baseball, basketball, bowling, cross-country, fencing, soccer, swimming, tennis, track, Ultimate Frisbee, volleyball

FEMALE

Basketball, bowling, cross-country, fencing, soccer, softball, swimming, tennis, track, Ultimate Frisbee, volleyball

% Students Who Play
Interscholastic Sports   40

Financial

Annual Tuition   None

*

COLLEGES THAT RECENT GRADS ARE ATTENDING

Brown University, Columbia University, Cornell University, Dartmouth University, Harvard University, Massachusetts Institute of Technology, Princeton University, University of Pennsylvania, Yale University

LA SCUOLA D'ITALIA "GUGLIELMO MARCONI"

12 East Ninety-sixth Street, New York, NY 10128

Phone Number: 212-369-3290 • **Website:** www.lascuoladitalia.org

Head of School: Bianca Maria Padolecchia Goodrich • **Director of Admissions:** Pia Pedicini

ABOUT LA SCUOLA D'ITALIA "GUGLIELMO MARCONI"

Founded in 1977 by the Italian Ministry of Foreign Affairs, La Scuola d'Italia "Guglielmo Marconi" is only English-Italian bilingual school in Northern America. Offering an international education to a diverse student body, the school's academically rigorous curriculum develops a strong foundation in the humanities and sciences that is combined with total immersion in the Italian language and culture.

The bilingual curriculum is open to English-speaking students, as the languages of learning are both Italian and English (though knowledge of the Italian language is a requirement after 8th grade). School diplomas are honored both in the United States and in the European Union, and students can transfer from and to other schools in both countries. La Scuola is legally recognized by the Italian Ministry of Education, chartered by the Regents of the University of the State of New York as a private, independent, coeducational American school, and also a provisional member of the New York State Association of Independent Schools.

MISSION STATEMENT

According to the school's website, La Scuola d'Italia provides its students with the multicultural, educational, and social tools necessary to become understanding and open "citizens of the world."

General

Type of School	Private
Religious Affiliation	None
Coeducational	Yes
Boarding	No
Day School	Yes
Dress Code	Yes
Founded	1977

Students

Enrollment (Grades 9–12)	23
% African American	1
% Hispanic/Latino	1
% Caucasian	98

Academics

REQUIRED CLASSES

Areas of study include art, art history, biology, chemistry, computers, economics, English, French, geography, history, Italian, Latin (language & literature), law, math, philosophy, physical education, physics

Student/Faculty Ratio	6:1

Financial

Annual Tuition	$17,000
**	

COLLEGES THAT RECENT GRADS ARE ATTENDING

The school's graduates attend a variety of universities in the United States, Canada, and Europe.

LITTLE RED SCHOOL HOUSE AND ELISABETH IRWIN HIGH SCHOOL

40 Charlton Street, New York, NY 10014

Phone Number: 212-477-5316 • **Website:** www.lrei.org

Head of School: Phil Kassen • **Director of Admissions:** Samantha Caruth

General	
Type of School	Private
Religious Affiliation	None
Coeducational	Yes
Boarding	No
Day School	Yes
Dress Code	Yes
Founded	1921

Students	
Enrollment (Grades 9–12)	167

ABOUT THE LITTLE RED SCHOOL HOUSE AND ELISABETH IRWIN HIGH SCHOOL

LREI was founded in 1921 by Elisabeth Irwin, a progressive educator who, along with colleagues such as John Dewey, spearheaded the development of new learning strategies and educational innovations. The LREI curriculum continues to reflect and build upon this tradition, offering problem-based, inquiry-driven, and student-centered classes. The goal is to motivate students to become active learners and decision-makers by offering broad and meaningful intellectual and artistic experiences with a solid foundation in the academic skills and disciplines required for admission to and success in college. LREI also has a special arrangement with NYU's College of Arts and Sciences which allows students may to take elective courses at the university, thereby providing high school students with valuable educational opportunities and a taste of college life.

LREI's faculty is selected for their scholarly expertise, teaching skills, and ability to relate to students outside the classroom. Among the teachers are authors, professors of graduate-level classes, and professionals in the visual and performing arts. Every high school teacher serves as an advisor to about seven students and designs a program that will both encourage students' individual interests and to satisfy college entrance requirements.

The student body reflects the city: All races, ethnic backgrounds, religions, and socioeconomic statuses come together to form one of the most diverse independent schools in New York. Students play a central role in the governance of the school community—performing school service, serving on the Student Government, participating in Town Meeting (the high school assembly), and serving on the Community Service Roundtable.

The high school's facilities include spacious classrooms, a computer/media center, a gymnasium, a cafeteria, a photo lab, an art studio, a theater, a music room, a technology center, and two science labs. The library has more than 10,000 books and 52 periodicals, and its computers provide access to the Lower and Middle School book collections, as well as the catalogs of the New York Public Library.

MISSION STATEMENT

"Our goal is to educate students to become independent thinkers and lifelong learners and pursue academic excellence and achievement in a context of respect for others and service to the community."

THE IDEAL APPLICANT

Little Red School House and Elisabeth Irwin High School enrolls students who "are bright, curious, motivated and show strong academic and personal promise. The successful student embraces our progressive curriculum and thrives on the connections made between experiential learning and the world. LREI prepares children to be independent thinkers and productive citizens. Our students gain a strong sense of self and citizenship, and our graduates continue on to become leaders in society."

WHERE STUDENTS COME FROM

Many come from the Greenwich Village, Soho, and Chelsea neighborhoods that surround the school, but students looking for progressive education come from throughout New York City, and also New Jersey.

Academics
REQUIRED CLASSES
4 years: English, history, math, art, physical education
3 years: Foreign language, science
2 years: Technology, life issues

ADDITIONAL REQUIREMENTS
Community Service, Senior Project

Student/Faculty Ratio   15:1

Extracurricular
MOST POPULAR
INTERSCHOLASTIC SPORTS
MALE
Basketball, cross-country, golf, soccer, softball, tennis, track, volleyball
FEMALE
Basketball, cross-country, golf, soccer, softball, tennis, track, volleyball
% Students Who Play
Interscholastic Sports   65

Financial
Annual Tuition $27,035–$27,200
*

ORIENTATION PROCESS FOR NEW STUDENTS

All new students attend a new student orientation before the school year begins. At this time students meet their classmates and teachers, review their schedule, and learn about the culture of the school. Students will meet with their advisors and take a tour of the campus. Freshmen will also meet their senior Peer Leaders. In mid-September the ninth grade goes on a three-day, two-night trip. Tenth graders join the ninth grade for the second half of the trip.

COLLEGES THAT RECENT GRADS ARE ATTENDING

Adelphi University, Bard College, Barnard College, Boston College, Boston University, Brandeis University, Bucknell University, Columbia University, Connecticut College, City University of New York—City College, City University of New York—Hunter, Dartmouth College, Drexel University, Emerson College, Eugene Lang College, Goucher College, Hampshire College, Hartwick College, Hobart and William Smith College, Hofstra University, Johnson & Wales University, London Metropolitan University, Loyola University New Orleans,

Manhattanville College, Miami University, Muhlenberg College, New York University, Northeastern University, Pennsylvania State University, Pepperdine University, Queensborough College, Quinnipiac University, Rhode Island School of Design, Santa Clara University, Sarah Lawrence College, School of the Museum of Fine Arts Boston, School of Visual Arts, Skidmore College, Smith College, Spelman College, St. Joseph College, State University of New York at Binghamton, State University of New York—Geneseo, State University of New York—Purchase (Music Conservatory), State University of New York—Stony Brook, Susquehanna University, Temple University, University College for the Creative Arts in Rochester, University of Bristol, University of Connecticut, University of Hartford, University of Massachusetts—Amherst, University of Richmond in London, University of the Arts, Yale University

Students Say

Students love their teachers who they "can talk to at any time" and are always "there for us." These open channels of communication encourage the "great community feeling" and the educational freedom to "try everything" and "put your own spin" on projects. Also garnering high marks is the "strong focus on the arts." And quality extends far beyond the classroom, as one student explains, "I love the cafeteria food—lunch is my favorite part of the day other than history class." Ultimately, LREI students gain an education from more than just books as they "learn about the world from the world and about life by living."

Parents Say

Parents appreciate the "small class size, quality of faculty, and progressive education" that LREI offers to children. The school provides "interesting and challenging classes" and takes a "hands-on, experiential approach" to teaching, encouraging students to "be inquisitive, active and engaged citizens." Most importantly, students "feel at home" thanks to "friendly teachers" who understand "how each child learns and how to help each child be successful." Parents also praise the school's "commitment to community service" and "good college advisory and placement programs"—all of this going a long way to foster "a philosophy of lifelong learning" in students.

Alumni Say

Alumni recall teachers who would "listen to what students had to say and emphasize that their opinions matter," who had "respect for students' ideas" and were always "more than happy to take the time to talk." Though the teachers had "high standards" and the "demanding but fair" curriculum proved to challenging, alumni excelled at their schoolwork and were taught "the importance of paying attention to the environment, world events and politics." This commitment to community has carried on long after graduation. In the words of one former student, "I learned at LREI that a single person, or two people, can make a difference, but only if they get involved."

LOYOLA SCHOOL

980 Park Avenue, New York, NY 10028

Phone Number: 212-228-3522 • **Website:** www.loyola-nyc.org

Head of School: James Lyness • **Director of Admissions:** Lillian Diaz-Imbelli

ABOUT THE LOYOLA SCHOOL

Loyola decided to become coeducational in 1973, making it the first Jesuit high school in the country to do so and the school remains the only Jesuit coeducational option in the New York area. In the spirit of the school's motto, "Men and women for others," the school runs weekend Christian Service trips to the Romero Center in Camden, New Jersey, a service trip every year to Kentucky during spring break, and another trip to Belize at the beginning of the summer. The school also takes great pride in its students and encourages activities, whether by adorning the walls of their historic 1900 building with student artwork, hosting Talent Night, Sports Night, and student literary readings, trips to Bear Mountain, or a spring break trip in Italy, students become not only an integral part of the academic environment but the community as well.

MISSION STATEMENT

"As a Catholic, independent, coeducational, college preparatory, urban, secondary day school, rooted in the Jesuit tradition, Loyola School challenges its young men and women to become intellectually fulfilled, open to growth, religious, loving, and committed to doing justice. Loyola School is committed to challenging its students religiously, intellectually, aesthetically, physically, and socially. Opportunities for personal study, reflection, and leadership allow students to expand their knowledge, develop their skills, mature as individuals and community members, and realize the goodness inherent in themselves and all God's creation. In keeping with the Ignatian spirit of cura personalis (care for the whole person), Loyola School strives to develop the diverse and unique talents of each member of the Loyola

General

Type of School	Private
Religious Affiliation	Roman Catholic
Coeducational	Yes
Boarding	No
Day School	Yes
Dress Code	Yes
Founded	1900

Students

Enrollment (Grades 9–12)	206
% African American	4
% Hispanic/Latino	17
% Asian	5
% Caucasian	73
% Other	1
% International Students	2
% Out-of-State Students	5
# Countries Represented	4
# States Represented	3

Admissions Selectivity

Applications Received	197
# Applicants Accepted	118
# Accepted Applicants Who Enrolled	52
Requires Standardized Test Scores	Yes
Application Essay	Yes
Median SAT	1240

COMPARABLE SCHOOLS

Browning; Convent of the Sacred Heart; Fordham Prep; Marymount; Regis; Trinity

community, and encourages the use of these talents to serve others for the greater glory of God."

THE IDEAL APPLICANT

The ideal Loyola applicant demonstrates an "enjoyment of learning and a commitment to intellectual growth, both in school and out." The student is also "exploring and developing other gifts and talents, and may even have understand that these gifts and talents are best used in service to others."

WHERE STUDENTS COME FROM

Most of Loyola's students are "residents of the five boroughs of New York City, with a sizable representation from Westchester County, and a few from New Jersey and Connecticut."

ORIENTATION PROCESS FOR NEW STUDENTS

Incoming students participate in a one-day orientation program in the first week of September where they meet with and participate in presentations from their "mentor" teachers, members of the administration, and senior students who function as "peer leaders."

COLLEGES THAT RECENT GRADS ARE ATTENDING

Amherst College, Boston College, Bowdoin College, Bucknell University, Carnegie Mellon University, Catholic University, Colgate University, College of Mt. St. Vincent, College of the Holy Cross, Colorado University, Columbia University, Cornell University, Dartmouth University, Emory University, Fairfield University, Fordham University, Georgetown University, George Washington University, Gonzaga University, Harvard University, Indiana, Lehigh University, Lesley College, Long Island University, Loyola University—Maryland, Loyola University—New Orleans, Marist College, Massachusetts Institute of Technology, New York University, Northeastern University, Northwestern University, Peabody Conservatory of Johns Hopkins, Pennsylvania State University, Skidmore College, Smith College, St. Louis University, Stanford University, Syracuse University, St. Joseph's University, St. Michael's College, St. Peter's College, University of Maine,

University of New Brunswick, University of Notre Dame, University of Scranton, University of the South, University of Wisconsin, University of Vermont, United States Naval Academy, Vanderbilt University, Vassar College, Villanova University, Webb Institute, Yale University

Students Say

Students agree Loyola is "a welcoming place" with "such a family feeling" that no one ever feels left out or "shunned for their beliefs." The school encourages independent thought, never dictating that students "follow one path in terms of how we view the world, politics, or religion." Simply put, in the words of one student, "Loyola can't be described in words, it needs to be experienced."

LYCÉE FRANÇAIS DE NEW YORK

505 East Seventy-fifth Street, New York, NY 10021

Phone Number: 212-369-1400 • **Website:** www.lfny.org

Head of School and Director of Admissions: Martine Lala

General	
Type of School	Private
Religious Affiliation	None
Coeducational	Yes
Boarding	No
Day School	Yes
Dress Code	Yes
Founded	1935

Students	
Enrollment (Grades 9–12)	233
% Male/Female	50/50
% African American	13
% Hispanic/Latino	4
% Asian	1
% Caucasian	82
# Countries Represented	63

ABOUT LYCÉE FRANÇAIS DE NEW YORK

First opening its doors in October 1935, the Lycée Français de New York is a nonprofit independent private coeducational institution, chartered by the Regents of the University of the State of New York, and accredited by both the French Ministry of National Education and The New York State Association of Independent Schools.

Located on the Upper East Side of Manhattan, LFNY educates some 1,300 students, representing over sixty nationalities, from early childhood through high school. Keeping in line with its dual-language and culture curriculum, it awards the New York State High School Diploma and prepares its students to pass the French baccalaureate.

The school charges itself with educating multicultural students to be responsible citizens, well-equipped for the future. The Lycée's academic program is a unique combination of the rigorous and comprehensive French program with a strong English curriculum. The blending of the French and American programs distinguishes the Lycée Français de New York and creates graduates who have a deeper understanding of both the European culture in which they are educated and the American culture in which they live. Although the primary language of instruction is French, many classes are team taught in French and English. This cross-disciplinary approach ensures that students are equally prepared to continue their course of study at either North American or European institutions of higher education.

MISSION STATEMENT

"Our mission comprises three basic objectives, each one equally crucial to our students' complete education: academic excellence; physical, psychological, and emotional equilibrium; and responsible citizenship. By pursuing these objectives with a demanding and rigorous curriculum that includes a rich program of artistic and cultural activities, the Lycée Français de New York endeavors to foster the development of independent, creative minds and a strong work ethic."

Where Students Come From

Students come to the Lycée from "sixty-three different countries."

Colleges that Recent Grads Are Attending

Bard College, Belmont University, Boston College, Bowdoin College, Brown University, Clark University, Concordia University, Cornell University, Dartmouth College, Drexel University, Emerson College, Fashion Institute of Technology, Massachusetts Institute of Technology, McGill University, New York University, Pratt School of Design, Princeton University, Rochester Institute of Technology, School of the Museum of Fine Arts, State University of New York at Binghamton, State University of New York—Purchase College, Swarthmore College, Tufts University, University of California—Berkeley, University of Chicago, University of Edinburgh, University of Pennsylvania, University of Virginia, Wheaton College, Yale University

Academics

Required Classes

All courses required for the New York State High School Diploma and preparation for the French baccalaureate

Additional Requirements

Community Service

Student/Faculty Ratio   9:1

Extracurricular

Most Popular Interscholastic Sports

Male

Basketball, cross-country, golf, soccer, softball, track & field, volleyball

Female

Basketball, cross-country, golf, soccer, softball, track & field, volleyball

Financial

Annual Tuition $14,000–$19,000
% Students Receiving
   Financial Aid   25

*

THE MASTERS SCHOOL

49 Clinton Avenue, Dobbs Ferry, NY 10522

Phone Number: 914-479-6400 • **Website:** www.themastersschool.com

Head of School: Maureen Fonesca • **Director of Admissions:** Lindsay Murphy

General

Type of School	Private
Religious Affiliation	None
Coeducational	Yes
Boarding	Yes
Day School	Yes
Dress Code	Yes
Founded	1877

Students

Enrollment (Grades 9–12)	412
% Male/Female	44/56
% African American	8
% Hispanic/Latino	5
% Asian	17
% Caucasian	70
% International Students	17
# Countries Represented	13
# States Represented	14

Admissions Selectivity

Applications Received	484
# Applicants Accepted	156
# Accepted Applicants Who Enrolled	81
Requires Standardized Test Scores	Yes
Application Essay	Yes

ABOUT THE MASTERS SCHOOL

Founded in 1877 as a girls' school, The Masters School has since grown into "a vibrant and diverse" coeducational institution. Located in Westchester County on nearly a hundred acres of woodland, lawns, and Hudson River views, the school provides a place of solitude and inspiration for students to learn, while still being only a short train ride away from socially dynamic New York City. Staffed with a "distinguished and dedicated" faculty, the school employs Harkness tables (oval-shaped to promote a low student-teacher ratio and inclusive environment) in classrooms, which encourage in-depth discussions of course material and "help students grow in their ability to listen, collaborate, and articulate their views while respecting those of others." This method plays a key role in developing students' confidence and self-assuredness personally and academically, effectively preparing them for college studies.

The Masters School is quick to single out its exemplary faculty for praise, noting that "more than 70 percent hold advanced degrees from leading universities," and thanks to their interaction with students in "a variety of roles—as instructors, coaches, advisors, and dorm parents—they have a true understanding of each student's interests, talents, and goals." Campus facilities include the Pittsburgh Library, Morris Hall (a state-of-the-art science and technology center), a separate middle school building, ten new faculty apartments, a digital language laboratory, and the completely refurbished academic areas of Masters Hall.

Mission Statement

"The mission of The Masters School is to provide the challenging academic environment that, for over a century, has encouraged critical, creative and independent habits of thought as well as a lifelong passion for learning. The Masters School promotes and celebrates academic achievement, artistic development, ethical awareness, technological literacy, athletic endeavor and personal growth. The school strives to maintain a diverse community that encourages students to participate actively in decisions affecting their lives and to develop an appreciation of their responsibilities in the larger world."

The Ideal Applicant

The Admission Committee selects students who are academically successful and are excited about learning, have strong (outside) interests and are involved in extracurricular activities, and will become enthusiastic, active participants in The Masters School community.

Where Students Come From

Students come to The Masters School from "sixteen states and fourteen countries, with an international population of 17 percent."

Orientation Process for New Students

Students attend an orientation meeting before the school year begins.

Academics
Required Classes
4 years: English, physical education
3 years: Foreign language, math, history
2 years: Lab science
1 year: Religion, health education, fine arts, computer science, speech

Student/Faculty Ratio   6:1

Extracurricular
Most Popular
Interscholastic Sports
Male
Baseball, basketball, cross-country (coed team), fencing, golf (coed team), lacrosse, soccer, tennis
Female
Basketball, cross-country (coed team), fencing, field hockey, golf (coed team), lacrosse, soccer, softball, tennis, volleyball

Financial
Annual Tuition	$25,850
Boarding Tuition	$35,500
Endowment	$21 million
% Students Receiving Financial Aid	26

*

Colleges that Recent Grads Are Attending

American University, Bard College, Barnard College, Bates College, Bennington College, Berkley College of Music, Boston University, Catholic University, Colby College, Columbia University, Cornell University, Denison University, Drew University, Eugene Lang College, Fordham University, George Washington University, Goucher College, Harvard University, Hobart & William Smith Colleges, Ithaca College, Johns Hopkins University, Kenyon College, Lake Forest College, Macalester College, Manhattan School of Music, McGill University, Middlebury College, Mount Holyoke College, New York University, Northeastern University, Oberlin College and Conservatory of Music, Occidental College, Parsons School of Design, Pennsylvania State University—Erie, Pitzer College, Purdue University, Rensselaer Polytechnic Institute, Rice University, Roger Williams University, Savannah College of Art and Design,

School of the Art Institute of Chicago, School of the Museum of Fine Arts, State University of New York—Fashion Institute of Technology, State University of New York—Purchase College, Swarthmore College, Syracuse University, Trinity College, University of California—Santa Barbara, University of California—Santa Cruz, University of Chicago, University of Hartford, University of Illinois, University of Miami, University of Richmond, University of San Francisco, University of Washington, University of Wisconsin, Washington University in St. Louis, Wesleyan University, Wheaton College, Yale University

STUDENTS SAY

Students mention that their favorite aspect of The Masters School is "the people" and "community" who embody "diversity in every sense." The multitude of "cultures and lifestyles" the school welcomes encourages students "to expand their beliefs" and "interests," and "if you want to try something new, there is always something interesting to learn here." Students also cite the "friendly faculty" who are "always there to help" as a hallmark of a Masters experience. Simply put, in the words of one student, "If you have a passion, Masters can help you dig deeper into it."

PARENTS SAY

Parents note that a major factor in choosing The Masters School for their child's education was "the caliber and overall concern for the students," along with the "multicultural" environment and "engaging setting." They appreciate that students "share a real desire to learn," which is bolstered by the "care displayed by faculty and administrators." As one parent explains, "We are comforted by the knowledge that my child's individual talents and ability will be nurtured at The Masters School." And this goes hand-in-hand with the school's vision of "broadening horizons" and "building upon students' core values through involvement in community service."

ALUMNI SAY

Many alumni recall the sense of "freedom" and "responsibility" The Masters School offered them, noting the excitement and eagerness students felt being part of "such an exceptional community." Former students felt "honored" to attend the school and note ultimately that "The Masters School taught me how to love learning."

MONSIGNOR SCANLAN HIGH SCHOOL

915 Hutchinson River Parkway, Bronx, NY 10465

Phone Number: 718-430-0100 • **Website:** www.scanlanhs.edu

Head of School: Sister Marie O'Donnell • **Director of Admissions:** Monsignor Thomas B. Derivan

ABOUT MONSIGNOR SCANLAN HIGH SCHOOL

Founded in 1949, Monsignor Scanlan High School is a Catholic, coeducational high school that offers a solid educational program rooted in the Catholic tradition and faith. With a focus on community service, the school endeavors to help students develop into keen and compassionate-minded individuals. The school is part of the educational services of the Parish of St. Helena, staffed by the Dominican Sisters of Sparkill and dedicated lay teachers, many of whom are Scanlan graduates. It is also accredited by the Middle States Association of Colleges and High Schools

MISSION STATEMENT

According to the school's website, Monsignor Scanlan High School is a school where "God is honored, praised, and loved." Its administration and faculty strive to "help our students to grow in the image of Jesus Christ, Our Lord and Our Savior," by challenging them to "grow in age, wisdom, and grace before God and men (Luke 1:49)."

WHERE STUDENTS COME FROM

The majority of Monsignor Scanlan High School's students come from Manhattan and the Bronx.

General

Type of School	Private
Religious Affiliation	Catholic
Coeducational	Yes
Boarding	No
Day School	Yes
Dress Code	Yes
Founded	1949

Students

Enrollment (Grades 9–12)	570
% African American	36
% Hispanic/Latino	58
% Asian	1
% Caucasian	5

Admissions Selectivity

Requires Standardized Test Scores	Yes; TACHS

COMPARABLE SCHOOLS

Cardinal Hayes; Fordham; Loyola; Monsignor; Regis; Rice; St. Agnes Boys; Xavier

Academics

Student/Faculty Ratio   15:1

Extracurricular
MOST POPULAR
INTERSCHOLASTIC SPORTS
MALE
Baseball, basketball, volleyball
FEMALE
Basketball, softball, volleyball

Financial

Annual Tuition $4,800
      **

COLLEGES THAT RECENT GRADS ARE ATTENDING

Cornell University, University of Rochester, Boston College, Johns Hopkins University, Rensselaer Polytechnic Institute, Syracuse University, Columbia University, Notre Dame University, Old Dominion University, University of Virginia, Dartmouth University, Brown University, Duke University, State University of New York—University at Buffalo, New York University, State University of New York at Binghamton, State University of New York at Albany, Fordham University, St. John's University, Marymount University, State University of New York—Maritime, Manhattan College, State University of New York—Stony Brook, College of New Rochelle, Iona College

MOTHER CABRINI HIGH SCHOOL

701 Fort Washington Avenue, New York, NY 10040

Phone Number: 212-923-3540 • **Website:** www.cabrinihs.com

Head of School: Brian Donahue • **Dean of Academics:** Joan Close

ABOUT MOTHER CABRINI HIGH SCHOOL

Mother Cabrini High School was founded in 1899 by St. Frances Xavier Cabrini and is sponsored by the Missionary Sisters of the Sacred Heart of Jesus, the order she founded. Mother Cabrini High School's peaceful campus overlooking the Hudson River provides a safe and enriching learning environment in which students receive an education of "the mind, character, heart, and soul." Mother Cabrini High School stands as a model of dedication and excellence in secondary education for young women, and 100 percent of MCHS graduates are accepted into colleges and universities, many receiving awards and scholarships. Mother Cabrini High School is among the nation's award-winning schools and the only Catholic High School in New York State to twice receive the U.S. Department of Education's "Blue Ribbon School of Excellence" award in 1986–1987 and 1997–1998.

MISSION STATEMENT

"As a Catholic high school and following the example of our foundress, Saint Frances Xavier Cabrini, we pledge ourselves to provide for our students a spiritual atmosphere promoting a love of God and recognition of the dignity of each individual. Echoing her words, we work for the "education of the heart," education as an act of love. This is best done in an atmosphere that engenders and supports affective and interactive relationships. As an educational institution, we are committed to fostering a love for learning and the achievement of academic excellence by the recognition of our professional roles and responsibilities. As educators we are committed, in the words of St. Frances Xavier Cabrini, 'to form the intellect in truth and to educate the heart in such a way that what is held within the intellect will become the norm of life.'"

General

Type of School	Private
Religious Affiliation	Catholic
Coeducational	No
Boarding	No
Day School	Yes
Dress Code	Yes
Founded	1899

Students

Enrollment (Grades 9–12)	415
% Male/Female	0/100
% African American	21.9
% Hispanic/Latino	74.8
% Asian	.6
% Caucasian	2.7
% International Students	15
% Out-of-State Students	.1
# States Represented	2

Admissions Selectivity

Requires Standardized Test Scores	Yes; TACHS
Application Essay	None

Academics

REQUIRED CLASSES

4 years: Religion, English, social studies, physical education

3 years: Math, science

2 years: Foreign language

1 year: Art/music

1 semester: Health

ADDITIONAL REQUIREMENTS

40 hours of work with the Cabrini Community Service Program

Student/Faculty Ratio   15:1

Extracurricular

MOST POPULAR

INTERSCHOLASTIC SPORTS

FEMALE

Basketball, cheerleading, High Voltage Energy Up Program, softball, volleyball

% Students Who Play Interscholastic Sports   19

Financial

Annual Tuition $6,185

% Students Receiving
  Financial Aid   55

Average Financial Aid/Scholarship
          $600–$5,000 anually
              *

THE IDEAL APPLICANT

The ideal applicant is "a young woman who is eager to begin a journey of self-discovery leading to academic success, a promising future, and a life of service to others. She should seek an education of not only the mind, but also of the character, heart, and soul. The ideal applicant to Mother Cabrini High School should also aspire to use Cabrini's strong college preparatory curriculum to ready herself for higher education."

WHERE STUDENTS COME FROM

Mother Cabrini High School attracts students from "all over New York City and Westchester, with a large concentration of students from Manhattan and the Bronx."

ORIENTATION PROCESS FOR NEW STUDENTS

Orientation lasts for two days and is designed to introduce students to the building, faculty, and peers. For the first six weeks of class, the guidance department assists students in their adjustment to high school. Each student is assigned a senior or junior to be their peer counselor. All new students have individual meetings with a guidance counselor, followed by weekly group meetings.

COLLEGES THAT RECENT GRADS ARE ATTENDING

Adelphi University, Babson College, Barnard College, Berkeley College, Boston College, Brandeis University, Cabrini College, City University of New York—Brooklyn College, City University of New York—City College, City University of New York—Hunter College, Clark Atlanta University, College of Mount St. Vincent, College of New Rochelle, Columbia University, Cornell University, Fairfield University, Fairleigh Dickinson University, Fordham University, Hampton University, Hofstra University, Iona College, Lafayette College, Long Island University, Marymount College, New York University, Northeastern University, Pace University, Pennsylvania State University, Quinnipiac University, Saint Bonaventure University, St. John's University, St. Joseph's College, St. Peter's College, St. Thomas Aquinas College, Siena College, Skidmore College, State University of New York at Buffalo, State University of New York at Stony

Brook, Syracuse University, University of Hartford, University of Maryland, University of Scranton, University of South Carolina, Vassar College, Wells College

Students Say

Cabrini students appreciate "the quality of the teachers and their deep knowledge of their subject material," noting that their "hands-on and fun methods" help not only to instruct but to inspire. Also mentioned are "the wide variety of co-curricular activities and the impressive amount of study materials available to students on campus." "Close friendships" abound thanks to the "interesting and fun" clubs and activities. As one student says, "The school gives me all the skills I will need to be successful in life."

Parents Say

For parents, Mother Cabrini High School "just gets better and better." The decision to enroll their daughters at Mother Cabrini High School is more than easy due to its "welcoming atmosphere" and "exceptionally high rate of college-bound graduates." They report that teachers "truly care about their students and see the unique potential in every young woman that passes through their doors." One parent singles out the "confidence" and high "academic performance" of students, also mentioning the peace of mind the "safe, tranquil campus" offers.

Alumnae Say

Alumnae note their "amazing metamorphosis" as students at Cabrini, successfully making the transition from "unsociable introvert to outgoing public speaker" and from "girl to young woman of knowledge." They fondly remember the "loving and respectful" environment and the teachers and staff who provided "so much encouragement and extra help to make sure you completely understood the material." In the end, alumnae explained they received not only "more than a diploma," but also "happiness, education, and fun!"

NIGHTINGALE-BAMFORD SCHOOL

20 East Ninety-second Street, New York, NY 10128

Phone Number: 212-289-5020 • **Website:** www.nightingale.org

Head of School: Dorothy A. Hutcheson • **Director of Admissions:** Barbara H. Scott

General	
Type of School	Private
Religious Affiliation	None
Coeducational	No
Boarding	No
Day School	Yes
Dress Code	Yes
Founded	1920

Students	
Enrollment (Grades 9–12)	160
% Male/Female	0/100
% Caucasian	74
% Other	26

ABOUT NIGHTINGALE-BAMFORD SCHOOL

The Nightingale-Bamford School curriculum allows each student to obtain a strong foundation in the basic disciplines through small, structured classes and faculty advisors—whom the student selects—who help balance both curricular and extracurricular demands while meeting responsibilities in a healthy and efficient manner. The school is committed to imbuing students with a strong sense of self and passion for learning, thus ensuring current and future success.

Nightingale students are challenged to delve more deeply into their studies and challenge themselves both in and out of the classroom. Seniors may take Advanced Placement college-level work in an area of interest, or pursue a Senior Independent Study Project involving in-depth study on a project of their own design. There are also a bevy of extracurricular opportunities, including sports, drama, music, art, and a variety of clubs. Students may also take part in a variety of educational exchange and travel opportunities, and all students must complete a minimum of sixty hours of social service to graduate.

MISSION STATEMENT

According to the school's website, Nightingale-Bamford's founding motto—Veritas, Amicitia, Fides (Truth, Friendship, Loyalty)—encapsulates Miss Nightingale and Miss Bamford's desire to offer students the educational ideals of "academic rigor with an abiding commitment to each student's personal and moral development." The school is committed to providing students with a strong academic foundation in a supportive and welcoming environment that offers every opportunity to grow, learn, and succeed.

THE IDEAL APPLICANT

The school's website states that the Nightingale-Bamford School seeks intelligent, determined, and curious students with "strong academic and personal promise."

WHERE STUDENTS COME FROM

Nightingale students come from all parts of the city, including all of the boroughs (except Staten Island), Connecticut, New Jersey, and Westchester County.

COLLEGES THAT RECENT GRADS ARE ATTENDING

Brown University, University of Chicago, Columbia University, Connecticut College, Cornell University, Dartmouth College, Emory University, Georgetown University, George Washington University, Grinnell College, Hamilton College, Harvard University, Lehigh University, Middlebury College, New York University, Oberlin College, University of Pennsylvania, Syracuse University, Trinity College, Wesleyan University, University of Wisconsin

Academics

Student/Faculty Ratio	7:1

Extracurricular
MOST POPULAR
INTERSCHOLASTIC SPORTS
FEMALE

Badminton, basketball, lacrosse, gymnastics, soccer, softball, swimming, tennis, track, volleyball

Financial

Annual Tuition	$22,485–$24,450
	**

NOTRE DAME SCHOOL

327 West Thirteenth Street, New York, NY 10014

Phone Number: 212-620-5575 • **Website:** www.cheznous.org

Head of School: Sister Mary Dolan, S.U. • **Director of Admissions:** Robert Grote

General

Type of School	Private
Religious Affiliation	Catholic
Coeducational	No
Boarding	No
Day School	Yes
Dress Code	Yes
Founded	1912

Students

Enrollment (Grades 9–12)	300
% Male/Female	0/100

Admissions Selectivity

Applications Received	500
# Applicants Accepted	250
# Accepted Applicants Who Enrolled	85
Requires Standardized Test Scores	Yes; TACHS

About Notre Dame School

Notre Dame School was founded in 1912 by the Sisters of St. Ursula in their home, hence the nickname "chez nous." The school is a private, Catholic secondary school for girls with an enrollment of 300 and a student-faculty ratio of 14:1. Located in historic Greenwich Village, Notre Dame has been recognized by U.S. News and World Report as one of the "outstanding high schools" in the country.

Since its founding, education at Notre Dame has been characterized "by close, family-like relationships between students and faculty." The educational program at Notre Dame is college preparatory and directed toward the development of each student as a whole person. Notre Dame "seeks to help to meet the needs of each student intellectually, physically, socially, and spiritually."

Mission Statement

"Notre Dame School of Manhattan offers a Catholic education for young women in the tradition of Anne de Xainctonge. Inspired by the seventeenth-century pioneer in women's education, Notre Dame promotes academic excellence for girls, an awareness of God in their lives, and engagement in the world around them.

"At Notre Dame in the twenty-first century, the school's small, nurturing environment encourages each student to be open to personal and intellectual growth. The rich cultural, racial, and ethnic mosaic of Notre Dame's community and its urban location enhance global awareness. A challenging curriculum prepares talented young women for college and for lives of leadership and service."

The Ideal Applicant

Notre Dame seeks "smart, college-bound students who are eager to learn and who enjoy a small-school atmosphere."

Where Students Come From

Students come from "all over the New York Metropolitan area and more than half live in Manhattan."

Orientation Process for New Students

Incoming 9th graders attend a one-day orientation each September.

Colleges that Recent Grads Are Attending

Adelphi University, American University, Amherst College, Barry University, Bennington College, Boston College, Brown University, Carnegie Mellon University, Colgate University, College of the Holy Cross, College of Mount Saint Vincent, College of New Rochelle, Columbia University, Cornell University, City University of New York—Baruch College, City University of New York—Hunter College, Dartmouth University, Fairfield University, Fordham University, Franklin & Marshall College, Gettysburg College, Hampton University, Hofstra University, Howard University, Ithaca College, Le Moyne College, Loyola College, Manhattan College, Marist College, Marymount College, Middlebury College, Mount Holyoke College, New York University, Niagara University, Northeastern University, Northwestern University, Pace University, Pennsylvania State University, Princeton University, Quinnipiac University, Rochester Institute of Technology, Rutgers University, Seton Hall University, Smith College, St. Francis College, St. John's University, Stanford University, State University of New York at Albany, State University of New York at Binghamton, State University of New York—University at Buffalo, State University of New York—Oneonta, State University of New York—Oswego, State University of New York—Stony Brook, Syracuse University, Temple University, Trinity College, University of Chicago, University of Delaware, University of Hartford, University of Miami, University of Michigan, University of Pennsylvania, University of Scranton, Vassar College, Villanova University, Wellesley College, Wells College, Wesleyan University, Yale University

Academics

Required Classes

4 years: Religion, English, physical education, social studies

3 years: Foreign language, math, laboratory science

1 year: Art, American Studies, Latin

1 semester: Health education

Additional Requirements

40 hours of Community Service

Student/Faculty Ratio   14:1

Extracurricular

Most Popular Interscholastic Sports

Basketball, soccer, softball, volleyball

Financial

Annual Tuition	$7,200
Fees	$385

*

THE PACKER COLLEGIATE INSTITUTE

170 Joralemon Street, Brooklyn, NY 11201

Phone Number: 718-250-0288 • **Website:** www.packer.edu

Head of School: Susan Feibleman • **Director of Admissions:** Noah Reinhardt

General	
Type of School	Private
Religious Affiliation	None
Coeducational	Yes
Boarding	No
Day School	Yes
Dress Code	No
Founded	1845

ABOUT THE PACKER COLLEGIATE INSTITUTE

Founded in 1845, The Packer Collegiate Institute is the oldest independent school in Brooklyn. The curriculum is designed to encourage students to reach their full potential. Adding to this is a challenging academic program, a vibrant community, and an array of artistic and athletic programs.

According to the school's website, "a Packer education involves more than teachers motivating students to conquer academic milestones." The faculty is charged with broadening the definition of success to accommodate and promote the every aspect of a student. This process guides students in recognizing and enhancing their academic, emotional, and physical talents and skills. The school finds this balanced approach to be very helpful when attempting to identify different types of intelligence and in accommodating a wider variety of learning styles.

Packer is committed to diversity and the development of an educational environment that best prepares students to become contributing members of a multicultural and interconnected society. This goal is supported through a substantial support network that includes teachers, administrators, students, and parents who work toward excellence, respect, and success.

MISSION STATEMENT

According to the school's website, Packer Collegiate Institute offers a challenging academic program that involves and engages their students by pushing them to fully develop their talents and capabilities. The school believes that "a rich and varied educational experience fosters creative problem-solving, develops confident use of the intellect, and encourages personal growth and exploration." In this, its goal is to prepare its students not only for academic success, but also for a "fulfilling and meaningful life."

Colleges that Recent Grads Are Attending

American University, Amherst College, Bard College, Barnard College, Bates College, Berklee College of Music, Boston College, Boston University, Bowdoin College, Brown University, Bryn Mawr College, Carnegie Mellon University, Claremont McKenna College, Colgate University, Colorado College, Columbia University, Cornell University, Dartmouth College, Davidson College, Duke University, Emerson College, Emory University, Franklin & Marshall College, George Washington University, Georgetown University, Goucher College, Hampshire College, Harvard University, Haverford College, Howard University, John Hopkins University, Kenyon College, Lewis & Clark College, Maryland Institute College of Art, Massachusetts Institute of Technology, McGill University, Middlebury College, Mount Holyoke College, New York University, Northwestern University, Oberlin College, Oxford University, Pitzer College, Pomona College, School of Visual Arts, Skidmore College, Smith College, Stanford University, State University of New York—Geneseo, State University of New York-Purchase College, Swarthmore College, Trinity College, Tufts University, Tulane University, University of Chicago, University of Colorado—Boulder, University of Delaware, University of Maryland, University of Massachusetts—Amherst, University of North Carolina—Chapel Hill, University of Pennsylvania, University of Southern California, University of Vermont, University of Wisconsin, Vassar College, Washington University in St. Louis, Wesleyan University, Yale University

Academics

REQUIRED CLASSES

4 years: English, physical education
3 years: History, math, science, foreign language
2 years: Art
1 year: Health education

ADDITIONAL REQUIREMENTS

45 hours of school and community service

Student/Faculty Ratio   7:1

Extracurricular

MOST POPULAR INTERSCHOLASTIC SPORTS

MALE

Baseball, basketball, cross-country, soccer, squash, tennis, track & field

FEMALE

Basketball, cross-country, soccer, softball, squash, tennis, track & field, volleyball

Financial

Annual Tuition $22,000
                **

POLY PREP COUNTRY DAY SCHOOL

9216 Seventh Avenue, Brooklyn, NY 11228

Phone Number: 718-836-9800 • **Website:** www.polyprep.org

Head of School: David B. Harman • **Director of Admissions:** Lori W. Redell

General	
Type of School	Private
Religious Affiliation	None
Coeducational	Yes
Boarding	No
Day School	Yes
Dress Code	Yes
Founded	1854

Students	
Enrollment (Grades 9–12)	459
% Male/Female	54/46
% African American	12
% Hispanic/Latino	5
% Asian	6
% Caucasian	63
% International Students	0
% Out-of-State Students	1
# States Represented	2

Admissions Selectivity	
Requires Standardized Test Scores	Yes
Application Essay	No

ABOUT POLYTECHNIC PREP COUNTRY DAY SCHOOL

Opened in 1854 as the Brooklyn Collegiate and Polytechnic Institute, Poly Prep Country Day School has grown into a coeducational institution with a deliberate focus on instilling "the writing and critical thinking skills in students that will be vital to success in college, universities, and careers." The foundation of a liberal education, school administrators believe, is "to teach a respect for intellect, for the power of knowledge, and for the method of reason."

Grades 9 through 12 offer a wide variety of courses and programs in a strong college preparatory curriculum. The school's distribution requirements ensure that all students experience a challenging and balanced curriculum in the academic core subjects, including the arts and physical education.

In their junior and senior years, students may choose from an extensive array of electives that allow select individuals to study in depth their particular areas of interest. For those qualified, Advanced Placement courses are offered in all major disciplines, and students entering Form III may apply to take the Special Advanced Program in Science and Mathematics.

MISSION STATEMENT

"At Poly Prep, we believe in working toward the development of the whole person—health, mind, and character. We also believe that such an education can only be obtained within a diverse learning community. To this end, the school has dedicated itself to creating a genuinely heterogeneous student body, one that bridges differences and provides a vibrant and inclusive educational environment. When students from different backgrounds work, learn, and succeed together, individual learning is enhanced, as are the prospects for the well-being of the immediate community, and for our society as a whole."

THE IDEAL APPLICANT

"A Poly Prep education fosters an appreciation and understanding of our national and local diversity. With a curricular vision that promotes character, sounds values, and ethical choices, we set as our objective the development of students who are academically strong, morally centered, and personally committed to becoming citizens of a positive global future."

WHERE STUDENTS COME FROM

Students come primarily from Brooklyn, Manhattan, Queens, and Staten Island.

ORIENTATION PROCESS FOR NEW STUDENTS

Upon enrollment in March, students are welcomed to campus for an orientation day in late May. New students come to campus to take placement exams in late May or early June, and there is an additional one-day orientation program in September prior to the start of classes.

COLLEGES THAT RECENT GRADS ARE ATTENDING

American University, Amherst College, Bard College, Barnard College, Bates College, Berklee College of Music, Boston College, Boston University, Bowdoin College, Brandeis University, Brown University, Bryn Mawr College, Bucknell University, Carleton College, Carnegie Mellon University, City University of New York—Hunter College, Claremont McKenna College, Colgate University, College of William & Mary, Columbia University, Cornell University, Dartmouth College, Drexel University, Duke University, Emory University, Fairfield University, Fairleigh Dickinson University, Fordham University, Georgetown

Academics

ADDITIONAL REQUIREMENTS

Community Service

Student/Faculty Ratio	6:1

Extracurricular

MOST POPULAR INTERSCHOLASTIC SPORTS

MALE

Baseball, basketball, cross-country, football, golf, lacrosse, soccer, squash, tennis, track, volleyball, wrestling

FEMALE

Basketball, cross-country, golf, lacrosse, soccer, softball, squash, tennis, track, volleyball

% Students Who Play Interscholastic Sports	65

Financial

Annual Tuition	$25,150
Endowment	$15 million
% Students Receiving Financial Aid	28–30
Average Financial Aid/ Scholarship	$12,500

*

University, George Washington University, Hampshire College, Harvard University, Haverford College, Hobart and William Smith Colleges, Hofstra University, Indiana University, Ithaca College, Johns Hopkins University, Johnson & Wales University, Kenyon College, Lehigh University, London School of Economics, Muhlenberg College, New York University, Northeastern University, Northwestern University, Pomona College, Princeton University, Rensselaer Polytechnic Institute, Rochester Institute of Technology, Sarah Lawrence College, School of Visual Arts, Seton Hall University, Skidmore College, St. John's University, Stanford University, State University of New York at Albany, State University of New York at Binghamton, Swarthmore College, Syracuse University, Temple University, Tufts University, Tulane University, University of Aberdeen, University of Arizona, University of California—Berkeley, University of Chicago, University of Miami, University of Michigan, University of Notre Dame, University of Pennsylvania, University of San Francisco, University of Virginia, United States Military Academy, United States Naval Academy, Vanderbilt University, Vassar College, Villanova University, Wesleyan University, Wheaton College, Williams College, Xavier University, Yale University

STUDENTS SAY

Poly Prep students are keen on the "amazing" facilities and "friendly" environment, noting that "students, teachers, and staff are always bright and welcoming." The school's diversity is "promoted not only in the student body but in the countless academic, athletic, and extracurricular arenas." Naturally, this lends itself to "a solid community" where "all members have a mutual desire to learn." Students form "very close bonds" with all their teachers and deeply "value these relationships" that encourage them to do their best. This "constant support" is what, in the words of one student, "makes going to Poly such a pleasure."

PARENTS SAY

Parents appreciate Poly Prep's "philosophy of developing 'the whole child'" and their focus on developing "solid morals and a good set of ethics" in their children. The "wonderfully diverse community" stands out, as does the "beautiful campus" and "excellent program" that offers "a niche for every child" by being "open to every interest and "encouraging creativity." Combine all this with the "excellent reputation" in college advising and "the open and frequent dialogue between faculty and students," and it's easy to understand why parents found the school "hard to resist."

ALUMNI SAY

Alumni fondly recall the "many challenging and vigorous" times they experienced in the classroom and on the sports field at Poly Prep. Even to this day they still have "an intense feeling of accomplishment and pride" when reflecting on their student days. They cite the school's focus on "the uniqueness in each individual student" and the "uncommon respect and spirit" Poly had for its students as major factors in the successful production of "confident and extremely well-prepared college-bound young adults." Former students feel "lucky to have gone there and still do!"

PROFESSIONAL CHILDREN'S SCHOOL

132 West Sixtieth Street, New York, NY 10023

Phone Number: 212-582-3116 • **Website:** www.pcs-nyc.org

Head of School: James Dawson • **Director of Admissions:** Sherrie Hinkle

ABOUT THE PROFESSIONAL CHILDREN'S SCHOOL

The Professional Children's School was founded in 1914 by Jane Harris Hall and Jean Greer Robinson, whose vision it was to deliver an education to children already engaged in careers in the arts and who, due to their schedules, had been until then unable to gain an education.

The program at PCS provides a challenging college preparatory education, and its liberal arts curriculum serves students preparing for college work as well as those whose academic education will end after high school. Approximately 80 percent of PCS students attend college on a full- or part-time basis immediately after high school, while the remainder—who don't already have professional careers—choose to continue their professional training. The school is committed to providing a rounded education to students regardless of their professional goals.

Concessions are made to students who, although still enrolled, have commitments to their careers. And while such busy schedules tend to interfere with a student's time and interests, PCS's diploma requirements provide for a solid background in a wide range of academic disciplines.

General	
Type of School	Private
Religious Affiliation	None
Coeducational	Yes
Boarding	No
Day School	Yes
Dress Code	No
Founded	1914

Students	
Enrollment (Grades 9–12)	149
% African American	7
% Hispanic/Latino	3
% Asian	25
% Caucasian	65

Admissions Selectivity	
Application Essay	Yes

COMPARABLE SCHOOLS

Fiorello H. LaGuardia High School of Music & Art and Performing Arts

MISSION STATEMENT

According to the school's website, the Professional Children's School is dedicated "to providing challenging academics for young people working in or studying for careers in the performing and visual arts, competitive sports, and modeling." Faculty and administration alike strive to meet the diverse needs of their students while offering an exemplary college preparatory education. The school also serves as a training ground for students looking to "balance the demands of their professional, personal, and academic lives" and who are often subject to professional pressures as well as adolescent ones. All of this is done in an environment that promotes respect for ethnic, economic, geographic, racial, and artistic diversity. At Professional Children's School, students are taught in a tight-knit community that welcomes artistic expression while instilling academic excellence and social responsibility.

COLLEGES THAT RECENT GRADS ARE ATTENDING

American University, Amherst College, Barnard College, Bennington College, Boston Conservatory, Boston University, Bowdoin College, Brown University, Columbia University, Connecticut College, Cornell University, Curtis Institute of Music, Dartmouth College, Duke University, Eastman School of Music, Emerson College, Fairleigh Dickinson University, Fordham University, George Washington University, Georgetown University, Goucher College, Harvard University, Indiana University, Ithaca College, Johns Hopkins University, The Juilliard School, Manhattan College, Manhattan School of Music, Marymount College, Marymount Manhattan College, Michigan State University, Middlebury College, Mills College, Montclair State University, New England Conservatory, New York University, Northwestern University, Oberlin College, Oklahoma City University, Peabody Conservatory of Music, Princeton University, San Francisco Conservatory of Music, Sarah Lawrence College, Seton Hall University, Skidmore College, State University of New York—Purchase, Syracuse University, Tufts University, Tulane University, University of Arizona, University of the Arts, University of California—Berkeley, University of Central Florida, University of Chicago, University of Cincinnati, University of Maryland, University of Miami—Florida, University of Michigan—Ann Arbor, University of Southern California, University of Tampa, Vassar College, Williams College, Yale University

PROFESSIONAL PERFORMING ARTS SCHOOL

328 West Forty-eighth Street, New York, NY 10036

Phone Number: 212-247-8652 • **Website:** www.ppasinfo.org

Head of School: Keith Ryan • **Director of Admissions:** Carole Lunney

ABOUT PROFESSIONAL PERFORMING ARTS SCHOOL

Since 1990, when the school was founded to offer exceptional educational and vocational opportunities to students in the arts, the Professional Performing Arts School has dedicated itself to producing some of the nation's finest actors, dancers, and musicians (20 percent of students already work professionally in their respective artistic fields). In its own words, "PPAS is committed to nurturing each student's passion for the performing arts and thirst for knowledge by providing a safe, supportive community that inspires lifelong learning and commitment to social change."

The school features a flexible schedule that involves academic study in the morning, followed by professional instruction in the afternoon in the student's chosen art. Students are also able to gain valuable insight into the professional world thanks to the school's partnerships with the Actors Studio for Drama and Musical Theater, the Ailey School of Dance, the Harlem School of the Arts for Instrumental and Vocal Music, and the School of American Ballet. Entrance into this school is extremely competitive and based largely on performance during open auditions (check the school's website for exact audition dates as they vary depending on which borough the student lives in). Also worth mentioning is that at 98 percent, PPAS has the third highest graduation rate of all New York City public schools.

General

Type of School	Public
Religious Affiliation	None
Coeducational	Yes
Boarding	No
Day School	Yes
Dress Code	No
Founded	1990

Students

Enrollment (Grades 9–12)	375
% Male/Female	30/70
% African American	28
% Hispanic/Latino	16
% Asian	5
% Caucasian	51
% Out-of-State Students	0
# States Represented	1

Admissions Selectivity

COMPARABLE SCHOOLS

Fiorello H. LaGuardia High School of Music & Art and Performing Arts, Frank Sinatra School of Arts, Professional Children's School

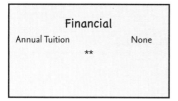

Financial	
Annual Tuition	None
**	

MISSION STATEMENT

According to the school's website, PPAS seeks to provide students with a "vigorous, meaningful academic curriculum" in a supportive and personalized environment that allows individual development in dance, drama, musical theater, and vocal music to coincide with preparing for and receiving a Regents-endorsed diploma.

WHERE STUDENTS COME FROM

Students come from all five boroughs of New York City.

COLLEGES THAT RECENT GRADS ARE ATTENDING

Carnegie Mellon University, Columbia University, Harvard University, New York University

QUEENS HIGH SCHOOL FOR THE SCIENCES AT YORK COLLEGE

94-50 159th Street, Jamaica, NY 11451

Phone Number: 718-657-3181 • **Website:** www.qhssyc.org

Head of School: Brian Jetter

ABOUT QUEENS HIGH SCHOOL FOR THE SCIENCES AT YORK COLLEGE

The Queens High School for the Sciences provides a rigorous technology-based college preparatory curriculum in collaboration with York College that features an emphasis in the study of science, mathematics, and biotechnology. Specializations in these subject areas expose students to potential careers in medicine or other scientific fields through opportunities such as the "Bridge to Medicine" program, a NASA "SEMAA" program, and partnerships with Mt. Sinai School of Medicine, the Academy of Medicine, and York College and the City University of New York system. Students also have the chance to enroll in college-level courses, and truly exceptional students may also complete many of their high school Regents requirements in three years. Students at QHSS are constantly encouraged by faculty and parents alike to achieve recognition and reach their full academic potential. For example, a research advisor helps guide students in entering research projects for science, math, or technology fairs, and enrichment courses are offered after school and on weekends. As is the case with nearly all selective public schools, admission to the school is selective and based on required exam performance.

General

Type of School	Public
Religious Affiliation	None
Coeducational	Yes
Boarding	No
Day School	Yes
Dress Code	No
Founded	2002

Students

Enrollment (Grades 9–12)	377
% Male/Female	51/49
% African American	28
% Hispanic/Latino	12
% Asian	47
% Caucasian	13

Admissions Selectivity

Requires Standardized Test Scores	Yes
Application Essay	None

COMPARABLE SCHOOLS

Bronx High School of Science; Brooklyn Latin School; Brooklyn Technical High School; High School of American Studies at Lehman College; High School for Mathematics, Science and Engineering at City College; Staten Island Technical High School; Stuyvesant High School

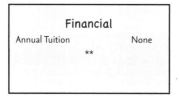

Financial	
Annual Tuition	None
**	

MISSION STATEMENT

According to the school's website, QHSS believes that students are "successful when nurtured in a small learning community where they can be challenged to expand their intellect through inquiry-based learning, problem-solving, research, and presentation-making."

WHERE STUDENTS COME FROM

Students come to the school from all five boroughs of New York City.

RAMAZ—THE RABBI JOSEPH F. LOOKSTEIN UPPER SCHOOL

60 East Seventy-eighth Street, New York, NY 10021

Phone Number: 212-774-8070 • **Website:** www.ramaz.org

Head of School: Rabbi Haskel Lookstein • **Director of Admissions:** Danielle Gorlin Lassner

ABOUT RAMAZ—THE RABBI JOSEPH F. LOOKSTEIN UPPER SCHOOL

Founded in 1937 by the Rabbi Joseph F. Lookstein, the Ramaz School is a coeducational yeshivah day school that offers Judaic and general courses. The school is a religious educational institution whose student body is composed of every section of the Jewish community. Consistent with the mission of Ramaz and its commitment to provide its students with the opportunity to grow in Torah learning and in practical observance, a diverse student body abounds. In the school's own words, "Our educational programs are most effective in an environment where children from all social and economic segments of the Jewish community grow together and learn from each other."

MISSION STATEMENT

According to the school's website, the Ramaz School's mission is to "educate its students in the two civilizations of which they are a part." With equal emphasis, the school simultaneously instructs its students in all aspects regarding the culture, history, values, and heritage of both Judaism and the United States.

General	
Type of School	Private
Religious Affiliation	Jewish
Coeducational	Yes
Boarding	No
Day School	Yes
Dress Code	Yes
Founded	1937

Students	
Enrollment (Grades 9–12)	494
% Caucasian	100

Admissions Selectivity	
Requires Standardized Test Scores	Yes; BJE
Application Essay	No

COMPARABLE SCHOOLS

The Abraham Joshua Heschel High School; Solomon Schechter High School; Yeshiva of Flatbush

Academics

Student/Faculty Ratio　　　8:1

Extracurricular
MOST POPULAR
INTERSCHOLASTIC SPORTS
MALE
Baseball, basketball, fencing, soccer, tennis, track
FEMALE
Basketball, dance, fencing, soccer, softball, tennis, track, volleyball

Financial
Annual Tuition　　　$20,000
**

THE IDEAL APPLICANT

According to the school's website, the Ramaz School looks for students of "good character and strong educational promise" who will grow in their dedication to Judaism, become actively engaged in their learning experiences, "be stimulated by the rigorous double curriculum, pursue independent work and contribute to the academic and co-curricular life of the learning community."

WHERE STUDENTS COME FROM

The school attracts students from the greater New York Metropolitan area, including Queens, Nassau and Westchester counties, as well as from New Jersey and Connecticut.

REGIS HIGH SCHOOL

55 East Eighty-fourth Street, New York, NY 10028

Phone Number: 212-288-1100 • **Website:** www.regis-nyc.org

Head of School: Dr. Gary J. Tocchet • **Director of Admissions:** Eric DiMichele

ABOUT REGIS HIGH SCHOOL

Regis High School was founded in 1914 as a tuition-free Jesuit college preparatory institution for young men. Its academic program is based on a traditional liberal arts curriculum that affirms that "education should be more than the acquisition of facts and the primary purpose of education is to train the intellect as fully as possible."

The requirements of the curriculum are also shaped by the nature of the Regis student body. Courses are intensive and accelerated in accordance with the fact that all admitted are, by national standards, intellectually gifted. In other words, the school does not 'track' students according to ability; all students take essentially the same courses through junior year.

While encouraging students to fulfill their academic goals, the school also aims to assist them in becoming "a committed Christian whose love for Jesus Christ and his people motivates him to share his gifts and himself in the service of others." As school officials say, "Within the limits proper to any schooling experience, we hope to exercise a positive and constructive influence on these young men during four of the most formative years of their lives."

MISSION STATEMENT

"As a Jesuit school, Regis is committed to both academic excellence and fostering a spirit of generosity and service to those in need. With an emphasis on academic rigor and Catholic formation, the school's program is designed to promote each student's intellectual and spiritual growth grounded in a deepening relationship with Jesus Christ. Regis seeks to inspire and train the ethnically diverse young men in its care to become imaginative leaders committed to promoting justice and exerting leadership in the Church, in the civic community, and in their chosen profession."

General	
Type of School	Private
Religious Affiliation	Catholic
Coeducational	No
Boarding	No
Day School	Yes
Dress Code	Yes
Founded	1914

Students	
Enrollment (Grades 9–12)	535
% Male/Female	100/0
% African American	4
% Hispanic/Latino	15
% Asian	9
% Caucasian	72
% Out-of-State Students	16
# States Represented	3

Admissions Selectivity	
Applications Received	800
# Applicants Accepted	135
# Accepted Applicants Who Enrolled	130
Requires Standardized Test Scores	Yes
Application Essay	Yes
Median SAT	1420

THE IDEAL APPLICANT

Regis High School looks for "Roman Catholic young men from the New York metropolitan area who demonstrate superior intellectual and leadership" potential.

WHERE STUDENTS COME FROM

The majority of Regis High School students come "from the five boroughs of New York City, with a substantial number from Westchester County, Upstate New York, Long Island, New Jersey, and Connecticut."

ORIENTATION PROCESS FOR NEW STUDENTS

Several evening and day events are held for accepted students and their families. Also, upperclassmen are assigned to mentor new freshmen.

COLLEGES THAT RECENT GRADS ARE ATTENDING

American University, Amherst College, Babson College, Boston College, Boston University, Brandeis University, Carleton College, Carnegie Mellon University, Catholic University, Chicago University, City University of New York—Queens College, Colgate University, Columbia University, Connecticut College, The Cooper Union for the Advancement of Science and Art, Cornell University, Dartmouth University, Davidson College, Duke University, Emory University, Fairfield University, Fordham University, George Washington University, Georgetown University, Hamilton College, Harvard University, Harvey Mudd University, Hofstra University, Holy Cross College, Ithaca College, Johns Hopkins University, Lafayette, LaSalle University, Lehigh University, Loyola University—Chicago, Loyola University—Maryland, Loyola University—Marymount, Loyola University—New Orleans, Massachusetts Institute of Technology, McGill University, Middlebury College, Muhlenberg College, New York University, Northeastern University, Northwestern University, Notre Dame University, Oberlin College, Olin College, Pennsylvania State University, University of Pennsylvania, Pomona College, Princeton University, Quinnipiac University, Rice University, Rose-Hulman Institute of Technology, Rutgers University, St. Francis College, Stanford University, State University of New York at Albany, State University of New York at Binghamton, State University of New York—University at Buffalo, State University of New York—Geneseo, State University of New York—Purchase, State University of New York—Stony Brook,

Swathmore College, Syracuse University, Temple University, Tufts University, Tulane University, University of Michigan, University of Rochester, United States Military Academy, United States Naval Academy, University of Southern California, Vanderbilt University, Vassar College, Villanova University, University of Virginia, Washington University in St. Louis, Wesleyan University, Yale University

STUDENTS SAY

Students praise "the overwhelming sense of community" at Regis High School, saying that a shared "level of intelligence and faith" informs the "overall feeling of camaraderie" and "brotherhood" that distinguishes this learning institution. Teachers here are involved in every facet of student life" and they take "active roles in developing well-rounded young men." And it is this sense of "generosity and gratitude that continues to mold young men into compassionate leaders intent on positively changing the world."

PARENTS SAY

Parents of Regis students have nothing but high marks for the school and the sense of community it creates, praising the "impressive academic curriculum, the preparation given to the boys for college, and how many alumni returned and were part of the faculty and staff." This dedication to excellence is bolstered by a program that "teaches by example, not just books," and located in an environment that fosters "the growth and well-being of its students," creating "independent, well-versed, and morally aware" young men.

ALUMNI SAY

Regis alumni rank their years spent at the school as some of the most important and influential of their lives, instilling in them "a deep commitment to serve mankind" by following the school's example of "dedication to public service." Others recall the "great and selfless teachers" who taught "the value of optimism over pessimism" and encouraged students "to work hard and think." Ultimately, the lasting legacy of Regis is that of its students, who seek to carry on the school's mission by harboring "the desire to always do the greater good."

RICE HIGH SCHOOL

74 West 124th Street, Harlem, NY 10027

Phone Number: 212-369-4100 • **Website:** www.ricehighschool.com

Head of School: Brother John M. Walderman, CFC • **Director of Admissions:** Anthony Ashe

General

Type of School	Private
Religious Affiliation	Catholic
Coeducational	No
Boarding	No
Day School	Yes
Dress Code	Yes
Founded	1938

Students

Enrollment (Grades 9–12)	400
% Male/Female	100/0
% African American	75
% Hispanic/Latino	25

Admissions Selectivity

Requires Standardized Test Scores	Yes; TACHS

COMPARABLE SCHOOLS

Cardinal Hayes; Fordham; Loyola; Monsignor Scanlan; Regis; St. Agnes Boys; Xavier

ABOUT RICE HIGH SCHOOL

In 1938, Rice High School was founded by the Congregation of Christian Brothers as a community of religious and laity in Central Harlem. They cherish the opportunity to educate young men intellectually, physically, emotionally, socially, and most of all, spiritually.

The school's goal is to nurture and encourage the uniqueness of each student by cultivating a caring but structured learning environment in which each student can emerge as a confident and disciplined young adult.

By expecting each student to strive to academic excellence, they challenge them to fulfill their own potential by becoming a critical user of all forms of information and a lifelong learner. Students are rewarded in this through scholarships (worth half the current tuition) that are doled out based on TACHS entrance exam performance. These scholarships may be renewed annually so long as a student maintains at least an 85 percent grade on their final report card.

Mission Statement

The school's website states that the school shares a dedication to Catholic-Christian values in its devotion to the academic and spiritual development of young men who possess "strong character and Christian values." Rice strives to lead each student along a path of "ethical and moral behavior that will sustain him in the roles he enacts in his family, vocation, community, church and society." Leadership, responsibility, and accountability are stressed in the curriculum since the faculty and administration make it clear that they expect all Rice men to enter into college and complete their respective degrees "with the intention to be leaders of their communities."

Academics

REQUIRED CLASSES

Religion, English, math, Spanish, science, social studies, art, music, physical education, electives

ADDITIONAL REQUIREMENTS

Community service

Student/Faculty Ratio   11:1

Extracurricular

MOST POPULAR

INTERSCHOLASTIC SPORTS

Baseball, basketball, bowling, track

Financial

Annual Tuition $5,350

**

RIVERDALE COUNTRY SCHOOL

5250 Fieldston Road, Riverdale, NY 10471

Phone Number: 718-519-2715 • **Website:** www.riverdale.edu

Head of School: Dr. John R. Johnson • **Director of Admissions:** Jenna C. Rogers

General	
Type of School	Private
Religious Affiliation	None
Coeducational	Yes
Boarding	No
Day School	Yes
Dress Code	None
Founded	1907

Students	
Enrollment (Grades 9–12)	465
% Male/Female	50/50
# Countries Represented	1
# States Represented	2

Admissions Selectivity	
# Accepted Applicants Who Enrolled	125
Requires Standardized Test Scores	Yes
Application Essay	Yes

ABOUT RIVERDALE COUNTRY SCHOOL

Since its inception in 1907, Riverdale has been shaped by the commitment of its founder, Frank S. Hackett, to what he called "scholarly, intimate teaching, rigorous, uncompromising academic standards, abundant play in the open and a care for the best influences." These values are still the keystone of Riverdale's character, which features the devotion of its faculty, the spirit and diversity of its students, the excellence of its facilities, and the atmosphere of its beautiful campus.

Riverdale offers a liberal arts education and a traditional college preparatory curriculum. Art, music, and drama are integral parts of all students' programs. Riverdale also offers a full range of intramural and interscholastic sports, including baseball, basketball, fencing, field hockey, football, gymnastics, lacrosse, soccer, softball, track and cross-country running, wrestling, tennis on outdoor courts, and swimming in our six-lane, twenty-five-meter pool.

Riverdale is constantly seeking to affirm "its commitment to the development of courage, responsibility, integrity, and civilized intelligence in the girls and boys and young women and men who attend the school," through the numerous activities and clubs that heighten students' awareness of the larger community.

MISSION STATEMENT

"The mission of Riverdale Country School is to offer students the foundations of a liberal education that will enable them to lead rewarding, worthwhile lives. Such an education demands the cultivation of the varied talents of our students and active attention to their intellectual, artistic, physical, moral, emotional, and social development from childhood through adolescence. We seek to foster habits of mind that will make learning an enduring part of their lives."

The Ideal Applicant

Riverdale Country School seeks students who have "a wide variety of talents and interests, and in addition to our rigorous academic program, they participate in the arts, athletics, and many student activities. What all our students have in common is curiosity, a willingness to try new things, and an appreciation for the community."

Where Students Come From

According to the school, "60 percent of students live in Manhattan; 30 percent live in the Bronx and Westchester County; and the last 10 percent live in New Jersey and other parts of the New York metro area."

Orientation Process for New Students

Riverdale holds a variety of orientation events for new students and their classmates at the start of the school year.

Colleges that Recent Grads Are Attending

Amherst College, Bard College, Barnard College, Boston College, Boston University, Bowdoin College, Brandeis University, Brown University, Carleton College, Carnegie Mellon University, Colby College, Colgate University, Columbia University, Connecticut College, Cornell University, Dartmouth College, Duke University, Emory University, George Washington University, Georgetown University, Harvard College, Haverford College, Kenyon College, Johns Hopkins University, Middlebury College, New York University, Northwestern University, Oberlin College, Princeton University, Radcliffe College, Skidmore College, Stanford University, Swarthmore College, Trinity College, Tufts University, Tulane University, University of Chicago, University of Colorado, University of Michigan, University of Pennsylvania, University of Wisconsin, Vanderbilt University, Vassar College, Washington University, Wesleyan University, Williams College, Yale University

Academics
Required Classes
4 years: English, physical education
3 years: History, math, foreign language, art
2 years: Science
1 year: Integrated liberal studies, health education

Student/Faculty Ratio   8:1

Extracurricular
Most Popular
Interscholastic Sports
Male
Baseball; basketball; cross-country, fencing, football, golf, lacrosse, soccer, swimming, tennis, track, wrestling
Female
Basketball, cross-country, fencing, field hockey, golf, gymnastics, lacrosse, soccer, softball, swimming, tennis, track, volleyball

Financial
Annual Tuition $31,200
% Students Receiving
Financial Aid   20
*

Students Say

For students, Riverdale is all about the "cohesiveness and friendliness" that inform "the feeling of community" and "openness and desire to accept new people into their lives" that makes the school so extraordinary. This welcoming atmosphere goes hand in hand with "the supportive students and faculty," a dean who is "always there to talk to anyone about anything," and "wonderful academic and athletic opportunities"—not to mention the "fantastic benefit" of being in a scenic, peaceful area but close enough to the city "to go home and have dinner with your family."

Parents Say

Parents chose Riverdale for its "outstanding campus" and "intelligent, inspirational, and involved" teachers, not to mention the "stellar science labs, beautiful ball-fields, and terrific theater program." They note "students share a sense of place and intellectual curiosity" that is fostered by the "warm, caring environment" and "bucolic setting." Parents also appreciate the bounty and balance of academic, athletic, arts, extracurricular, and community service programs. With a "challenging yet engaging" curriculum that "encourages critical thinking," it's no wonder many parents are saying "Viva Riverdale!"

Alumni Say

In retrospect, alumni appreciate "the great teachers" at Riverdale who inspired them. They note the "classical liberal arts education" and "extensive community service" in shaping who they were and who they have become. And it is this "sense of your place in the larger world" that has continued to inform them long after leaving the school.

ROBERT LOUIS STEVENSON SCHOOL

24 West Seventy-fourth Street, New York, NY 10023

Phone Number: 212-787-6400 • **Website:** www.stevenson-school.org

Head of School: B. H. Henrichsen

ABOUT ROBERT LOUIS STEVENSON SCHOOL

The Robert Louis Stevenson School offers a welcoming environment for students who have experienced great difficulty in achieving academic excellence in a traditional school environment. It does so by providing a safe haven for students, making them feel comfortable asking for help and giving them the guidance needed to succeed.

While sensitive to individual needs, teachers at Stevenson also understand the importance of providing the leadership and direction necessary for students to feel secure. While setting clear limits, they encourage their students sincerely and are quick to give recognition to every sign of effort and achievement. It is their marked commitment to their student's intellectual and psychological development that is the hallmark of this school.

MISSION STATEMENT

According to the school's website, Stevenson is committed to preparing "bright underachieving adolescents academically and developmentally for college." Students here are welcomed regardless of the difficulties they may have had at previous institutions, and the school prides itself on removing the academic, emotional, and social pressures often associated with high school. Stevenson offers refuge and rehabilitation for students who may have struggled with "adjustment difficulties, problems with peers, mild depression, or anxiety," while others have been diagnosed as learning disabled, Attention Deficit Disordered, unmotivated, or uninterested. At Stevenson, "the explicit purpose is academic; the implicit purpose is therapeutic and remedial, as necessary to enable our students to achieve academic goals."

General	
Type of School	Private
Religious Affiliation	None
Coeducational	Yes
Boarding	No
Day School	Yes
Dress Code	No

Students	
Enrollment (Grades 9–12)	59
% African American	8
% Hispanic/Latino	10
% Asian	8
% Caucasian	74

Admissions Selectivity	
Applications Received	200
# Applicants Accepted	30
Requires Standardized Test Scores	No
Application Essay	No

COMPARABLE SCHOOLS	
The Child School; The Churchill School	

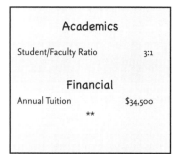

Academics	
Student/Faculty Ratio	3:1
Financial	
Annual Tuition	$34,500
**	

THE IDEAL APPLICANT

Students at Stevenson are bright and have the potential for successful high school and college work, work well with others in a small classroom environment, and are welcoming of their peers regardless of their appearance and manner.

WHERE STUDENTS COME FROM

The Robert Louis Stevenson School serves students from all five boroughs of New York City, as well as Long Island, Westchester County, New Jersey, and Connecticut.

ORIENTATION PROCESS FOR NEW STUDENTS

Orientation meetings for new students are held before and after classes start.

SAINT AGNES BOYS HIGH SCHOOL

555 West End Avenue, New York, NY 10024

Phone Number: 212-873-9100 • **Website:** www.staghs.org

Head of School: Brother Richard Van Houten, FMS • **Director of Admissions:** David J. Dinora

ABOUT SAINT AGNES BOYS HIGH SCHOOL

Founded by the parish of Saint Agnes in 1892, Saint Agnes Boys High School is a Roman Catholic secondary school which endeavors to form a respectful and caring educational community grounded in the spiritual tenets of the Catholic faith. Located on West End Avenue at West 87th Street on the Upper West Side of Manhattan, the school is perfectly positioned to reap all of Manhattan's rich cultural and educational benefits.

The school charges itself with achieving a sense of community and belonging in the school by acknowledging and understanding talents and needs of students while developing their spiritual, mental, and emotional growth, and also by encouraging each individual to accept responsibility for building a moral and charitable society. Recently, the school has taken steps to improve its students eating habits by removing all vending machines from the school premises and no longer offering unhealthy snack items in the cafeteria.

MISSION STATEMENT

The school's website states that the fundamental mission of Saint Agnes Boys High School is to ensure the "academic, personal, and spiritual growth" of each student under the guidance of the Catholic Archdiocese of New York. This is achieved through a supportive environment where students are taught to "appreciate diversity and honor God's presence in all people" while undertaking a challenging course of study that prepares these young men for future academic and personal success, and "leads them to place their talents at the service of others in the spirit of the Gospel."

General	
Type of School	Private
Religious Affiliation	Catholic
Coeducational	No
Boarding	No
Day School	Yes
Dress Code	Yes
Founded	1892

Students	
Enrollment (Grades 9–12)	407
% Male/Female	100/0
% African American	22
% Hispanic/Latino	54
% Asian	4
% Caucasian	19

Admissions Selectivity	
Requires Standardized Test Scores	Yes; TACHS
Application Essay	None

COMPARABLE SCHOOLS

Cardinal Hayes; Fordham; Loyola; Regis; Rice; Xavier

Academics

REQUIRED CLASSES

4 years: Religion, English, math, social studies

3 years: Spanish, science, physical education

1 year: Fine arts

1 semester: Health education, computers

Student/Faculty Ratio   18:1

Extracurricular

MOST POPULAR
INTERSCHOLASTIC SPORTS

Baseball, basketball, soccer, track

Financial

Annual Tuition $5,550

★★

WHERE STUDENTS COME FROM

Students from all five boroughs of New York City are enrolled at Saint Agnes.

COLLEGES THAT RECENT GRADS ARE ATTENDING

Boston College, Boston University, Brown University, Duke University, Fairfield University, Fordham University, Marist College, New York University, Pennsylvania State University, St. John's University, State University of New York

SAINT ANN'S SCHOOL

129 Pierrepont Street, Brooklyn, NY 11201

Phone Number: 718-552-1660 • **Website:** www.saintannsny.org

Head of School: Dr. Larry Weiss • **Director of Admissions:** Diana Lourask

About Saint Ann's School

Founded in 1965 by the Vestry of Saint Ann's Episcopal Church, Saint Ann's School was created as a nonsectarian school dedicated to academic excellence. Under the guidance of founding headmaster Stanley Bosworth, the school flourished with a commitment to psychometrics, a challenging and varied curriculum, and a community that reflected its location. Most interestingly, Saint Ann's is gradeless—there are neither marked grades nor age-group classes.

The school prides itself on flexibility matched with a constant emphasis on academic achievement. The goal in this is to sustain a positive environment in which students can attain their highest promise and potential without sacrificing their unique talents and interests. Students are involved in many diverse activities, fostering their interests while building a welcoming educational community. Add to this mix a unique faculty and environment founded on mutual respect and freedom, and it's clear that the academic excellence and singular educational vision of Saint Ann's leaves much to be admired.

General	
Type of School	Private
Religious Affiliation	None
Coeducational	Yes
Boarding	No
Day School	Yes
Dress Code	No
Founded	1965

Students	
% Caucasian	81
% Other	19

Admissions Selectivity	
Requires Standardized Test Scores	Yes
Application Essay	Yes

Mission Statement

The school's website states: "At Saint Ann's it is hard to distinguish curriculum from community. A curriculum is traditionally thought of as a sequence of concepts and details, assumed to be related to each other, and thought to be learnable in a given period. For us, however, the curriculum is pervasive: a vehicle for learning skills as well as facts; the medium of our friendship with children; a source of humor and poetry; a focus for activities across the disciplines and for formalisms from art to algebra. It is also a way for our students to reach us. As we share enthusiasm, it becomes our common ground, the center around which a group can be built, in the classroom and beyond it."

Academics
REQUIRED CLASSES
4 years: English, history, math, foreign language
3 years: Science
2 years: Art/music/theater, recording arts

Extracurricular
MOST POPULAR
INTERSCHOLASTIC SPORTS
MALE
Baseball, track
FEMALE
Gymnastics, softball, track

Financial
Annual Tuition $21,300–$22,500
*

THE IDEAL APPLICANT

According to the school's website, "Saint Ann's seeks students who show evidence of the intellectual motivation and aptitude that will enable them to handle both freedom and rigorous academic requirements."

COLLEGES THAT RECENT GRADS ARE ATTENDING

American University, Amherst College, Bard College, Barnard College, Boston University Brandeis University, Brown University, Bucknell University, Carleton College, The Cooper Union for the Advancement of Science and Art, Cornell University, Dartmouth University, Duke University, Emerson College, Franklin & Marshall Colleges, George Washington University, Georgetown University, Hamilton Ithaca College, Johns Hopkins University, Lewis & Clark College, Macalester College, Manhattanville College, The New School, New York University, Northwestern University, Oberlin College, Princeton University, Quinnipiac University, Sarah Lawrence University, Skidmore College, Smith College, Stanford University, Trinity College, Tufts University, University of Chicago, University of Michigan, University of Pennsylvania, University of Rochester, University of Vermont, University of Wisconsin, Vassar College, Wesleyan University, Wheaton College, Whittier College, Yale University

SAR HIGH SCHOOL

5900 Netherland Avenue, Riverdale, NY 10471

Phone Number: 718-548-2727 • **Website:** www.saracademy.org

Head of School: Rabbi Tully Harcsztark • **Director of Admissions:** Nancy Lerea

ABOUT SAR HIGH SCHOOL

Founded in 2004, the SAR High School is part of the SAR Academy, and it seeks to provide students with an innovate experience that balances its curriculum between secular studies, Torah learning, and the modern world. Housed within an impressively designed building, the school has developed a unique and independent program of study that covers subjects both general and Judaic in order to offer children an expansive while personal education. It is this dedication to moving forward while remembering the past that infuses students and faculty alike with an enthusiasm for learning and growing as a community where they grow and succeed together.

General	
Type of School	Private
Religious Affiliation	Jewish
Coeducational	Yes
Boarding	No
Day School	Yes
Dress Code	No
Founded	2004

Students	
Enrollment (Grades 9–12)	350

SAR High School takes a keen interest in each student's personal, educational, and spiritual development through the attentive nature of its teachers as well as its bounty of special programs. These include the Beit Midrash Fellows Program, which merges the traditional chavruta system with a modern educational angle to form small groups of students and post-college men and women who study Torah together, and also Challenge Options, a voluntary course of study that strengthens and deepens students' understanding of key educational subjects. Other programs include an Artist-in-Residence position and "Advisories"—small groups of students who meet regularly with teachers so as to encourage academic advancement and personal attention.

MISSION STATEMENT

According to the school's website, SAR relishes the opportunity to encourage and inspire each student's individual talents through the fusion of Torah and secular studies, "where a love for Medinat Yisrael and Jewish tradition are fostered, where study is probing and meaningful, and where students discover the beauty of their heritage." SAR displays an evident commitment to Jewish pride and the State of Israel as well as the United States and its history, founding a unique sense of appreciation and education between these two cultures. The school's dedicated teachers and administrators work actively with students to "inspire a love of learning and academic excellence."

WHERE STUDENTS COME FROM

The school's website explains that their students come from "a wide range of geographic locations," including Connecticut, Riverdale, Westchester, New Jersey, Rockland County, and all five boroughs of New York City.

THE SMITH SCHOOL

131 West Eighty-sixth Street, New York, NY 10024

Phone Number: 212-879-6354 • **Website:** www.smithschool.net

Head of School: Karen Smith • **Director of Admissions:** Cristina Martinez

ABOUT THE SMITH SCHOOL

Diversity is a key component of The Smith School, whose student body varies from the gifted to the special-needs student, from the college-bound to those desiring a postgraduate year. Students are placed in classes according to their level of ability, "in order to nurture their strengths, while appropriately addressing any academic weaknesses." The small class size—which ranges between one to six pupils, with an average of four—allows for close observation, comprehensive instruction, and personal engagement in every aspect of the student's learning process. To further implement this, supervised study halls, a homework assistance program, and (at the parent's request) the EXCEL! Program are incorporated into each student's day to aid with homework, organization, and study skills. What distinguishes The Smith School from traditional institutions is its "capacity to address a wide assortment of individual needs such as learning disabilities, attention disorders, phobias, and many other emotional issues." The school takes pride in "its ability to assist each student in achieving his or her academic potential and in developing a more confident sense of self."

MISSION STATEMENT

"In the pursuit of our core goal of excellence in alternative education, the operating philosophy of The Smith School was developed organically from the collective experience of the faculty and administration. As our team strives to ensure the success of every student in our community, we remember always the diversity of strengths and styles, of backgrounds and histories that Smith School students bring to us every year. Thus, pragmatism and adaptiveness are emphasized throughout classroom instruction and curriculum development. Informed experimentation and instruc-

General

Type of School	Private
Religious Affiliation	None
Coeducational	Yes
Boarding	No
Day School	Yes
Dress Code	Yes
Founded	1990

Students

Enrollment (Grades 9–12)	60
% Male/Female	60/40
% African American	25
% Hispanic/Latino	16
% Asian	4
% Caucasian	55
% International Students	0
% Out-of-State Students	0
# Countries Represented	1
# States Represented	1

Admissions Selectivity

Applications Received	50
# Applicants Accepted	21
# Accepted Applicants Who Enrolled	21
Requires Standardized Test Scores	No
Application Essay	No

COMPARABLE SCHOOLS

Birch Wathen Lenox; York Preparatory School

tional flexibility are encouraged, always with the settled purpose of realizing each student's potential for academic success, personal growth, and social maturation."

THE IDEAL APPLICANT

The ideal applicant is "someone who is a looking to improve their academic, social, or emotional history; sensitive and tolerant of other student's differences; a good role model for younger peers; and a student who is willing to work diligently to improve their academic standing."

WHERE STUDENTS COME FROM

"The majority of our students come from New York City."

ORIENTATION PROCESS FOR NEW STUDENTS

Each student meets with the vice-principal on the first day of school to discuss the school's policies on attendance, lateness, absences, discipline, behavior, dress code, academic programs, and policies. At the conclusion of this meeting, each student is required to sign a contract with the school, acknowledging the guidelines and rules.

COLLEGES THAT RECENT GRADS ARE ATTENDING

City University of New York—Hunter College, Fordham University, Hofstra University, Mitchell College, Sarah Lawrence University, State University of New York—Fashion Institute of Technology, University of Connecticut, University of Vermont

STUDENTS SAY

Students report "never having felt so welcome" as they do at The Smith School. Many note that "Smith gave me a chance to get good grades and to feel like I was really learning for the first time," while the teachers "really care about the kids and want them to do well." With "grades way up" and an environment where "everyone gets along well," students resoundingly agree that "here I can learn, and when I need help, I can always get it."

Parents Say

Parents of Smith students have no qualms about recommending the school "with confidence and pleasure," noting that any "serious academic and personal problems" on the student's part are met with "professional and personal attention" and "generosity" by faculty and administration alike, in turn "improving grades and self-esteem." Graced with "a perfect academic setting" and "patiently persistent and very accommodating" teachers, The Smith School is renowned for giving students and parents alike "the stability and support needed to get back on track" both academically and emotionally. In the words of one parent, "How lucky these youngsters are to have The Smith School in their corner."

Alumni Say

Alumni count themselves "lucky" to have attended Smith, recalling fondly the extracurricular activities, field trips, and most importantly, graduation. "Without The Smith School, I don't know what would have happened to me," says one student. The school was filled with teachers who were "always around to give help when you needed it" and "good people who will do what it takes to help." As one graduate explains, the school "prepared me for college and made me believe I could do it. And I have!"

THE SPENCE SCHOOL

22 East Ninety-first Street, New York, NY 10128

Phone Number: 212-289-5940 • **Website:** www.spenceschool.org

Head of School: Arlene Joy Gibson • **Director of Admissions:** Susan Parker

General	
Type of School	Private
Religious Affiliation	None
Coeducational	No
Boarding	No
Day School	Yes
Dress Code	Yes
Founded	1892

Students	
% Male/Female	0/100
% Caucasian	71
% Other	29
# States Represented	3

ABOUT THE SPENCE SCHOOL

Founded by Clara B. Spence in 1892, The Spence School is one of the preeminent independent, college-preparatory day schools for young women in New York City. The school is committed to maintaining a positive and supportive academic environment that fosters diversity, creativity, and high moral standards. The curriculum is not just designed to give students a solid liberal arts foundation in preparation for future success in college, but also to help young women become the strong and confident leaders of tomorrow—or as the school's founder put it, "not for school, but for life we learn." Spence encourages self-expression as a tool for nurturing confidence and also as a means to becoming independent thinkers and resourceful individuals of great promise. Teachers here support a welcoming environment by recognizing each student's talents and fostering a sense of community and friendship with their roles as educators and mentors. Students have a range of extracurricular activities including athletics, clubs, field trips, and every educational opportunity imaginable thanks to its location in one of the most vibrant cities in the world.

MISSION STATEMENT

According to the school's website, The Spence School's mission is to offer young women the highest quality of education in a welcoming environment that will provide them with all the necessary tools to become women with high academic and personal standards. By graduation, Spence students will successfully entertain their pursuit of higher education as "responsible and effective" citizens.

THE IDEAL APPLICANT

According to the school's website, The Spence School encourages applications from eager and dedicated students who love to learn and will contribute "ability, vitality, and personal integrity to the school community."

Where Students Come From

According to the school's website, the majority of students come from Manhattan, though recently they have come from all five boroughs of New York City, as well as Long Island, Connecticut, and New Jersey.

Colleges that Recent Grads Are Attending

Amherst College, Bard College, Barnard College, Bates College, Boston College, Boston University, Bowdoin College, Brown University, Bucknell University, Carleton College, Carnegie Mellon University, City University of New York—Hunter College, Colgate University, Colorado College, Columbia University, Connecticut College, Cornell University, Dartmouth College, Duke University, Emory University, Fordham University, Franklin & Marshall College, Georgetown University, George Washington University, Harvard University, Haverford College, Johns Hopkins University, Kenyon College, Lehigh University, Macalester College, McGill University, Middlebury College, New York University, Northeastern University, Northwestern University, Notre Dame College, Oberlin College, Pace University, Pomona College, Princeton University, Rhode Island School of Design, Rice University, Rollins College, Sarah Lawrence College, Skidmore College, Spelman College, Stanford University, Swarthmore College, Syracuse University, Trinity College, Tufts University, Tulane University, Union College, University of Chicago, University of Connecticut, University of Michigan, University of Pennsylvania, University of Rochester, University of St. Andrews, University of Vermont, University of Virginia, University of Wisconsin, Vanderbilt University, Vassar College, Washington and Lee University, Washington University in St. Louis, Wesleyan University, Williams College, Yale University

Academics

Required Classes

4 years: English, math, physical education

3 years: History, science, fine arts

2 years: Foreign language

1 year: Computer science, health

Extracurricular

Most Popular Interscholastic Sports

Tennis, track, volleyball

Financial

Annual Tuition $27,000

% Students Receiving Financial Aid 17

**

ST. JEAN BAPTISTE HIGH SCHOOL

173 East Seventy-fifth Street, New York, NY 10021

Phone Number: 212-288-1645 • **Website:** www.stjean.org

Head of School: Sister Ona B. Bessette, CND PhD • **Director of Admissions:** Flora Lugo

General

Type of School	Private
Religious Affiliation	Roman Catholic
Coeducational	No
Boarding	No
Day School	Yes
Dress Code	Yes
Founded	1929

Students

Enrollment (Grades 9–12)	420
% Male/Female	0/100
% African American	30
% Hispanic/Latino	60
% Asian	5
% Caucasian	5
% International Students	5
% Out-of-State Students	1

Admissions Selectivity

Applications Received	450
# Applicants Accepted	350
# Accepted Applicants Who Enrolled	115
Requires Standardized Test Scores	Yes
Application Essay	No
Median SAT	950

COMPARABLE SCHOOLS

Cathedral High School; St. Michael Academy; St. Vincent Ferrer High School

ABOUT ST. JEAN BAPTISTE HIGH SCHOOL

St. Jean Baptiste High School welcomes "young women of varied abilities and diverse ethnic backgrounds, and encourages in these students a strong faith in God and a life lived according to Christian principles." St. Jean's community recognizes the value of each person and commits itself to the development of each student's talents through an academic, religious, and social educational program.

It is the mission of the St. Jean Baptiste community to "actively participate in the transformation of society for a more just world." Because of its moderate size, students report a feeling of belonging and engaging rapport with their teachers. An excellent guidance department is at the service of students with personal needs, problems, conflicts, and difficulties. School officials note that of the "98 percent of students who graduate, over 90 percent move on to postsecondary education with a large number receiving full or partial college scholarships."

MISSION STATEMENT

"The goal of the faculty and administration is to nurture in each incoming student the qualities and characteristics of womanhood. Our mission is to empower each student to become five things: *Woman of Personal Strength and Courage*—A young woman coming to St. Jean Baptiste High School has already exhibited considerable strength and courage because of the exigencies of urban life. By graduation, we want to ensure that these qualities have been developed and refined. *Woman of Academic Achievement*—The graduate of St. Jean's should recognize that her high school education is not an end in itself, but rather, a stepping stone to continued education. *Woman of Faith*— The young woman who comes to St. Jean's has already acquired knowledge of her faith. By graduation, we want her to have deepened her faith and to have grown spiritually. *Woman for Others*—By graduation we want to insure that the qualities necessary for living and interacting effectively and respectfully, with a view to justice and peace, are an integral part of her personal attributes. *Woman Oriented to the Future*—By graduation we hope that the student will have developed attitudes and behaviors that enable her to live a life of continuing commitment to the transformation of society for a more just world."

THE IDEAL APPLICANT

The ideal applicant is "a young woman eager to learn and share her talents with the school community."

WHERE STUDENTS COME FROM

"The majority of our students come from Manhattan and the surrounding boroughs (Bronx, Brooklyn, Queens, and Staten Island)."

ORIENTATION PROCESS FOR NEW STUDENTS

Incoming students attend a three-week summer program that helps them build skills and orient themselves in the school. Three days in September are also given for orientation into the school program.

Academics
REQUIRED CLASSES

4 units: Religion, English, math, social studies (including U.S. history, economics, government)

3 units: Science, foreign language, electives

2 units: Fine arts

1 unit: Computer, health, physical education, service (half unit)

ADDITIONAL REQUIREMENTS

140 hours of Christian Service in 12th grade

Student/Faculty Ratio	12:1

Extracurricular
MOST POPULAR INTERSCHOLASTIC SPORTS

Basketball, soccer, softball, track

% Students Who Play Interscholastic Sports	10

Financial

Annual Tuition	$5,800
% Students Receiving Financial Aid	65
Average Financial Aid/ Scholarship	$2,000

*

COLLEGES THAT RECENT GRADS ARE ATTENDING

Clark Atlanta University, College of Mt. St. Vincent, The College of St. Rose, City University of New York—Brooklyn College, City University of New York—City College, City University of New York—Hunter College, City University of New York—John Jay College of Criminal Justice, Dominican College, Farleigh Dickinson University, Fordham University, Iona College, Lincoln University, Long Island University—Brooklyn, Long Island University—C. W. Post, New York University, Northeastern University, Pace University, Pennsylvania State University, St. Francis College, St. John's University, State University of New York at Albany, State University of New York at Binghamton, State University of New York—University at Buffalo, State University of New York—Oswego College, State University of New York—Stony Brook, Syracuse University, Temple University, Union College, Vassar University

Students Say

For students, St. Jean Baptiste High School is nothing less than a second home thanks to its "warm and loveable faculty" who provide not only "personal academic assistance," but also "a strong family environment." The school places an "emphasis on educational success," using a "competitive but friendly spirit" to drive students to thrive both academically and emotionally. Students appreciate the "open communication between students and teachers," as well as the "motivational praise, encouragement, and awards" that are offered during liturgies and assemblies, and the "fun extracurricular activities"—especially "sports!"—which add to the deep-rooted sense of community. Several students single out the counselors for praise, noting the "confidence and influence" they imbue by providing the students with the "inspiration to accomplish their goals." In short, everything is a team effort at St. Jean's. In the words of one student, "Everyone in the school has someone to count on."

Parents Say

Parents are quick to mention St. Jean's "warm, welcoming atmosphere" as a key component in their decision to send their child there. The school is not just "an educational institution, but an extended family" that offers young women "a solid education, religious guidance, and a true sense of community." With a small student body that enables faculty "get to know the whole student" and give "individual attention when needed," it's no wonder "the young ladies of St. Jean's are very happy and proud of their school" and parents equally proud of their children's accomplishments.

Alumni Say

Alumni agree: St. Jean Baptiste School is all about family. Whether it is "the unquestionable cohesiveness of the student body and faculty," "the diverse environment of cultures and ethnicities," or the "academic excellence and lasting friendships," former students recall fondly the school that gave them "the skills to succeed in life." From their classroom studies to plays they performed in to sports they participated in, the "unbreakable bonds" that students formed with each other as well as the "caring and nurturing" faculty remain as strong now as when they were when formed, leaving alumni confident that the education that began at St. Jean's didn't end after graduation, but has guided them toward becoming "open, compassionate, and successful individuals."

ST. MICHAEL ACADEMY

425 West Twenty-third Street, New York, NY 10001

Phone Number: 212-563-2547 • **Website:** www.stmichaelsnyc.org

Head of School: Sister Kathleen Cusack • **Director of Admissions:** Giselle Brown

ABOUT ST. MICHAEL ACADEMY

Founded by the Presentation Sisters of the Blessed Virgin Mary in 1874, St. Michael Academy is an all-girls high school that offers a college preparatory curriculum designed to satisfy and exceed New York State Regents requirements. In addition, the school encourages students to earn college credits in English and history through Advanced Placement and college-sponsored courses.

St. Michael Academy also offers several extracurricular programs to supplement its academic courses, such as the Sunrise Tutoring Program (which allows students to receive tutoring from business people before school and work hours), the Homework Helpers Program, (which addresses specific instructional needs after school and increased student grades by an average of ten points in its first two years), and the St. Michael Academy Business Partnerships Horizon (in which students participate in internships at a number of companies throughout New York City, effectively preparing them for future careers). In addition, St. Michael's offers a wide spectrum of student activities, including a student council, dramatic productions, athletics and a variety of clubs.

General	
Type of School	Private
Religious Affiliation	Catholic
Coeducational	No
Boarding	No
Day School	Yes
Dress Code	Yes
Founded	1874

Students	
Enrollment (Grades 9–12)	416
% Male/Female	0/100
% African American	33
% Hispanic/Latino	61
% Asian	3
% Caucasian	3

Admissions Selectivity	
Requires Standardized Test Scores	Yes

COMPARABLE SCHOOLS

Convent of the Sacred Heart; Dominican Academy; Mother Cabrini High School; Notre Dame School

MISSION STATEMENT

With a philosophy "rooted" in the Catholic tradition and Spirit of the Presentation Sisters, St. Michael Academy's mission is to educate young women in a "loving and caring community," guiding each student in their educational and spiritual development, encouraging her "unique gifts and talents" and helping her to live "a fully Christian life."

THE IDEAL APPLICANT

According to the school's website, St. Michael Academy seeks exemplary young women who have shown strong academic achievement along with "a desire to mature into women guided by Catholic Christian values."

Academics

REQUIRED CLASSES

4 years: English, religion
3 years: Science, math
2 years: Foreign language, social
 studies
1 year: Art, music, business

Student/Faculty Ratio   13:1

Extracurricular

MOST POPULAR
INTERSCHOLASTIC SPORTS

Basketball, cheerleading, step

Financial

Annual Tuition $5,400
              **

WHERE STUDENTS COME FROM

Students come from all five boroughs of New York City and also New Jersey.

COLLEGES THAT RECENT GRADS ARE ATTENDING

Allentown College, Amherst College, Barnard College, Boston College, Boston University, Carnegie Mellon University, Colgate University, College of the Holy Cross, College of New Rochelle, College of Mt. St. Vincent, Columbia University, Cornell University, Dartmouth University, D'Youville College, Dominican College, Fordham University, Hampton College, Howard University, Iona College, Knox College, Laboratory Institute of Merchandising, La Salle University, Long Island University, Manhattan College, Marymount College, Mount St. Mary College, New York University, Niagara University, Northeastern University, Ohio University, Pace University, Princeton University, Rochester Institute of Technology, Rutgers University, Sacred Heart University, Skidmore College, St. Francis College, St. John's University, St. Joseph's College, St. Peter's College, Spelman University, Syracuse University, Temple University, Tufts University, Tuskegee School, University of Bridgeport, University of Hartford, University of Massachusetts, University of Pittsburgh, University of Scranton, Wesleyan University

STATEN ISLAND ACADEMY

715 Todt Hill Road, Staten Island, NY 10128

Phone Number: 718-987-8100 • **Website:** www.statenislandacademy.org

Head of School: Diane J. Hulse • **Director of Admissions:** Linda Schuffman

ABOUT STATEN ISLAND ACADEMY

Founded in 1884, Staten Island Academy is a coeducational college-preparatory day school educating students from kindergarten through high school. The school is also the oldest—and only—independent school on Staten Island. As the principal explains, the Academy is "committed to the education of the whole child through a rigorous academic program, innovative performing and visual arts programs, and a comprehensive athletics and health and wellness program."

The curriculum is "intense and challenging," designed to prepare students for college starting from the first day of classes. Beginning in the 9th grade, students meet with college advisors to embark on their journey to college admissions. In addition, students have a bounty of Advanced Placement, independent study, and honors courses at their disposal, allowing for students of high performance and potential "to take advanced courses that give them a solid foundation for college-level courses." The scenic twelve-acre campus contains several outstanding facilities, including a new fitness center and renovated library, athletics fields, state-of-the art classrooms and computer labs, science labs, tennis courts, and two outdoor swimming pools.

General	
Type of School	Private
Religious Affiliation	None
Coeducational	Yes
Boarding	No
Day School	Yes
Dress Code	No
Founded	1884

Students	
Enrollment (Grades 9–12)	142
% African American	4
% Hispanic/Latino	2
% Asian	8
% Caucasian	87

Admissions Selectivity	
Requires Standardized Test Scores	Yes
Application Essay	No

MISSION STATEMENT

The school's website states, Staten Island Academy is committed "to providing a child-centered education of superior quality." "Our objective is educating the whole child, and encouraging intellectual, creative, social and physical development. Within a collegial campus environment, in small classes, and through extracurricular activities, the school's students are expected to participate actively in an educational community that promotes ethical leadership, self-reliance, and critical thinking." Believing in the exceptional strength of a diverse student body, Staten Island Academy celebrates the "cultural differences, individual interests, and personal talents of our student body."

Academics	
Student/Faculty Ratio	10:1

Extracurricular

MOST POPULAR
INTERSCHOLASTIC SPORTS
MALE

Baseball, basketball, cross-country, golf, lacrosse, soccer, tennis, volleyball

FEMALE

Basketball, cross-country, golf, lacrosse, softball, tennis, volleyball

% Students Who Play Interscholastic Sports	75

Financial

Annual Tuition	$21,900
**	

THE IDEAL APPLICANT

The ideal applicant to Staten Island Academy is one who welcomes a challenging academic environment and dedicates themselves to continued academic success.

COLLEGES THAT RECENT GRADS ARE ATTENDING

Allegheny College, American University, Barnard College, Boston College, Boston University, Brandeis University, Brown University, Carnegie Mellon University, College of the Holy Cross, College of William & Mary, Columbia University, Cornell University, City University of New York—Hunter College, Davidson College, Dickinson College, Drexel University, Duke University, Emory University, Fairfield University, Fairleigh Dickinson University, Fordham University, George Washington University, Georgetown University, Gettysburg College, Harvard University, Ithaca College, Johns Hopkins University, Lafayette College, Loyola College—Maryland, Loyola University—Los Angeles, Loyola University—New Orleans, Marist College, Marymount Manhattan College, McGill University, Moravian College, New Jersey Institute of Technology, New York Institute of Technology, New York University, Northeastern University, Oberlin College, Pace University, Pennsylvania State University, Pepperdine University, Princeton University, Quinnipiac University, Seton Hall University, Skidmore College, St. Thomas Aquinas College, Stevens Institute of Technology, State University of New York at Albany, State University of New York at Binghamton, State University of New York—University at Buffalo, Swarthmore College, Syracuse University, Temple University, Trinity College, Tufts University, United States Military Academy, University of Central Florida, University of Chicago, University of Connecticut, University of Delaware, University of Hartford, University of Illinois, University of Massachusetts—Amherst, University of Miami, University of New Hampshire, University of North Carolina—Greensboro, University of Pennsylvania, University of Notre Dame, University of Rhode Island, University of Rochester, University of Tampa, University of Virginia, University of Wisconsin—Madison, Ursinus College, Vassar College, Villanova University, Wesleyan University, Wheaton College, Yale University

STATEN ISLAND TECHNICAL HIGH SCHOOL

485 Clawson Street, Staten Island, NY 10306

Phone Number: 718-657-3181 • **Website:** www.siths.org

Head of School: Vincent A. Maniscalco • **Director of Admissions:** Mark Erlenwein

ABOUT STATEN ISLAND TECHNICAL HIGH SCHOOL

Founded in 1988, the Staten Island Technical High School is a highly competitive college preparatory public institution that provides a demanding and challenging curriculum with an emphasis on engineering, mathematics, humanities, science, computers, and athletics. The school is committed to building community by involving parents in their child's education, encouraging them to join with teachers in guiding students through their current educational and future professional development. This dedication to excellence has proven itself time and time again, most recently in 2004 when SITHS students had perfect Regent Exams scores as well as graduation rates. The school takes a particular interest in the global community, marked by its renowned exchange programs with Russia—to add to this, all students must take Russian language courses. Admission to the school is based solely on the Specialized High School Admissions Test (SHSAT), which is open to all 8th and 9th grade New York City students.

MISSION STATEMENT

According to the school's website, SITHS nurtures and challenges students in a welcoming and rigorous educational setting that places a premium on "exemplary character, scholarship, service, leadership, and citizenship." The school's goal is to produce a student body that through dedication and ingenuity will succeed in their college studies in fields as diverse as engineering, mathematics, science, foreign language, social science, and liberal and performing arts. The school's friendly community encourages all facets of a student's development through athletics, community service, and student activities.

General	
Type of School	Public
Religious Affiliation	None
Coeducational	Yes
Boarding	No
Day School	Yes
Dress Code	No
Founded	1988

Students	
Enrollment (Grades 9–12)	788
% African American	2
% Hispanic/Latino	4
% Asian	14
% Caucasian	81

Admissions Selectivity	
Requires Standardized Test Scores	Yes
Application Essay	No

COMPARABLE SCHOOLS

Bronx High School of Science; Brooklyn Latin School; Brooklyn Technical High School; High School of American Studies at Lehman College; High School for Mathematics, Science and Engineering at City College; Queens High School for the Sciences at York College; Stuyvesant High School

Extracurricular

Most Popular Interscholastic Sports

Male

Baseball, basketball, bowling, cross-country, fencing, football, golf, handball, track, soccer, swimming, tennis, volleyball, wrestling

Female

Basketball, bowling, cross-country, fencing, golf, handball, track, soccer, softball, swimming, tennis, volleyball

Financial

Annual Tuition   None

**

The Ideal Applicant

Students at Staten Island Technical High School tend to be bright and inquisitive, involved in extracurricular activities, and take schoolwork seriously—that means good attendance and dedication to homework, as well as a respectful attitude in the classroom. One of the most important factors in such a child is equally dedicated parents.

Where Students Come From

Students come to the school from all five boroughs of New York City.

STUYVESANT HIGH SCHOOL

345 Chambers Street, New York, NY 10282

Phone Number: 212-312-4800 • **Website:** www.stuy.edu

Head of School: Stanley Teitel

ABOUT STUYVESANT HIGH SCHOOL

Founded in 1904, Stuyvesant High School has since served as a key school in New York City for the development of talent in science, mathematics, and technology. Each year during the school's selection process (based upon performance on the Specialized Science High Schools Admissions Test), of the nearly 20,000 students who apply, approximately 800 of those are accepted into this vibrant and academically challenging environment. The diverse student body is composed of individuals from all over the world who fill the halls with a gamut of native languages.

The school's multimillion-dollar building houses twelve laboratories, twelve shops (including robotics, energy, and digitally controlled machines), and also more than 450 computers in thirteen networks, to which each student and teacher has individual access. Student athletic teams also flourish despite the school having no field to call its own—instead relying on the New York City park system to provide them with ample ground to practice on.

MISSION STATEMENT

According to the school's website, its mission is to supply students with a friendly academic environment that encourages and enhances the special talents of Stuyvesant students. The educational heritage of Stuyvesant is "deeply rooted in the tradition of Science, Mathematics and Technology." These areas have served as the foundation of the school's educational success and "remain the cornerstones" of Stuyvesant's educational program. With this in mind, the school's goal is to cultivate the moral,

General	
Type of School	Public
Religious Affiliation	None
Coeducational	Yes
Boarding	No
Day School	Yes
Dress Code	No
Founded	1904

Students	
Enrollment (Grades 9–12)	3,200
% Male/Female	58/42
% African American	3
% Hispanic/Latino	3
% Asian	51
% Caucasian	43

Admissions Selectivity	
# Applicants Accepted	800
Requires Standardized Test Scores	Yes
Application Essay	No
Median SAT	1400

COMPARABLE SCHOOLS

Bronx High School of Science; Brooklyn Latin School; Brooklyn Technical High School; High School of American Studies at Lehman College; High School for Mathematics, Science and Engineering at City College; Queens High School for the Sciences at York College; Staten Island Technical High School

Academics
REQUIRED CLASSES
4 years: English, history, science, physical education
3 years: Math, foreign language
1 semester : Art, music, health education, computers, technology

Extracurricular
MOST POPULAR
INTERSCHOLASTIC SPORTS
MALE
Baseball, basketball, bowling, cross-country, fencing, golf, gymnastics, handball, soccer, swimming, tennis, track, volleyball
FEMALE
Basketball, bowling, cross-country, fencing, golf, gymnastics, handball, soccer, softball, swimming, tennis, track, volleyball

Financial
Annual Tuition   None

**

intellectual, and humanistic values necessary for each child to "achieve his or her maximum potential as a student and as a caring citizen of the world."

WHERE STUDENTS COME FROM

Students travel to the school from all five boroughs of New York City to the school.

TOWNSEND HARRIS HIGH SCHOOL

149-11 Melbourne Avenue, Flushing, NY 11367

Phone Number: 718-575-5580 • **Website:** www.thhs.qc.edu

Head of School: Thomas Cunningham

ABOUT TOWNSEND HARRIS HIGH SCHOOL

Originally founded 1848 as the New York Free Academy, and then reopened in 1984, Townsend Harris High School is a selective magnet academic institution located on the Queens College campus. The school prides itself on a "rigorous humanities-focused academic curriculum" that encompasses at a minimum 10 credits in English, 8 credits in social studies, and 6 credits in math, science, and 2 foreign languages (one of which must be Latin or Greek). In the words of one school official, "It is our expectation that a strong base in the humanities, bolstered by mathematics, science, and the integration of current technology, will equip students to tackle the ethical and intellectual challenges of the next generation." Townsend Harris is also distinguished by its association with Queens College, making it part of the City University of New York system. Thanks to this partnership, students in their senior year enroll in college courses and earn twelve free college credits. It is worth mentioning that admissions are extremely competitive—every year over 7,000 New York City students apply for entrance.

General	
Type of School	Public
Religious Affiliation	None
Coeducational	Yes
Boarding	No
Day School	Yes
Dress Code	Yes
Founded	1984

Students	
Enrollment (Grades 9–12)	1,200
% Male/Female	30/70
% African American	6.2
% Hispanic/Latino	8.9
% Asian	42.3
% Caucasian	42.6
# Countries Represented	63
# States Represented	1

Admissions Selectivity	
Applications Received	7,000+
# Applicants Accepted	290
Requires Standardized Test Scores	Yes

MISSION STATEMENT

"The mission established for our special high school is to maintain a school of ethnically integrated, highly motivated students, who represent all parts of our diverse urban population. Our major educational priorities are to insure academic excellence in the humanities tradition, but accommodated to the needs of the twenty-first century; to incorporate into all aspects of school life respect and regard for people and ideas; and, to realize these priorities by emphasiz-

Academics

REQUIRED CLASSES

4 years: English, social studies, physical education

3 years: Math, science, foreign language

2 years: Classical Greek or Latin

1 semester: Health, music, art

ADDITIONAL REQUIREMENTS

1 year: Humanities seminar

Student/Faculty Ratio   23:1

Extracurricular

MOST POPULAR

INTERSCHOLASTIC SPORTS

MALE

Baseball, basketball, bowling, cross-country, fencing, handball, soccer, softball, track, tennis, volleyball

FEMALE

Basketball, bowling, cross-country, fencing, handball, soccer, softball, swimming, track, tennis, volleyball

Financial

Annual Tuition   None

*

ing clear thinking, precision of language, and sensible decision-making."

THE IDEAL APPLICANT

Townsend Harris High School looks for students "who enjoy a rigorous learning environment, are highly motivated, and have a commitment to their community."

WHERE STUDENTS COME FROM

Our student body is selected from a citywide pool of applicants and includes public, private, and parochial school students.

ORIENTATION PROCESS FOR NEW STUDENTS

Enrolled students are provided with two days of orientation prior to classes, and parents participate in one day of orientation in the spring.

COLLEGES THAT RECENT GRADS ARE ATTENDING

American University, Barnard College, Berklee College of Music, Boston College, Boston University, Brandeis University, Brown University, Bryn Mawr University, Carnegie Mellon University, Colgate University, Columbia University, The Cooper Union for the Advancement of Science and Art, Cornell University, City University of New York—Baruch College, City University of New York—Brooklyn College, Dartmouth College, Duke University, Eugene Lang College, Fordham University, George Washington University, Hampshire College, Harvard University, Lehigh University, Loyola College of Maryland, Michigan State University, New York University, Northeastern University, Oberlin College, Pace University, Pennsylvania State University, Polytechnic University, Rutgers University, Sarah Lawrence University, Skidmore College, State University of New York at Albany, State University of New York at Binghamton, Swarthmore College, Tufts University, University of Connecticut, University of Florida, University of Maryland, University of Michigan, University of Pennsylvania, Vanderbilt University, Vassar College, Washington University in St. Louis, Wesleyan University

Students Say

Students cite college preparation as a massive benefit of attending Townsend Harris High School. With "teachers who are always available to help" and a "dedicated alumni association," students report that the attention and guidance they receive goes a long way in securing their college of choice. Make no bones about it, though "the stories of four hours of homework a night are a bit exaggerated," the curriculum at Townsend Harris is "difficult." This, however, is appreciated as students find themselves "prepared for college to a high degree." Also mentioned is the wide array of extracurricular activities, such as a "fencing team and economics club." Ultimately, in the words of one student, "Townsend Harris is hard, yes. But it is worth it."

Parents Say

Parents call Townsend Harris High School "the crown jewel of the New York City public school system," and praise its high graduation rate, excellent faculty and staff, and impressive curriculum. In the words of one parent, "It's like being enrolled in a top private high school without paying for it." Though Townsend Harris' rigorous curriculum might have worried some that little room would be left for their children's "creative side to shine," they soon found the "welcoming atmosphere" provided an impressive breadth extracurricular opportunities and creative enterprises. Parents also note the sense of "camaraderie amongst students," and appreciate the small school size "that creates an intimacy and excellent learning environment where teachers, administrators and students get to know each other very well."

Alumni Say

Townsend Harris alumni fondly recall their teachers, "who knew every single student personally" and were of the "highest caliber" not because of their resumes or publications, but "because they cared so much about the students." Alumni also note the "sense of priority" they developed due to the large workload, which in turn served them well in the professional world. On a more personal level, a former student mentions the school "instilled core values that I treasure to this day...values I intend to pass on to my children." As another explains, "I continue to look back on the lessons I learned while in school and continue to grow because of them."

TREVOR DAY SCHOOL

1 West Eighty-eighth Street, New York, NY 10024

Phone Number: 212-426-3360 • **Website:** www.trevor.org

Head of School: Pamela J. Clarke • **Director of Admissions:** Elizabeth Mitchell

General

Type of School	Private
Religious Affiliation	None
Coeducational	Yes
Boarding	No
Day School	Yes
Dress Code	No
Founded	1930

Students

Enrollment (Grades 9–12)	260
% Male/Female	50/50

Admissions Selectivity

Applications Received	221
# Applicants Accepted	17
# Accepted Applicants Who Enrolled	8
Requires Standardized Test Scores	Yes
Application Essay	Yes

ABOUT TREVOR DAY SCHOOL

Founded in 1930, Trevor Day School is "an intellectual community dedicated to academic excellence." Through its serious, rigorous, and visionary program, Trevor teaches traditional content, demands responsibility and promotes the power of collaboration, creativity, and critical thinking. Trevor students actively participate in their learning, often engaging in challenging, small-group projects

Trevor supports its students' intellectual and social growth with a unique advisory program and a school life that is centered in the Common Room, which is shared by students and faculty. Students participate in a rich visual and performing arts program while also pursuing a vigorous college-preparatory program that cultivates independent thought and imaginative problem-solving.

The school boasts several new facilities, including a state-of-the-art science center for grades 8 through 12. Students are also encouraged to take part in community building with an eighty-hour community service requirement. As a member of several athletic leagues, Trevor teams compete in soccer, volleyball, basketball, softball, tennis, track and field, and baseball.

MISSION STATEMENT

"Trevor Day School builds an activity-based setting to educate each student for academic excellence and personal integrity in a diverse coeducational community that emphasizes responsibility, stimulates collaboration, and promotes mutual respect."

THE IDEAL APPLICANT

Trevor Day School looks for students with "a passion for learning" and "a diversity of ideas, experiences, and cultures."

Where Students Come From

Students come from "all five boroughs of New York City, as well as from New Jersey."

Orientation Process for New Students

Incoming students participate in group exercises and a class trip.

Colleges that Recent Grads Are Attending

Bard College, Bennington College, Boston College, Boston University, Bowdoin College, Brandeis University, Clark University, Colby-Sawyer College, Colorado College, Colorado State University, Columbia University, Connecticut College, Cornell University, Davidson College, Emory University, Harvard University, Lehigh University, Eugene Lang College, Middlebury College, Mount Holyoke College, Muhlenberg College, New York University, Oberlin College, Pitzer College, Princeton University, Sarah Lawrence University, Skidmore College, Smith College, Stanford University, Swarthmore University, Syracuse University, Tufts University, University of Chicago, University of Colorado—Boulder, University of Michigan, University of Southern California, University of Wisconsin, Vassar College, Washington University in St. Louis, Wesleyan University, Williams College

Academics

REQUIRED CLASSES

4 years: English, physical education

3 years: History, math, lab science, foreign language, art

ADDITIONAL REQUIREMENTS

80 hours of community service

Student/Faculty Ratio 5:1

Extracurricular

MOST POPULAR INTERSCHOLASTIC SPORTS (COED)

Baseball, basketball, soccer, track & field

FEMALE

Softball, volleyball

% Students Who Play Interscholastic Sports 67

Financial

Annual Tuition $29,400

% Students Receiving Financial Aid 20

*

Students Say

Students at Trevor Day School appreciate the "focused yet relaxed learning environment" that places a special emphasis on teacher/student interaction through its Common Room, "where students and teachers hang out during their free periods either to do work or talk." As one student explains, "What's so great about this is that the students and teachers can easily communicate and get to meet anytime during the day because they are all in the same room." Also garnering high marks are the "advanced" science courses which students feel are "a great part of Trevor."

Parents Say

Parents are quick to cite the "progressive, nurturing, and welcoming" environment at Trevor along with its "independent approach to mentoring" as the key factors behind their decision to enroll their children. They value the school's many facilities, including the "paperless classwork" (thanks to each student using a PC) and the "inviting and unique" student lounge. Ultimately, as one parent says, "learning is encouraged, but in a less pressured, more open way," which lends both to the comfort and success of Trevor's students.

Alumni Say

Alumni note that they chose Trevor because of its focus on "a tight-knit community and hands-on learning inside the classroom." They remember their "involved" teachers who "wanted the students to do as best as possible," as well as the "great setup" and "convenience" of "every student and faculty member having a laptop," which makes taking notes, communicating, and learning extremely effective.

TRINITY SCHOOL

139 West Ninety-first Street, New York, NY 10024

Phone Number: 212-873-1650 • **Website:** www.trinityschoolnyc.org

Head of School: Henry C. Moses • **Director of Admissions:** Jan Burton

About Trinity School

Founded in 1709, the school's motto, *Labore et virtue*—"hard work and excellence"—encompasses all that Trinity School believes is necessary to pursue the promise and joy of its students. Trinity is committed to educating, inspiring, and preparing students not only for college, but for life. Featuring a rich and varied curriculum that allows students to explore any area of interest, along with a dedicated staff of instructors and administrators, it's of little wonder that Trinity's student body is an enthusiastic one, committed to learning and thereby also to academic and personal success.

General	
Type of School	Private
Religious Affiliation	None
Coeducational	Yes
Boarding	No
Day School	Yes
Dress Code	No
Founded	1709

The Upper School building houses a science lab, the Chapel (which doubles as a performance space), study areas, computer labs, and two swimming pools. With a long-standing reputation as not only one of the most prestigious high schools in New York City but also the nation, and an enviable alumni roster (John McEnroe and Larry Hagman, among others), Trinity has shown no signs of slowing and continues to honor its illustrious history with current and future excellence in education.

Mission Statement

According to the school's website, the focal point of a Trinity education is "the conversation between student and teacher." This relationship forms the foundation of students' academic experience and informs their development wherein Trinity "challenges the minds, fires the imaginations, and trains the bodies of the young people who have been entrusted to [them]." The school believes that learning is a lifelong experience and in that, students are encouraged to broaden their spiritual lives and capacity for caring and self-respect. With the support of a friendly school community, students are taught to "learn confidently" and "give generously and joyfully to others."

Academics

Student/Faculty Ratio   6:1

Extracurricular
MOST POPULAR
INTERSCHOLASTIC SPORTS
MALE

Baseball, basketball, cross-country, lacrosse, soccer, swimming, tennis, track, wrestling

FEMALE

Basketball, cross-country, lacrosse, soccer, softball, swimming, tennis, track, volleyball

Financial

Endowment $29 million

⋆⋆

THE IDEAL APPLICANT

According to the school's website, Trinity School seeks students who have a demonstrated record of high academic achievement both in and out of the classroom, as well as being "highly motivated and self-disciplined," with a marked interest in their education and attitude of respect and compassion. Trinity students are expected to "maintain its tradition of excellence in academics, as well as in the arts, in athletics, and in service to the community." Simply put, the more adaptable and promising the student, the more likely it is that they will thrive at Trinity.

COLLEGES THAT RECENT GRADS ARE ATTENDING

Amherst College, Brown University, Colgate University, Columbia University, Cornell University, Dartmouth College, Duke University, Emory University, Harvard Univesity, Johns Hopkins University, Oberlin College, Princeton University, Skidmore College, Tufts University, University of Chicago, University of Pennsyvania, University of Wisconsin, Wesleyan University, Yale University

UNITED NATIONS INTERNATIONAL SCHOOL

24-50 FDR Drive, New York, NY 10010

Phone Number: 212-684-7400 • **Website:** www.unis.org

Head of School: Dr. Kenneth Wrye • **Director of Admissions:** Anne Alexander

ABOUT UNITED NATIONS INTERNATIONAL SCHOOL

Founded in 1947 by a group of parents who wanted to educate their children while preserving cultural identity, the United Nations International School has grown into a challenging, well-defined, standards-based, international curriculum drawing on "a strong academic curriculum which fosters the acquisition of knowledge, development of skills and attitudes, and complex problem-solving application across a range of disciplines." The school's written curriculum and assessment plan is developed and reviewed through an ongoing renewal process.

MISSION STATEMENT

"Inspired by the ideals of the United Nations, our school serves children and youth from the UN community, the diplomatic corps, the nongovernmental international sector and local New York families. Every day students and staff from all over the world teach, learn, and grow here together. Lessons learned and friendships made are long lasting, as our alumni regularly assure us. And the excitement and stimulation of this international, culturally diverse environment never becomes dulled by familiarity. Day after day, year after year, it remains a fresh experience."

General	
Type of School	Private
Religious Affiliation	None
Coeducational	Yes
Boarding	No
Day School	Yes
Dress Code	No
Founded	1947

Students	
Enrollment (Grades 9–12)	450
% Male/Female	49/51
% International Students	78
# Countries Represented	115

Admissions Selectivity	
Requires Standardized Test Scores	Yes
Application Essay	Yes
Median SAT	1210

Academics

REQUIRED CLASSES

4 years: English, foreign language,
  math, science, humanities
2 years: Physical education
1 year: UN studies
1 semester: Music, health, art, individual
  project

ADDITIONAL REQUIREMENTS

30 hours of community service per
  year

Student/Faculty Ratio   10:1

Extracurricular

MOST POPULAR
INTERSCHOLASTIC SPORTS
MALE

Baseball, basketball, soccer, track,
  volleyball

FEMALE

Basketball, soccer, softball, track,
  volleyball

Financial

Annual Tuition

  $20,370 (9–10th grades)
  $20,580 (11th grade)
  $21,000 (12th grade)
  *

THE IDEAL APPLICANT

The school looks for students "who can follow the program of study, are socially mature, intellectually curious and whose parents are supportive of the school's mission."

COLLEGES THAT RECENT GRADS ARE ATTENDING

American University of Beirut, American University of Paris, Amherst College, Automona de Madrid, Bard College, Barnard College, Boston College, Boston University, Brown University, Bryn Mawr College, Carnegie Mellon University, City University of New York—Brooklyn College, Colgate University, Columbia University, The Cooper Union for the Advancement of Science and Art, Copenhagen Business School, Cornell University, Dartmouth College, Dickinson College, Drexel University, Duke University, Emerson College, Fordham University, French Culinary Institute, George Washington University, Georgetown University, Goucher College, Hamilton College, Hampshire College, Harvard University, Johns Hopkins University, Lafayette College, London School of Economics, Moscow State University, Marymount College, McGill University, Massachusetts Institute of Technology, Moscow State University, Mount Holyoke College, New York University, Northeastern University, Northwestern University, Oberlin College, Pennsylvania State University, Politecnico di Milano, Pomona College, Princeton University, Rice University, Rutgers University, Sarah Lawrence College, Skidmore College, Smith College, Trinity College—Dublin, Tsukuba University, University of Bath, Universidad de Buenos Aires, University of Michigan, University of Notre Dame, University of Pennsylvania, University of Redlands, Utrecht University, Vanderbilt University, Vassar College, Wellesley College, Wesleyan University, Williams College, Yale University

XAVIER HIGH SCHOOL

30 West Sixteenth Street, New York, NY 10011

Phone Number: 212-924-7900 • **Website:** www.xavierhs.org

President: Reverend Daniel J. Gatti, S.J. • **Head of School:** Michael LiVigni

Director of Admissions: Thomas Wierzbowski

About Xavier High School

Founded in 1847 by Father John Larkin, Xavier High School is "a vital part of a vibrant Jesuit community" that includes forty-six high schools and twenty-eight colleges and universities across the country. Committed to academic excellence with a curriculum that cultivates rigor, critical thinking, and reflection, the school is one of only four Jesuit high schools in New York City and it prides itself on its dedication to the principles and ideals of a spiritual life in education. The faculty and programs are responsive to individual needs and changing times. Its active campus ministry department stresses the importance of ministering to those less fortunate. Service trips and projects are organized in the United States and abroad which are bolstered by student who raise funds and participate in these humanitarian ventures.

The curriculum is "challenging and engaging," encouraging students to push themselves in their pursuit of education. In addition to the standard course of study, Xavier offers twelve Advanced Placement classes which students can start taking as early as sophomore year. An optional JROTC program is also available to interested students. Xavier's dedication to excellence bears results—99 percent of its graduates go on to four-year colleges. Part of that success is due to the competitive application process. To apply to Xavier, students take the TACHS (Test for Admission into Catholic High Schools) and list Xavier as one of their three choices. Students who score in the top 25 percent on the exam, and who have above-average grades are strongly considered for admission.

General

Type of School	Private, Independent
Religious Affiliation	Catholic, Jesuit
Coeducational	No
Boarding	No
Day School	Yes
Dress Code	Yes

Students

Enrollment (Grades 9–12)	940
% Male/Female	100/0
% African American	5
% Hispanic/Latino	15
% Asian	7
% Caucasian	73
% International Students	2
% Out-of-State Students	2
# States Represented	2

Admissions Selectivity

Applications Received	1,300–1,400
# Accepted Applicants Who Enrolled	260
Requires Standardized Test Scores	Yes; TACHS
Application Essay	None
Median SAT	1127

Comparable Schools

Fordham Prep, Loyola, Regis

MISSION STATEMENT

"Xavier High School endeavors to prepare students for the twenty-first century who will be per-
sons of competence, conscience, and compassion.
As a Catholic, college preparatory school for young
men, Xavier accomplishes this goal in the context of
a multicultural, urban community dedicated to
learning, faith, and service."

THE IDEAL APPLICANT

The ideal Xavier student is "one who is open to
learning and maturing as a person intellectually,
physically, emotionally, and spiritually through hard
work and a dedication to excellence. Xavier prepares
students to continue their studies in college and,
more importantly, to lead a faith-filled life in a world
in need of greater peace and justice."

WHERE STUDENTS COME FROM

The school draws students from "all five bor-
oughs of New York City, as well as New Jersey,
Nassau County, Westchester County, and Orange
County."

ORIENTATION PROCESS FOR
NEW STUDENTS

Incoming freshmen attend a three-day orientation during which they are introduced to the administration, faculty, upperclassmen, and facilities. Prior
to the formal orientaion to Xavier policies and procedures, freshmen are invited to spend a "Fun Day"
at Xavier where activities and lunch are planned. It
is a great way for new students to get introduced to Xavier.

COLLEGES THAT RECENT GRADS ARE ATTENDING

American University, Boston College, Boston University, The Citadel, Clark Atlanta
University, College of the Holy Cross, Cornell University, City University of New York—Honors
College, City University of New York—Brooklyn, City University of New York—John Jay College
of Criminal Justice, Drexel University, Fairfield University, Florida A&M University, Fordham
University, George Washington University, Georgetown University, Gettysburg College, Hobart
and William Smith Colleges, Ithaca College, Le Moyne College, Lehigh University, Loyola
College—Maryland, Loyola Marymount University, Loyola University—New Orleans, Marist
College, Massachusetts Institute of Technology, New School University, New York University,

Northeastern University, Pace University, Pennsylvania State University, Purdue University, Sacred Heart University, Saint Joseph's University, School of Visual Arts, St. Francis College, Stanford University, State University of New York at Albany, State University of New York at Binghamton, State University of New York—Fashion Institute of Technology, State University of New York—University at Buffalo, Syracuse University, United States Naval Academy, University of Delaware, University of Georgia, University of Massachusetts—Boston, University of Michigan, University of Notre Dame, University of San Diego, Villanova University, Xavier University, Yale University

STUDENTS SAY

Students call Xavier a "great academic institution" with "a very high standard of excellence," and many note the feeling of belonging thanks to "the brotherhood" the school provides. Combine that with "energetic" teachers, "challenging" subjects, "compassion for others," and a commitment to "human enrichment" and it's no wonder students say they are "proud to be part of the Xavier community." In the words of one student, "At Xavier, you are never alone" and because of this students are encouraged to always "strive to do better than the day before."

PARENTS SAY

According to parents, Xavier "continually challenges and encourages" students to "see things from different perspectives," to "ask questions," and "excel in everything" they do, which in turn leads to "confidence," "independence," and the "skills needed to succeed in the world today." "Enthusiasm" is a key component to the "rigorous education" Xavier offers, and thanks to this, students gain "a sense of personal responsibility" that nurtures the development of these "mature" and "generous" young men.

ALUMNI SAY

Alumni appreciate the Jesuit philosophy that informed not only their time at Xavier, but also their lives. As one former student explains, "Xavier showed me what it means to put others first." The school's "large family" environment provided students with a solid support network and imbued a sense of "respect" that functioned independent of grade level or disagreements. The emphasis on "work ethic and skills" also played a large role in make the transition to college a smooth one, effectively preparing students to "face university and the world."

YESHIVAH OF FLATBUSH

1609 Avenue J, Brooklyn, NY 11230

Phone Number: 718-377-1100 • **Website:** www.flatbush.org

Head of School: Rabbi Raymond Harari • **Director of Admissions:** Rabbi Ronald J. Levy

General

Type of School	Private
Religious Affiliation	Jewish
Coeducational	Yes
Boarding	No
Day School	Yes
Dress Code	No
Founded	1927

Students

Enrollment (Grades 9–12)	766
% African American	1
% Hispanic/Latino	1
% Caucasian	98

Admissions Selectivity

Requires Standardized Test Scores	Yes; BJE

COMPARABLE SCHOOLS

The Abraham Joshua Heschel High School; Ramaz—The Rabbi Joseph F. Lookstein Upper School; Solomon Schechter High School

Academics

Student/Faculty Ratio	13:1

Extracurricular

MOST POPULAR
INTERSCHOLASTIC SPORTS

MALE
Basketball, soccer, swimming, tennis

FEMALE
Basketball, soccer, swimming, tennis, volleyball

Financial

Endowment	$26 million

*

ABOUT YESHIVA OF FLATBUSH

Since its inception in 1927, the Yeshiva of Flatbush has "imbued its students with a thirst for knowledge, a commitment to Zionism, a love of the Hebrew language, and the dedication to serve the greater Jewish and secular communities." The yeshiva features a challenging curriculum of Judaic studies, liberal arts, and extracurricular activities that holds firmly to its fundamental tenet of teaching Judaic studies classes in Hebrew, regardless of a student's level of proficiency. While proving for a heavy workload, this approach is successful and students are quick to become fluent in Hebrew thanks to a "dedicated and highly qualified" faculty. Also worth mentioning is that 80 percent of the yeshiva's $26 million budget is "allocated towards an investment in teachers and staff," ensuring a dedicated and talented faculty.

MISSION STATEMENT

"The school philosophy is a synthesis of Judaic studies, liberal arts, and extracurricular activities that places great emphasis on the students' character development. It has evolved into a unique complement of Jewish and American values that focuses on all aspects of education and enables our graduates to meet the challenges of college and life."

COLLEGES THAT RECENT GRADS ARE ATTENDING

City University of New York—Honors College, Columbia University, New York University, University of Pennsylvania, Yeshiva University

YESHIVA UNIVERSITY HIGH SCHOOL FOR BOYS

2540 Amsterdam Avenue, New York, NY 10033

Phone Number: 212-960-5337 • **Website:** www.yuhsb.org

Head of School: Rabbi Mark Gottlieb • **Director of Admissions:** Rabbi Gil Perl

ABOUT YESHIVA UNIVERSITY HIGH SCHOOL FOR BOYS

With a focus on both religious and educational instruction, Yeshiva University High School for Boys operates a challenging dual-program curriculum of the secular and spiritual, involving traditional high school subjects with the study of the Talmud, Tanach, Bekius, Halacha, and Hashkafa. As such, students find that both programs make "significant demands outside the classroom, including preparation for classes, exams, and written assignments," but ultimately this manner of study allows each child to achieve their educational, personal, and religious potential.

Despite the breadth of the program, students still find time to participate in "a variety of educationally-enriching programs, events, and extracurricular activities." The faculty is made up of "a very diverse group of professionals," the majority of whom hold master's degrees in the subject they teach. The rabbinical staff, too, holds an impressive wealth of experience and study, particularly in law, psychology, mathematics, and the pulpit rabbinate.

General	
Type of School	Private
Religious Affiliation	Jewish
Coeducational	No
Boarding	Yes
Day School	Yes
Dress Code	Yes

Students	
Enrollment (Grades 9–12)	300
% Male/Female	100/0
% Caucasian	100

Admissions Selectivity	
Requires Standardized Test Scores	Yes; BJE
Application Essay	Yes
Median SAT	1233

MISSION STATEMENT

The school's website states that Yeshiva University High School for Boys is committed to its students' academic, emotional, and spiritual development. The Yeshiva cherishes the opportunity to educate and inspire a group of "knowledgeable and committed Jews," as well as intelligent, curious, and caring individuals of promise. The High School's challenging academic curriculum encourages "adherence to the traditional ideals and practices of Orthodox Judaism." As such, it aspires to motivate Torah living—or, in the Yeshiva's own words, "striving to become ever more devoted to G-d, Torah learning, personal integrity, and ethical behavior basic to Jewish life and participation in contemporary society. Genuine concern for observance of mitzvot, love of the Jewish people, and pride in our Jewish heritage and values should characterize the intellectual goals and the daily behavior of our students." The Yeshiva's commitment to Torah U'Madda requires students to pursue their academic studies with an equal determination in hopes of becoming more understanding and compassionate world citizens, working hard "to maximize intellectual potential." It is the Yeshiva's endeavor to involve its students in all facets of school life, whether by studying in the classroom or participating in extracurricular activities, so that the students' academic experience "reflects the primacy of Torah, as well as the importance of secular studies."

THE IDEAL APPLICANT

According to the school's website, Yeshiva University High School for Boys seeks active young men who "identify wholeheartedly with the destiny of fellow Jews throughout the world, exhibit loyalty to Eretz Yisrael," and recognize Israel as the fruition of Zionism and as the homeland of the Jewish people. Students are also expected to be exemplary scholars and citizens, demonstrating respect and compassion at all times.

WHERE STUDENTS COME FROM

According to the school's website, Yeshiva draws approximately 85 percent of the student body from New York City's five boroughs and suburbs. The remaining 15 percent of students travel from throughout the U.S., Canada, Europe, and Israel.

ORIENTATION PROCESS FOR NEW STUDENTS

Orientation meetings are held for new students and their parents at the beginning of the school year.

YORK PREPARATORY SCHOOL

40 West Sixty-eighth Street, New York, NY 10023

Phone Number: 212-362-0400 • **Website:** www.yorkprep.org

Head of School: Ronald P. Stewart • **Director of Enrollment:** Elizabeth Norton

ABOUT YORK PREPARATORY SCHOOL

Though York Prep first appears to be a traditional school with an Ivy League look, what is immediately apparent is that it is home to an energetic and happy student body. Since its founding in 1969 by the present headmaster, Ronald Stewart, and his wife, Jayme Stewart, College Guidance Director and author of *How to Get Into the College of Your Choice*, York Prep has earned an enviable reputation as a school that cares about its students' success and works hard to ensure students receive the finest possible education in an challenging and supportive atmosphere.

At the heart of York students' success is the tracking system. This allows students to work at an advanced pace through Honors courses, AP classes, and the Scholars Program, in subjects in which they excel, and at a moderate pace in those subjects where they need more guidance. Also, York Prep's Jump Start Program enables students with different learning styles to function successfully in an academically-challenging mainstream setting. Study skills, test-taking skills, and organizational skills are key components of this supplemental program. In addition to this, York Prep was chosen by VH-1 as the home of *Rap School*, a documentary which follows the educational journey of eight York students as they explore the history, music, dance, and art of hip hop, with rapper Ice T as their instructor.

York strives to be on the cutting edge of technology. In addition to computers in every classroom, each room is equipped with a projector and a screen for use by teachers and students alike. In September 2003, York Prep introduced Edline, a web-based service designed to seamlessly integrate this technology into the home.

General

Type of School	Private
Religious Affiliation	None
Coeducational	Yes
Boarding	No
Day School	Yes
Dress Code	Yes
Founded	1969

Students

Enrollment (Grades 6–12)	320
% Male/Female	55/45
% African American	18
% Hispanic/Latino	10
% Asian	5
% Caucasian	67
% International Students	8
% Out-of-State Students	4
# Countries Represented	9
# States Represented	3

Admissions Selectivity

Applications Received	400+
# Applicants Accepted	150
# Accepted Applicants Who Enrolled	100
Requires Standardized Test Scores	Yes
Application Essay	Yes

COMPARABLE SCHOOLS

Birch Wathen Lenox; Calhoun; Columbia Prep; Dwight; Trevor Day

The quiet strength of York is its faculty who imbue a sense of commitment and pride in a system that works and breeds success, which explains why some faculty have called York "home" for thirty years or more. With a student teacher ratio of 6:1, there is ample opportunity for students and teachers to engage in meaningful work together, and the school encourages students to find a balance between extracurricular activities within the school and the community at large.

Mission Statement

"York Preparatory School is a coeducational, independent, college preparatory day school offering a traditional curriculum for grades 6-12. In the belief that every student can succeed, we provide a supportive atmosphere that reflects and is enhanced by the diversity and richness of New York City. York Prep recognizes the student as the focus of the educational process. We guide our students to reach their optimum potential intellectually, physically, and socially. Each student is challenged to think critically and creatively in a structured environment where excellence is rewarded and individual effort is encouraged. We strive to develop responsible citizens by reinforcing respect for self and for others in the community."

The Ideal Applicant

The ideal applicant is an "above-average student prepared to join a close community of 320 other students who will contribute to and value that community."

Where Students Come From

Most students come from the five boroughs of New York as well as Westchester County and Long Island. There are "a handful" of students from New Jersey and Connecticut as well.

Orientation Process for New Students

In the fall new students attend a pre-school Orientation Program and party, during which the students have a chance to get acquainted with their new surroundings and daily routines.

Colleges that Recent Grads Are Attending

Bennington College, Boston University, Connecticut College, Cornell University, Fordham University, George Washington University, Hobart and William Smith Colleges, Northeastern University, New York University, Rhode Island School of Design, State University of New York at Binghamton, Syracuse University, Tulane University, University of Colorado at Boulder, University of Michigan, University of Rhode Island, University of Vermont, University of Wisconsin—Madison, Vanderbilt University, Vassar College, Wesleyan University, Wheaton College, Williams College

Students Say

Students are "grateful" to attend York Prep, saying that the school "maximized my academic potential." They note the "small community" and "wonderful faculty and staff" who dedicate themselves to supplying students with "a wealth of knowledge" and "the necessary tools to get into a top college." As one student explains, teachers at York do more than instruct in the classroom, but also "contribute immensely to our character and perspective on the world and each other."

Parents Say

Parents overwhelmingly agree that York Prep's "rigorous educational programs," "small class sizes," and "kind support of newcomers" go a long way in securing students' successful futures. Many praise the teachers who "are always available to guide students through class projects and to prepare for exams" and "communicate frequently with parents," which in turn fosters a "positive learning environment" and "sense of community." Students "blossom" in this supportive atmosphere, where they find constant encouragement in "applying for advanced honors courses, partaking in team sports and performing in talent shows," leading one parent to say, "we are so lucky to have found York Prep."

Alumni Say

Alumni recall the "outstanding education" and "supportive and nurturing environment" York Prep offered, noting that the values of "self-development, self-love, and self-motivation" that the school instilled gave them the "confidence to grow into a responsible, young adult." One student explains how Ronald and Jayme Stewart "were like parents," "nurturing and challenging" at the same time. And perhaps most tellingly, a large majority of former students hope to enroll their children at York so they can "obtain all the knowledge and wisdom" they received in their time there.

PART V
THE LOWDOWN ON ENTRANCE EXAMS

The following information on the SSAT and ISEE has been taken from The Princeton Review's *Cracking the SSAT & ISEE*, albeit in an abridged form (unfortunately, we don't have enough space to include it all!). It should prove a good start in your preparation for the admissions process at a private or selective public high school, but we highly recommend taking a look at *Cracking the SSAT & ISEE*—it provides invaluable information and techniques that will enhance your math and verbal skills, boost your vocabulary, and teach you how to dodge trap answers with the best of 'em.

What is the SSAT?

The Secondary School Admission Test (SSAT) is a standardized test made up of a writing sample, which is not scored but is sent along with each score report, and a series of multiple-choice questions divided into Quantitative (math), Verbal, and Reading sections. The entire test lasts about 155 minutes, during which you will work on five different sections.

Writing Sample (ungraded)	1 essay topic	25 minutes
Quantitative	25 questions	30 minutes
Verbal	60 questions	30 minutes
Reading	40 questions	40 minutes
Quantitative (a second section)	25 questions	30 minutes

Keep in mind that the sections will not necessarily appear in this order. The writing sample can come either before or after the multiple-choice sections, and within the multiple-choice portion of the test, the sections can appear in any order.

There are three different types of sections on the SSAT: Verbal, Reading, and Quantitative. You will receive four scores on the test, however. In addition to listing a score for each of these three sections, your score report will also show an overall score, which is a combination of your verbal and quantitative scores. Reading is not included in the computation of your overall score. You will also receive a percentile score of between 1 percent and 99 percent that compares your test scores with those of other test takers from the previous three years.

What's On the SSAT?

The Verbal section of the SSAT tests your knowledge of vocabulary using two different question types: synonyms and analogies. There are no sentence completions on the SSAT. The Reading section tests your ability to read and understand short passages. These reading passages include both fiction (including poetry and folklore) and nonfiction. The Math sections test your knowledge of general mathematical concepts, including arithmetic, algebra, and geometry. There are no quantitative comparison questions on the Math sections of the SSAT.

Tips on Taking the SSAT

Pacing

Most people believe that to do well on a test, it is important to answer every question. While this is true of most of the tests you take in school, it is not true of many standardized tests, including the SSAT. On this test, it is very possible to score well without answering all of the questions; in fact, many students can improve their scores by answering fewer questions, as you will be penalized only for the questions you answer incorrectly, not for skipping. So for the most part, give your attention to problems you think you can answer, and decide which questions are too thorny to waste time on. You'll decide based on your target score how many problems you should skip in each section (more on this in a minute). This test-taking approach is as necessary a factor in score improvement as your knowledge of vocabulary and math rules.

Guessing

When should you guess? Whenever you can eliminate even one wrong answer. Yes, really. Eliminating four definitely wrong answers out of five will give you the right answer. Be aggressive but remember: While educated guessing is always a good idea, random guessing will not improve your SSAT score.

Process of Elimination

While you won't see the following question on the SSAT, it will show you how powerful the process of elimination can be.

What is the capital of Malawi?
a)   New York
b)   Paris
c)   London
d)   Lilongwe
e)   Washington, DC

There are two ways to get this question right. First, you already know that the capital of Malawi is Lilongwe. (If you do, good for you!) The second is to know that the capital of Malawi is not New York, Paris, London, or Washington, DC. You don't get more points for knowing the right answer from the start, so one way is just as good as the other. Try to get in the habit of looking at a question and asking, "What are the wrong answers?" instead of, "What is the right answer?"

Math

The SSAT measures your basic math skills, so although you may feel a little frustrated reviewing things you have already learned, this type of basic review is the best way to improve your score. Remember that you will not be allowed to use a calculator on the SSAT, so if you have developed a habit of reaching for your calculator whenever you need to add or multiply a couple of numbers, take our advice and put it away. Start practicing your math homework without it. Also, do not try to do math in your head. You are allowed to write in your test booklet. Even when you are just adding a few numbers together, write them down and do the work on paper. It'll help to eliminate careless errors and give you something to refer to if you need to check over your work.

One Pass, Two Pass

Within any Math section, you will find three types of questions:

- Those you can answer easily without spending too much time

- Those that, if you had all the time in the world, you could do

- Some questions that you have absolutely no idea how to tackle

When you work on a Math section, start out with the first question. If you think you can do it without too much trouble, go ahead. If not, save it for later. Move on to the second question and decide whether to do that one. Once you've made it all the way through the section—working slowly and carefully to answer all the questions that you find easiest—then go back and try some of the ones that you think you can do but that will take a little longer to complete. You should pace yourself so that while you're finishing the second pass through the section, time will run out.

Practice Drills

1. The sum of five consecutive positive integers is 30. What is the square of the largest of the five positive integers?
   a) 25
   b) 36
   c) 49
   d) 64
   e) 81

2. How many factors does the number 24 have?
   a) 2
   b) 4
   c) 6
   d) 8
   e) 10

3. How many numbers between 1 and 100 are multiples of both 2 and 7?
   a) 7
   b) 49
   c) 51
   d) 56
   e) 63

4. If 3x–6=21, then what is x÷9?

    a) 0
    b) 1
    c) 3
    d) 6
    e) 9

5. One-half of the difference between the number of degrees in a square and the number of degrees in a triangle is

    a) 45
    b) 90
    c) 180
    d) 240
    e) 360

6. In a jar of lollipops, the ratio of red lollipops to blue lollipops is 3:5. If only red lollipops and blue lollipops are in the jar and if the total number of lollipops in the jar is 56, how many blue lollipops are in the jar?

    a) 35
    b) 28
    c) 21
    d) 8
    e) 5

7. An art club of 4 boys and 5 girls makes craft projects. If the boys average 2 projects each and the girls average 3 projects each, what is the total number of projects produced by the club?

    a) 14
    b) 23
    c) 26
    d) 54
    e) 100

8. During a severe winter in Ontario, the temperature dropped suddenly to 10 degrees below zero. If the temperature in Ontario before this cold spell occurred was 10 degrees above zero, by what percent did the temperature drop?

    a) 25%
    b) 50%
    c) 100%
    d) 150%
    e) 200%

9. If J is an odd integer, which of the following must be true?

    a) (J÷3)>1
    b) (J–2) is a positive integer.
    c) 2xJ is an even integer.
    d) J^2>J
    e) J>0

10. If $\$n=120$, then n=
    a) 11
    b) 12
    c) 13
    d) 120
    e) 130

Answers: Math

1. d)
2. d)
3. b)
4. b) Be careful of choosing answer choice c).
5. b)
6. a)
7. b)
8. e)
9. c)
10. c)

VERBAL

This test is designed for students in three or four different grade levels. There will be vocabulary in some of these questions that is aimed at students older than you, and almost no one in your grade will get those questions right. On the SSAT score report, you will be compared only with students in your own grade. The younger you are in your test level, the fewer questions you are expected to complete. This is good news for eighth graders: they are expected to do the least number of questions on the Upper Level test.

Which Questions Should I Do?

The questions are arranged roughly in order of difficulty—the harder synonyms tend to come toward the end of the synonym section, and the harder analogies tend to come at the end of the analogy section. However, everyone is different, and some questions are harder for certain people than they are for others. You know some words that your friends don't, and vice versa.

You get as many points for an easy question as you do for a hard one. So here's the plan: Do all the questions that are easy for you first. Easy questions are those without guesswork: You know the definitions of all the words involved. Then go back through and do the questions with words that sound familiar, even if you are not sure of their dictionary definitions—these are words you sort of know. As you work through these questions, you'll probably be concentrating mostly on the beginning and middle of each section, but don't be afraid to glance ahead—there may be some words you know toward the end. Remember to skip a number on the answer sheet when you skip a question.

Knowing your vocabulary is the key to quickly deciding if you can answer a question easily.

Know Yourself

Categorize the words you see in SSAT questions into

- Words you know

- Words you sort of know

- Words you don't really know

The easiest way to get a verbal question right is by making sure all the words in it fall into the first category—words you know. The best way to do this is by learning new vocabulary *every day*.

Eliminate Answer Choices

With math questions, there's always a correct answer; the other answers are simply wrong. With verbal questions, however, things are not that simple. Words are much more slippery than numbers. Verbal questions have *best* answers, not *correct* ones. The other answers aren't necessarily wrong, but the people who score the SSAT think they're not as good as the *best* ones. This means that your goal is to eliminate *worse* answer choices in the Verbal and Reading sections. And this is good news because there are many more of them than there are *best* answers, meaning *worse* answers are easier to find!

Should you guess if you can't narrow it down to one answer? Yes. If you can eliminate even one answer choice, you should guess from the remaining choices.

Practice Drills
Analogies & Synonyms

1. Chapter is to book as
   a) glass is to water
   b) lamp is to light
   c) scene is to play
   d) stew is to meat
   e) elevator is to building

2. Fish is to fin as
   a) fruit is to stem
   b) bird is to wing
   c) insect is to shell
   d) cod is to school
   e) dog is to tail

3. Rough is to cough as
   a) chapped is to sore
   b) flight is to fright
   c) sight is to fight
   d) seated is to sated
   e) lair is to liar

4. Swift is to fast as
   a) slow is to stopped
   b) beneficial is to detrimental
   c) athletic is to lithe
   d) bellicose is to warlike
   e) grumpy is to frowning.

5. Island is to _____ as
   a) castle is to moat
   b) star is to galaxy
   c) river is to delta
   d) bay is to peninsula
   e) earth is to hemisphere

6. _____ is to jury as
   a) eradicate is to problem
   b) quarantine is to patient
   c) elect is to politician
   d) liquidate is to opponent
   e) evacuate is to city

7. PRINCIPLE
   a) leader
   b) standard
   c) theory
   d) game
   e) chief

8. AUTOMATIC
   a) involuntary
   b) enjoyable
   c) forceful
   d) hapless
   e) independent

Answers: Verbal

1. c) Chapter is a section of a book.
2. b) Fish uses a fin to move itself (Get specific!).
3. c) Rough and cough are spelled the same except for the first letter (rearranged letters).
4. d) Swift and fast mean the same thing (synonyms).
5. a) or b) because a castle is surrounded by a moat and a galaxy is a group of stars.
6. b) or c) because quarantine means to isolate a patient or elect means to choose a politician.
7. b)
8. a)

Reading

You have to read the SSAT reading passages differently from the way you read anything else because the passages the test writers use are packed with information.

Passages are chosen precisely because there is a lot of information in only a few paragraphs. It's all bunched together. So if you read your normal way, here's what happens: You read the first sentence and you try to remember it. You read the second sentence and try to remember it. You read the third sentence and, as you try to remember it, forget the first two.

You have to read with a different goal in mind for the SSAT. This may sound crazy, but *don't* try to learn or remember anything. *You don't get any points for reading the passage well!* You get points for answering questions correctly. So slow down and make sure you're checking each answer carefully before eliminating it.

What are the Passages Like?

There are six to eight passages in the Reading section. The first two passages are the easiest—definitely do them.

After the first two, you can choose which to do. The Reading section purposely has far more passages and questions than most students can complete in 40 minutes—6 to 8 passages and 40 questions. Don't let the test writers choose which ones you'll finish. Choose for yourself by flipping through them and going with the types you do best. You'll do better on topics that interest you.

How Do I Read the Passages?

Quickly! Don't try to remember the details in the passage. Your goal is to read the passage quickly to get the main idea.

The SSAT Reading section is an open-book test—you can look back at the passage to answer questions about the details.

After you have read the entire passage, ask yourself two questions:

- **"What?"** What is the passage about?

- **"So what?"** What's the author's point about this topic?

The answers to these questions will show you the main idea of the passage. Scribble down this main idea in just a few words. The answer to "What?" is the thing that was being talked about—"bees" or "weather forecasting." The answer to "So what?" gives you the rest of the sentence—"Bees do little dances that tell other bees where to go for pollen," or "Weather forecasting is complicated by many problems."

Don't assume you will find the main idea in the first sentence. While often the main idea is in the beginning of the passage, it is not *always* in the first sentence or even the first paragraph. The beginning may just be a lead-in to the main point.

What is the ISEE?

The Independent School Entrance Examination (ISEE) is a standardized test made up of a series of multiple-choice questions and a writing sample. The entire test lasts a little less than three hours, during which you will work on five different sections.

Verbal Reasoning	40 questions	20 minutes
Quantitative Reasoning	35 questions	35 minutes
Reading Comprehension	40 questions	40 minutes
Mathematics Achievement	45 questions	40 minutes
Essay (ungraded)	1 essay topic	30 minutes

Keep in mind that the sections will not necessarily appear in this order. The essay comes after the multiple-choice sections, but the sections within the multiple-choice portion of the test can appear in any order. Some schools refer to the ISEE as the ERB. Actually, there is no test called the ERB; ERB stands for Educational Records Bureau, and they are the people who administer the ISEE.

What's on the ISEE?

The Verbal section of the ISEE tests your knowledge of vocabulary using two different question types: synonyms and sentence completions. There are no analogies on the ISEE. The Reading Comprehension section tests your ability to read and understand short passages. These reading passages include both fiction (including poetry and folklore) and nonfiction. The Math sections test your knowledge of general mathematical concepts through two different question types: problem-solving questions and quantitative comparison questions. The quantitative comparison questions ask you to compare two columns of data.

Tips on Taking the ISEE

Pacing

Most people believe that to do well on a test, it is important to answer every question. While this is true of most of the tests you take in school, it is not true of many standardized tests, including the ISEE. On this test, it is very possible to score well without answering all of the questions; in fact, many students can improve their scores by answering fewer questions as there is no penalty for wrong answers. So it is to your advantage to choose an answer for every question. This doesn't mean that you need to rush through the test to try to solve every question. Work at a pace that will maximize correct answers, and be ready to guess at the questions you don't have time to answer. You should *answer* every question, but that does not mean you should *do* every question.

Process of Elimination

Here's a question you will not see on the ISEE, but which will show you how powerful the process of elimination can be.

What is the capital of Malawi?
- a) New York
- b) Paris
- c) London
- d) Lilongwe
- e) Washington, DC

There are two ways to get this question right. First, you already know that the capital of Malawi is Lilongwe. (If you do, good for you!) The second is to know that the capital of Malawi is not New York, Paris, London, or Washington, DC. You don't get more points for knowing the right answer from the start, so one way is just as good as the other. Try to get in the habit of looking at a question and asking, "What are the wrong answers?" instead of, "What is the right answer?"

Guessing

When should you guess? Whenever you can when taking the ISEE. Yes, really. With no guessing penalty on the exam, you should be certain to choose an answer for every question, even if you don't have time to look at it.

In addition to this random guessing, you can also improve your score by taking educated guesses. If you encounter a verbal question, for instance, to which you do not know the right answer, don't just give up. Instead, look at the answer choices and try to identify wrong answers so you can eliminate them. Eliminating some answer choices turns guessing into a way to improve your score.

MATH

Remember that you will not be allowed to use a calculator on the ISEE, so if you have developed a habit of reaching for your calculator whenever you need to add or multiply a couple of numbers, take our advice and put it away. Start practicing your math homework without it. Also, do not try to do math in your head. You are allowed to write in your test booklet. Even when you are just adding a few numbers together, write them down and do the work on paper. It'll help to eliminate careless errors and give you something to refer to if you need to check over your work.

One Pass, Two Pass

Within any Math section, you will find three types of questions:

- Those you can answer easily without spending too much time

- Those that you could do if you had all the time in the world

- Some questions that you have absolutely no idea how to tackle

When you work on a Math section, start out with the first question. If you think you can do it without too much trouble, go ahead. If not, save it for later. Move on to the second question and decide whether to do that one. Once you've made it all the way through the section—working slowly and carefully to do all the questions that come easily to you—then go back and try some of the ones that you think you can do but that will take a little longer. You should pace yourself so that while you're finishing the second pass through the section, time will run out.

PRACTICE DRILLS

1. The sum of five consecutive positive integers is 30. What is the square of the largest of the five positive integers?
    a) 25
    b) 36
    c) 49
    d) 64
    e) 81

2. How many factors does the number 24 have?
    a) 2
    b) 4
    c) 6
    d) 8
    e) 10

3. How many numbers between 1 and 100 are multiples of both 2 and 7?
    a) 7
    b) 49
    c) 51
    d) 56
    e) 63

4. If 3x–6=21, then what is x÷9?
    a) 0
    b) 1
    c) 3
    d) 6
    e) 9

5. One-half of the difference between the number of degrees in a square and the number of degrees in a triangle is
    a) 45
    b) 90
    c) 180
    d) 240
    e) 360

6. In a jar of lollipops, the ratio of red lollipops to blue lollipops is 3:5. If only red lollipops and blue lollipops are in the jar and if the total number of lollipops in the jar is 56, how many blue lollipops are in the jar?

   a) 35
   b) 28
   c) 21
   d) 8
   e) 5

7. An art club of 4 boys and 5 girls makes craft projects. If the boys average 2 projects each and the girls average 3 projects each, what is the total number of projects produced by the club?

   a) 14
   b) 23
   c) 26
   d) 54
   e) 100

8. During a severe winter in Ontario, the temperature dropped suddenly to 10 degrees below zero. If the temperature in Ontario before this cold spell occurred was 10 degrees above zero, by what percent did the temperature drop?

   a) 25%
   b) 50%
   c) 100%
   d) 150%
   e) 200%

9. If J is an odd integer, which of the following must be true?

   a) $(J \div 3) > 1$
   b) $(J-2)$ is a positive integer.
   c) $2 \times J$ is an even integer.
   d) $J^2 > J$
   e) $J > 0$

10. If $\$n = 120$, then $n =$

    a) 11
    b) 12
    c) 13
    d) 120
    e) 130

Quantitative Comparison Plugging In

11.	Column A		Column B
1.	x	$x>1$	x^2
2.	$b/2$	b is an integer and $-1<b<1$	$b/8$
3.	p gallons		m quarts
4.	$x/4$	x is a positive integer	$x/5$
5.	pw	w is an integer less than 4	w
		p is an integer greater than 10	
6.	$4c+6$		$3c+12$

Answers: Math

1. d)
2. d)
3. b)
4. b) Be careful of choosing answer choice c).
5. b)
6. a)
7. b)
8. e)
9. c)
10. c)
11. b)

Verbal

This test is designed for students in two to four different grade levels. There will be vocabulary in some of these questions that is aimed at students older than you, and almost no one in your grade will get those questions right. The ISEE score you receive will be compared only with students in your own grade. The younger you are in your test level, the fewer questions you are expected to complete. This is good news for eighth graders: They are expected to do the least number of questions on the Upper Level test.

Which Questions Should I Do?

So here's the plan: Go through the first section, and do all the synonyms that are easy for you first. Easy questions are those without guesswork: You know the definitions of all the words involved. Then go back through and do the questions with words that sound familiar, even if you are not sure of their dictionary definitions—these are words you sort of know. As you work through these questions, you'll probably be concentrating mostly on the beginning and middle of each section, but don't be afraid to glance ahead—there may be some words you know toward the end. Remember to skip a number on the answer sheet when you skip a question.

Knowing your vocabulary is the key to quickly deciding if you can answer a question easily.

Know Yourself

Categorize the words you see in ISEE questions into

- Words you know

- Words you sort of know

- Words you don't really know

The easiest way to get a verbal question right is by making sure all the words in it fall into the first category—words you know. The best way to do this is by learning new vocabulary every day.

Eliminate Answer Choices

With math questions, there's always a correct answer; the other answers are simply wrong. With verbal questions, however, things are not that simple. Words are much more slippery than numbers. Verbal questions have best answers, not correct ones. The other answers aren't necessarily wrong, but the people who score the ISEE think they're not as good as the best ones. This means that your goal is to eliminate worse answer choices in the Verbal and Reading sections. And this is good news since there are many more of them than there are best answers, meaning worse answers are easier to find!

Should you guess if you can't narrow it down to one answer? Yes. If you can eliminate even one answer choice, you should guess from the remaining choices. And even if you can't eliminate any choices, a wrong guess won't hurt your score.

PRACTICE DRILLS

1. PRINCIPLE
   a) leader
   b   standard
   c) theory
   d   game
   e   chief

2. AUTOMATIC
   a) involuntary
   b) enjoyable
   c) forceful
   d) hapless
   e) independent

3. Once very —————————, computers are now found in almost every home.

4. After playing more than a dozen different concert halls, the orchestra was praised by critics for its ————————— rendition of Beethoven's famous *Fifth Symphony*.

5. Although Miles was unable to sleep the night before, he seemed remarkably ———————— when he gave his presentation.
   a) worn
   b) tired
   c) presentable
   d) alert

6. Julie was ———————— to have been in the right place at the right time; the drama coach gave her the lead in our class play.
   a) fortunate
   b) inspired
   c) dramatic
   d) impressive

7. Psychologists have long ———————— the connection between violence on television and actual crime; the wealth of different ———————— makes it very hard to reach a consensus.
   a) found...facts
   b) debated...opinions
   c) agreed...articles
   d) argued...criminals

8. Jason felt quite ———————— about his ability to score well; he had studied ———————— the night before.
   a) frightened...thoroughly
   b) happy...poorly
   c) confident...diligently
   d) resistant...lately

Answers: Verbal

1. b)
2. a)
3. rare
4. remarkable
5. d)
6. a)
7. b)
8. c)

Reading

You have to read the ISEE reading passages differently from the way you read anything else because the passages the test writers use are packed with information.

Passages are chosen precisely because there is a lot of information in only a few paragraphs. It's all bunched together. So if you read your normal way, here's what happens: You read the first sentence and you try to remember it. You read the second sentence and try to remember it. You read the third sentence and, as you try to remember it, forget the first two.

You have to read with a different goal in mind for the SSAT. This may sound crazy, but don't try to learn or remember anything. You don't get any points for reading the passage well! You get points for answering questions correctly. So slow down and make sure you're checking each answer carefully before eliminating it.

What Are the Passages Like?

There are around 9 passages in a Reading Comprehension section, and there are 40 questions. Of these, 20 questions are based on science passages, and 20 questions are based on social studies passages.

You can choose which passages to do. The Reading Comprehension section purposely has far more passages and questions than most students can complete in 40 minutes. Don't let the test writers choose which ones you'll finish. Choose for yourself by flipping through them and going with the types you do best. You'll do better on topics that interest you.

How Do I Read the Passages?

Quickly! Don't try to remember the details in the passage. Your goal is to read the passage quickly to get the main idea.

The ISEE Reading Comp section is an open-book test—you can look back at the passage to answer questions about the details.

After you have read the entire passage, ask yourself two questions:

- **"What?"** What is the passage about?

- **"So what?"** What's the author's point about this topic?

The answers to these questions will show you the main idea of the passage. Scribble down this main idea in just a few words. The answer to "What?" is the thing that was being talked about—"bees" or "weather forecasting." The answer to "So what?" gives you the rest of the sentence—"Bees do little dances that tell other bees where to go for pollen," or "Weather forecasting is complicated by many problems."

Don't assume you will find the main idea in the first sentence. While often the main idea is in the beginning of the passage, it is not always in the first sentence or even the first paragraph. The beginning may just be a lead-in to the main point.

What Is the SSHSAT/SHSAT?

The SSHSAT/SHSAT exams are given to measure breadth of thinking and ability in both English and mathematics. (Note: Don't get worried about the difference between the SSHAT and the SHSAT—there is none. SSHSAT was simply a distinction used for the science-focused schools in New York City.) It consists of multiple-choice questions and is offered only once a year to 8th and 9th graders living in any of New York City's five boroughs. Students who take the test in the 8th grade may retake it in the 9th if they wish. It is usually offered during the last week of October or the first week of November, and they are informed in February of the result. The exam has a time limit in total of 2 hours and 30 minutes (includes both sections) with no break in between. The breakdown is as follows:

- Verbal: 45 multiple-choice questions consisting of 30 reading comprehension, 10 logical reasoning, and 5 scrambled paragraph sets.

- Mathematics: 50 multiple-choice questions that involve basic math, pre-algebra, algebra, geometry, substitution, factoring, trigonometry, coordinate graphing, and logic and word problems.

Like the ISEE, there is no penalty for wrong answers or unanswered questions, so if you aren't sure, guess! You have nothing to lose.

Your score on the SHSAT is determined by the total number of correct answers (aka the "Raw" score) out of 100. From that, a scaled score of 200–800 is determined and students are ranked accordingly (high grades to low) with a cut-off score for schools established through overall scores, quantity of students selecting a school, and the number of spaces a school has available. Depending on your score and the availability of the schools you've chosen, you may or may not be placed where you want. The only guarantee for acceptance at your dream school is hard work and lots of studying. But remember, you can take this exam twice, so to ensure you get the best shot possible at an elite school, take the test as an 8th grader, and if that doesn't work out, try again in the 9th grade. It's a numbers game, to be sure, but if you play it right, you'll reap the benefits.

Getting Ready

Looking for the perfect word to describe the SHSAT? Try "competitive." The test is open to all New York City 8th and 9th grade students, which means that every year, over 26,000 students take pen to paper to qualify for entry to their dream high school. This means that every year, cut-off scores and student openings fluctuate. That's a lot of variables to deal with, so we recommend that you study, study, study. If you need some help, talk to your teachers and parents, or even sign up for a SHSAT prep course with The Princeton Review.

Also, there are several other programs run by the New York City Department of Education and certain selective public high schools that can help students get ready for the SHSAT. Staten Island Technical High School and Stuyvesant High School sponsor a free program for middle school students with high standardized test scores. For students who take the SHSAT and score just below the cut-off score, there is still hope. All it takes is a recommendation from their guidance counselor and they may be accepted into the Summer Discovery Program. If they do well and complete this program with flying colors, students gain admission to a specialized high school. For more information, contact the New York City Department of Education or check their website at http://schools.nyc.gov.

PART VI—FAMOUS ALUMNI

HEADS OF THE CLASS

Whether you consider it a magnet or nexus for the world's elite minds, New York City is undeniably a landscape rife with talented individuals, so it's no surprise that its schools alumni rosters offer a list of the best and brightest minds this nation has known. Take a look to see whose ranks you could well join.

Bronx High School of Science

Bruce Ames, Biologist
Judith Baumel, Poet
Stokely Carmichael, Activist
Dominic Chianese, Actor
Leon N. Cooper, Nobel Prize winner
Jon Cryer, Actor
Bobby Darin, Singer
Samuel Delany, Author
E. L. Doctorow, Author
Jon Favreau, Actor
Sheldon L. Glashow, Nobel Prize winner
Roy J. Glauber, Nobel Prize winner
Russell A. Hulse, Nobel Prize winner
Steve Lappas, College basketball coach
Jeanette Lee, Professional pool player
Joseph Lelyveld, Pulitzer Prize winner
Daniel Libeskind, Architect
Anthony Marx, President of Amherst College
Robert Moog, Inventor of the Moog synthesizer
Kevin Phillips, Author and political analyst
Frederik Pohl, Author
H. David Politzer, Nobel Prize winner
Richard Price, Author
William Safire, Pulitzer Prize winner
Melvin Schwartz, Nobel Prize winner
William Sherman, Pulitzer Prize winner
Bernard L. Stein, Pulitzer Prize winner
William Taubman, Pulitzer Prize winner
Gary Weiss, Author and journalist
Steven Weinberg, Nobel Prize winner
Wolf Wigo, Olympic water polo player

Brearley School

Blue Balliett, Author
Elizabeth Fishel, Author and Journalist
Betsy Gotbaum, New York City Public Advocate

Téa Leoni, Actress

Abby Rockefeller Mauzé, Philanthropist,

Caroline Kennedy Schlossberg, Author

Kyra Sedgwick, Actress

Gertrude Vanderbilt Whitney, Sculptor

William Von Arx, Scientist

Martha Denckla, Physician

Stephen Friedman, Dean of Pace Law School

Dan Hedaya, Actor

Robert Maccrate, Judge

Fisher Stevens, Actor

BROOKLYN TECHNICAL HIGH SCHOOL

Gary Ackerman, U.S. Congressman

Colonel Karol J. Bobko, Astronaut

Harry Chapin, Humanitarian

Frank A. Cipriani, President of State University of New York—Farmingdale

Kim Coles, Actress

Joseph M. Colucci, Executive director for General Motors' Research & Design Center

Lou Ferrigno, Actor and bodybuilder

Bernard Friedland, Author and engineer

Bernard Gifford, Vice President of Education for Apple Computers

Joseph J. Jacobs, Author and engineer

Marvin Kitman, Author and critic

Donald L. Klein, Inventor

Joseph J. Kohn, Mathematician

Harvey Lichtenstein, President of the Brooklyn Academy of Music

Conrad McRae, Professional basketball player

Saverio Morea, Engineer

Arno A. Penzias, Nobel Prize winner

Sal Restivo, Author

George Wald, Nobel Prize winner

Anthony Weiner, U.S. Congressman

CALHOUN SCHOOL

Mark-Paul Gosselaar, Actor

Ben Stiller, Actor, director, and writer

THE COLLEGIATE SCHOOL

Peter Bogdanovich, Actor, director, and writer

Ben Brewer, Musician

Edgar Bronfman Jr., Film producer

David Duchovny, Actor

Edward Glaeser, Economist

William Kristol, Speechwriter
Taylor Mali, Poet and teacher
Walter Murch, Film editor and sound mixer
Cesar Romero, Actor
Mark Ronson, Musican
Arthur Schlesinger Jr., Historian and social critic
Robert F.X. Sillerman, Media entrepreneur
Paul Weitz, Film director

THE DALTON SCHOOL

Anderson Cooper, Reporter
Claire Danes, Actress
Samuel R. Delany, Author
Maxim Dlugy, Chess Grandmaster
Jane Elliot, Actress
Noah Emmerich, Actor
Edgar de Evia, Author and photographer
Mark Feuerstein, Actor
Frances FitzGerald, Pulitzer Prize winner
Helen Frankenthaler, Painter
Jennifer Grey, Actress
Sean Lennon, Musician
Mary Stuart Masterson, Actress
Tracy Pollan, Actress
Tracee Ellis Ross, Actress
Melissa Russo, Television journalist
Eric Schlosser, Author and journalist
Christian Slater, Actor

DWIGHT SCHOOL

Truman Capote, Author
Julian Casablancas, Musician
Fiorello LaGuardia, Former Mayor of New York City
Herbert Lehman, Former Governor of New York
Roy Lichtenstein, Artist
Fabrizio Moretti, Musician
Henry Morgenthau, Former Secretary of the Treasury
Hal Prince, Theater director
Nick Valensi, Musician

THE FIELDSTON SCHOOL

Jill Abramson, Managing editor for *The New York Times*
Diane Arbus, Photographer
Sofia Coppola, Oscar-winning film director and writer

Andrew Delbanco, Author and critic

Nicholas Delbanco, Novelist

David Denby, Film critic for *The New Yorker*

Rita Gam, Film actress

Walter Koenig, Actor

Joseph Kraft, Public affairs columnist

Christopher Lehmann-Haupt, Author

Robert Levey, Columnist for *The Washington Post*

Doug Liman, Director

Andrew Litton, Conductor

Jeffrey Lyons, Film critic

Jane Mayer, Staff writer for *The New Yorker*

Jo Mielziner, Stage designer

Robert M. Morgenthau, New York County District Attorney

Howard Nemerov, Poet

J. Robert Oppenheimer, Pioneer in nuclear science

Gus Ornstein, Professional football player

Belva Plain, Author

Edward Pressman, Film producer

Dan Rottenberg, Author and editor

Muriel Rukeyser, Poet and playwright

Stewart Stern, Screenwriter

FIORELLO H. LAGUARDIA HIGH SCHOOL OF MUSIC & ART AND PERFORMING ARTS

Jennifer Aniston, Actress

Chastity Bono, Human and gay rights advocate

Adrien Brody, Actor

Eagle Eye Cherry, Musician

Dom DeLuise, Actor

Hector Elizondo, Actor

Omar Epps, Actor

Milton Glaser, Graphic designer

Erica Jong, Author

Michael Kamen, Composer

Kelis, Singer

Yunjin Kim, Actress

Eartha Kitt, Actress and singer

Warren Kremer, Comics artist and writer

Liza Minnelli, Actress and singer

Isaac Mizrahi, Designer

Al Pacino, Actor

Sarah Paulson, Actress

Freddie Prinze, Actor

Esmeralda Santiago, Author

Wesley Snipes, Actor

Paul Stanley, Musician

Marlon Wayans, Actor

Billy Dee Williams, Actor

FORDHAM PREPARATORY SCHOOL

Robert Abplanalp, Inventor

Esteban Bellan, Professional baseball player

Tim Brosnan, Executive Vice President for Business for Major League Baseball

Arthur Daley, Pulitzer Prize winner

Frankie Frisch, Professional baseball player

Mario J. Gabelli, CEO and Founder of Gabelli Asset Management

Robert Hackett, Olympic silver medalist

Theodore Cardinal McCarrick, Archbishop of Washington D.C.

Joseph Moglia, CEO of Ameritrade Inc.

Johnny Murphy, Professional baseball player

Sgt. Robert C. Murray, Medal of Honor recipient

Colonel Robert Gould Shaw, Civil War officer

George Stirnwiess, Professional baseball player

Donnie Walsh, President and CEO of the Indiana Pacers

Malcolm Wilson, Former Governor of New York

HORACE MANN SCHOOL

Peter L. Bernstein, Economist

Josh Bernstein, Television host

Jordy Bratman, Music producer

Robert Caro, Pulitzer Prize winner

Elliot Carter, Composer

Peter Cincotti, Pianist

Roy Cohn, Lawyer

Martin Duberman, Author and historian

Henry Geldzahler, Curator

E. J. Kahn, Author

Jack Kerouac, Author

August Kleinzahler, Poet

Richard Kluger, Pulitzer Prize winner

Ira Levin, Author

Anthony Lewis, Pulitzer Prize winner

Allard K. Lowenstein, Congressman

James Murdoch, Media executive

Samuel Newhouse, Media executive

Generoso Pope, Newspaper publisher

Bob Rafelson, Film director, writer, and producer

Barry Scheck, Attorney

James Schlesinger, Former Secretary of Defense

Gil Shaham, Violinist

Eliot Spitzer, New York State Attorney General

Peter Vierick, Pulitzer Prize winner

Paul Francis Webster, Oscar and Grammy Award–winning songwriter

William Carlos Williams, Pulitzer Prize winner

Lycée Français de New York

Nikolai Fraiture, Musician

Danielle Steele, Author

Dominique de Villepin, Politician

Michel David-Weill, Investment banker

Mount Saint Michael Academy

Sean John Combs, Designer, entrepreneur, and musician

Walter Murphy, Musician

Harry G. Pellegrin, Musician and author

Leon Robinson, Actor

Packer Collegiate Institute

Malcolm Lee, Film director

Lois Lowry, Author

Mary White Ovington, Co-founder of the NAACP

Rosanna Scotto, Television News Anchor

Professional Performing Arts School

Claire Danes, Actress

Jesse Eisenberg, Actor

Alicia Keys, Singer/musician

Alisa Reyes, Actress

Britney Spears, Singer

Lee Thompson Young, Actor

Ramaz—The Joseph F. Lookstein Upper School

Natasha Lyonne, Actress

Daphne Merkin, Author and journalist

Achinoam Nini, Musician

Baruch Shemtov, Designer

Elizabeth Wurtzel, Author

Regis High School

Vito Acconci, Artist

Edward Conlon, Author

Bill Condon, Film director and screenwriter

John Donvan, Television news correspondent

Anthony Fauci, AIDS researcher

Greg Giraldo, Comedian

Pete Hamill, Writer

Luc Sante, Author and critic

Jim Sciutto, Television news correspondent

Riverdale Country School

Bradley Abelow, State Treasurer of New Jersey

Dan Abrams, General Manager of MSNBC

Sean D. Altman, Musician

Richard Blumenthal, Attorney General of Connecticut

Neal Conan, Radio journalist

Richard Engel, Author and reporter

Jesse Harris, Musician

Calvin Hill, Professional football player

John Lahr, Theater critic

Dany Levy, Writer

Nick McDonell, Author

Philip Proctor, Actor

Edward Rendell, Governor of Pennsylvania

Tracee Ellis Ross, Actress

Carly Simon, Musician

Scott Snyder, Author

Joss Whedon, Television director, producer, and writer

Tim Zagat, Restaurant critic

Michael Zakarin, Musician

Spence School

Serena Altschul, Television journalist

Jade Jagger, Jewelry designer

Elizabeth Montgomery, Actress

Gwyneth Paltrow, Actress

Emmy Rossum, Actress

Kerry Washington, Actress

St. Ann's School

Jon Abrahams, Actor

Eva Amurri, Actress

Daniel Bergner, Journalist

Beth Bosworth, Author

Jennifer Connelly, Actress

Michael Diamond, Musician

Alexis Dziena, Actress

Nicholas Eanet, Violinist

Sasha Frere-Jones, Author

Tobias Frere-Jones, Artist

Akiva Goldsman, Screenwriter

Katherine Healy, Dancer

William Hogeland, Author

Curtis Moore, Painter

Rebecca O'Brien, Journalist

John Pomfret, Journalist

Zac Posen, Designer

Meredith Rainey, Olympic track & field athlete

Mia Sara, Actress

John Sifton, Lawyer

Judith Surkis, Historian

Elizabeth A. Wood, Historian

STUYVESANT HIGH SCHOOL

Richard Axel, Nobel Prize winner

Walter Becker, Musician

Arthur Blank, Founder of The Home Depot

Leroy Brown, Olympic silver medalist

Robert Fogel, Nobel Prize winner

Roald Hoffmann, Nobel Prize winner

Joshua Lederberg, Nobel Prize winner

Paul Levitz, President of DC Comics

David Lipsky, Author

Lucy Lui, Actress

Joseph L. Mankiewicz, Oscar-winning film director

Jerrold Nadler, U.S. Congressman

Tim Robbins, Actor

George Segal, Sculptor

Robert Siegel, Radio journalist

TOWNSEND HARRIS HIGH SCHOOL

Kenneth Arrow, Nobel Prize winner

Lawrence Cremin, Pulitzer Prize winner

Herbert Hauptman, Nobel Prize winner

Ira Gershwin, Pulitzer Prize winner

Sidney Kingsley, Pulitzer Prize winner

Eugene Lang, Philanthropist

Frank Loesser, Pulitzer Prize winner

Adam Clayton Powell, Jr., Politician

Edward G. Robinson, Actor

Richard Rodgers, Pulitzer Prize winner

Jonas Salk, Physician and researcher

Julian Schwinger, Nobel Prize winner

Herman Wouk, Pulitzer Prize winner

Trinity School

Julie Ann Blumberg, Television writer

Jim Carroll, Author and poet

David Faber, Television journalist

Jim Fixx, Author

Russell Gewirtz, Screenwriter

Ryo Goto, Violinist

Larry Hagman, Actor

Sophie B. Hawkins, Musician

Katrina vanden Heuvel, Editor of *The Nation*

Lloyd Kaufman, Filmmaker

Tracy Kidder, Pulitzer Prize winner

John McEnroe, Professional tennis player

Patrick McEnroe, Professional tennis player

Eric Schneiderman, New York State Senator

United Nations International School

Yasmine Bleeth, Actress

Vikram Chatwal, Hotelier

Sarah Jones, Actress

Xavier High School

Colonel Donald Cook, Medal of Honor recipient

Al Roker, Television weatherman

Antonin Scalia, Supreme Court Justice

Yeshiva of Flatbush

Robert J. Avrech, Screenwriter

Rabbi Dr. David Berger, Professor at City University of New York—Brooklyn College

Baruch Samuel Blumberg, Nobel Prize winner

Abraham Foxman, Director of the Anti-Defamation League

Dr. Judith Hauptman, Professor at the Jewish Theological Seminary

Eric R. Kandel, Nobel Prize Winner

Dennis Prager, Radio talk show host

Leon Wieseltier, Editor of *The New Republic*

PART VII—UPPER LEVEL ISEE PRACTICE TEST

How to Take a Practice Test

Here are some reminders for taking your practice test.

- Find a quiet place to take the test where you won't be interrupted or distracted, and make sure you have enough time to take the entire test.

- Time yourself strictly. Use a timer, watch, or stopwatch that will ring, and do not allow yourself to go over time for any section.

- Take a practice test in one sitting, allowing yourself breaks of no more than two minutes between sections.

- Use the attached answer sheets to bubble in your answer choices.

- Each bubble you choose should be filled in thoroughly, and no other marks should be made in the answer area.

- Make sure to double-check that your bubbles are filled in correctly!

SECTION 1

VERBAL REASONING

Time: 20 minutes
40 Questions

Part One and Part Two of this section consist of two different kinds of questions. Answer the questions in Part Two as soon as you have completed Part One.

Part One

Each question in Part One is made up of a word in capital letters followed by four choices. Choose the one word that is most nearly the same in meaning as the word in capital letters.

SAMPLE QUESTION: Sample Answer

SWIFT: (A) clean   (B) fast   Ⓐ ● Ⓒ Ⓓ
(C) quiet   (D) fancy

---

1. GRAVE: (A) deadly (B) open   (C) solemn
    (D) final

2. FOMENT: (A) instigate   (B) dissemble
    (C) articulate (D) praise

3. INARTICULATE: (A) tongue-tied
    (B) creative (C) overly sensitive   (D) friendly

4. JARGON: (A) fast speaking   (B) odor
    (C) definition (D) terminology

5. THESIS: (A) paper   (B) report   (C) belief
    (D) study

6. DEBUNK: (A) build (B) justify   (C) discredit
    (D) impress

7. DISDAIN: (A) hope (B) contempt   (C) find
    (D) annoy

8. RETICENT: (A) anxious   (B) aware
    (C) informed   (D) reserved

9. PREVALENT: (A) old-fashioned (B) minority
   (C) predominant (D) fascinating

10. SATIATE: (A) fill (B) starve (C) serve
    (D) deny

11. CANDID: (A) defiant (B) stingy (C) frank
    (D) dejected

12. EMULATE: (A) brush off (B) imitate
    (C) perplex (D) permit

13. TAINT: (A) master (B) infect (C) annoy
    (D) handle

14. CONFORM: (A) perpetuate (B) jar
    (C) harmonize (D) contract

15. DETRIMENTAL: (A) desolate (B) injurious
    (C) emphatic (D) considerate

16. METICULOUS: (A) finicky (B) maddening
    (C) favorable (D) gigantic

17. JUXTAPOSE: (A) place side by side
    (B) put behind (C) keep away (D) question

18. HETEROGENEOUS: (A) similar
    (B) generous (C) unusual (D) mixed

19. MITIGATE: (A) harden (B) bend
    (C) untangle (D) ease

20. ELUSIVE: (A) unhappy (B) real
    (C) treacherous (D) slippery

Each question below is made up of a sentence with one or two blanks. One blank indicates that one word is missing. Two blanks indicate that two words are missing. Each sentence is followed by four choices. Select the one word or pair of words that will best complete the meaning of the sentence as a whole.

SAMPLE QUESTIONS: Sample Answer

Ann carried the box carefully so that she   Ⓐ ● Ⓒ Ⓓ
would not ------- the pretty glasses.

(A) open
(B) break
(C) fix
(D) stop

When our boat first crashed into the rocks   ● Ⓑ Ⓒ Ⓓ
we were -------, but we soon felt -------
when we realized that nobody was hurt.

(A) afraid . . relieved
(B) sleepy . . sad
(C) happy . . confused
(D) sorry . . angry

---

21. Jane felt ------- about whether to go to the party
    or not; on one hand it seemed like fun, but on the
    other, she was very tired.
    (A) happy
    (B) ambivalent
    (C) apathetic
    (D) irritated

22. Even though the critics praised the author's
    ------- use of words, they found the text ------- at
    a mere 100 pages.

    (A) improper . . laconic
    (B) precise . . short
    (C) hackneyed . . threadbare
    (D) sure . . banal

23. Like the more famous Susan B. Anthony,
    M. Carey Thomas ------- feminism and women's
    rights.

    (A) defaced
    (B) gained
    (C) found
    (D) championed

24. It is unfortunate but true that some of the most
    ------- nations in the world are capable of some
    of the most brutal and barbaric acts.

    (A) advanced
    (B) ill-mannered
    (C) large
    (D) primitive

25. Although Marie was a talented and -------
    performer, her gifts were often ------- because
    she didn't know how to promote herself.

    (A) promising . . satisfied
    (B) faithful . . supported
    (C) insulting . . overlooked
    (D) versatile . . ignored

26. The ------- given on the Fourth of July was a tra-
    dition for years after the American Revolution;
    the ------- men in town would stand up in front
    of their communities and speak about what made
    America great.

    (A) invitation . . ordinary
    (B) concert . . musical
    (C) oration . . important
    (D) experiment . . famous

27. Thomas Jefferson was a man of ------- talents: he
    was known for his skills as a writer, a musician,
    an architect, and an inventor as well as a politi-
    cian.

    (A) overblown
    (B) diverse
    (C) mundane
    (D) professed

28. Monica could remain ------- no longer;
    the injustices she witnessed moved her to
    speak up.

    (A) diplomatic
    (B) active
    (C) furious
    (D) helpful

29. Louisa May Alcott's *Little Women* is really quite
------; much of the story is based on her experiences as a young woman growing up in Concord,
Massachusetts.

(A) moving
(B) visual
(C) autobiographical
(D) fictional

30. Although she was the daughter of a wealthy
slaveholder, Angelina Grimke ------- slavery and
------- her whole life for the cause of abolition.

(A) represented . . fought
(B) detested . . worked
(C) hated . . wasted
(D) desired . . picketed

31. Though his lectures could be monotonous,
Mr. Cutler was actually quite ------- when he
spoke to students in small, informal groups.

(A) prosaic
(B) vapid
(C) fascinating
(D) pious

32. Craig had ------- that the day would not go well,
and just as he'd thought, he had two pop quizzes.

(A) an interest
(B) a premonition
(C) an antidote
(D) a report

33. Morality is not -------; cultures around the world
have different ideas about how people should be
treated.

(A) debatable
(B) universal
(C) helpful
(D) realistic

34. Marshall's worst habit was that he -------, putting
off all his work until it was overwhelming.

(A) obfuscated
(B) procrastinated
(C) celebrated
(D) proliferated

35. Many of today's consumers are ------- expensive computer equipment, purchasing complicated machinery that they may not even need.

(A) captivated by
(B) jealous of
(C) sullen about
(D) misled by

36. Because Martha was naturally -------, she would see the bright side of any situation, but Jack had a ------- personality and always waited for something bad to happen.

(A) cheerful . . upbeat
(B) frightened . . mawkish
(C) optimistic . . dismal
(D) realistic . . unreasonable

37. Rhubarb is actually quite ------- requiring a large amount of sugar to make it -------.

(A) nutritious . . sickening
(B) bitter . . palatable
(C) flavorful . . fattening
(D) unpopular . . sticky

38. The panelist was extremely ------- to the other members of the discussion, referring to them as "ignorant demagogues."

(A) deferential
(B) contentious
(C) respectful
(D) garrulous

39. Coach Jones' feelings about the team were -------; he didn't need to explicitly state them.

(A) covert
(B) reasonable
(C) fractious
(D) tacit

40. Unwilling to commit to any field of study or type of work, Margie was labeled ------- by her advisors at school.

(A) a dilettante
(B) a firebrand
(C) a logician
(D) an opportunist

SECTION 2

QUANTITATIVE REASONING

Time: 35 minutes

35 Questions

Directions

Any figures that accompany questions in this section may be assumed to be drawn as accurately as possible EXCEPT when it is stated that a particular figure is not drawn to scale. Letters such as x, y, and n stand for real numbers. There are two types of questions:

(1) For Questions 1-20, work each in your head or on the space available on the test pages. Then look at the four choices and fill in the corresponding oval on the answer sheet.

Example 1	If $3 + x = 5$, what is the value of x? (A) 0 (B) 1 (C) 2 (D) 3	Answer Ⓐ Ⓑ ⬤ Ⓓ
Example 2	$1 + \dfrac{1}{3} =$ (A) $\dfrac{2}{3}$ (B) $\dfrac{4}{3}$ (C) $\dfrac{5}{3}$ (D) $\dfrac{7}{3}$	Answer Ⓐ ⬤ Ⓒ Ⓓ

(2) For Questions 21-35, note the given information, if any, and then compare the quantity in Column A to the quantity in Column B. On the answer sheet, fill in

    (A)   if the quantity in Column A is greater
    (B)   if the quantity in Column B is greater
    (C)   if the two quantities are equal
    (D)   if the relationship cannot be determined from the information given

	Column A	Column B	
Example 3	3^2	2^3	Answer ⬤ Ⓑ Ⓒ Ⓓ

The quantity in Column A (9) is greater than the quantity in Column B (8), so space A is marked.

	Column A	Column B	
Example 4	The cost of 8 apples at 7 cents apiece	The cost of 7 apples at 8 cents apiece	Answer

The quantity in Column A (56 cents) equals the quantity in Column B (56 cents), so space C is marked.

| Example 5 | 1 | $1 + x$ | Answer |

Since x can be any real number (including 0 or negatives), there is not enough information given to determine the relative sizes of the quantities in Columns A and B. Therefore, space D is marked.

1. Which of the following is greatest?

   (A) 0.0100
   (B) 0.0099
   (C) 0.1900
   (D) 0.0199

2. Which of the following is NOT the product of two prime numbers?

   (A) 33
   (B) 35
   (C) 45
   (D) 91

3. If x, y, and z are consecutive even integers, then what is the difference between x and z ?

   (A) 0
   (B) 1
   (C) 2
   (D) 4

Questions 4-5 refer to the following chart.

Clothing Close-out

Dresses	Originally $120	Now $90
Coats	Originally $250	Now $180
Shoes	Originally $60	Now $40
Hats	Originally $40	Now $20

4. Which of the items for sale has the greatest percent discount?

    (A) Dresses
    (B) Coats
    (C) Shoes
    (D) Hats

5. Purchasing which item will save the buyer the most dollars?

    (A) Dresses
    (B) Coats
    (C) Shoes
    (D) Hats

6. Amy is three years older than Beth and five years younger than Jo. If Beth is b years old, how old is Jo, in terms of b ?

    (A) $2b + 3$
    (B) $2b - 3$
    (C) $b + 4$
    (D) $b + 8$

7. If x is divided by 5, the remainder is 4. If y is divided by 5, the remainder is 1. What is the remainder when $(x + y)$ is divided by 5 ?

(A) 0
(B) 1
(C) 2
(D) 3

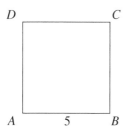

8. What is the perimeter of the square $ABCD$ shown above?

(A) 5
(B) 15
(C) 20
(D) 25

9. At a party, 4 pizzas with 8 slices each were served. If each of the 9 guests had 3 pieces of pizza each, how many slices remained?

(A) 4
(B) 5
(C) 6
(D) 7

10. Jamie had x dollars in the bank. He withdrew $\frac{1}{2}$ to buy a car. He withdrew $\frac{1}{3}$ of what was left to buy a couch. What fraction of the original amount remained in his account?

   (A) $\frac{1}{6}$

   (B) $\frac{1}{5}$

   (C) $\frac{1}{4}$

   (D) $\frac{1}{3}$

11. J is a whole number divisible by 4. J is also divisible by 3. Which of the following is NOT a possible value for J ?

   (A) 12
   (B) 24
   (C) 30
   (D) 36

12. The product of 0.48 and 100 is approximately

   (A) 0.5
   (B) 4.8
   (C) 5
   (D) 50

13. Which of the following is less than $\frac{6}{7}$?

   (A) $\frac{2}{3}$

   (B) $\frac{8}{9}$

   (C) $\frac{7}{6}$

   (D) $\frac{17}{19}$

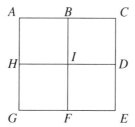

14. Square *ACEG* shown above is composed of 4 squares with sides of 1 meter each. Traveling only on the lines of the squares, how many different routes from *A* to *D* that are exactly 3 meters long are possible?

   (A) 2
   (B) 3
   (C) 4
   (D) 5

15. If, in triangle *ABC*, the measure of angle *B* is greater than 90°, and *AB* = *BC*, what is a possible measure for angle *C* in degrees?

   (A) 35
   (B) 45
   (C) 60
   (D) It cannot be determined from the information given.

16. Chumway Motors discounts the cost of a car by 10% and then runs another special one-day deal offering an additional 20% off the discounted price. What discount does this represent from the original price of the car?

   (A) 28%
   (B) 30%
   (C) 40%
   (D) 72%

17. David scored 82, 84, and 95 on his first three math
     tests. What score does he need on his fourth test to
     bring his average up to a 90 ?

     (A) 90
     (B) 92
     (C) 96
     (D) 99

18. $\dfrac{1}{3}$ is most nearly equivalent to

     (A) 0.13
     (B) 0.3
     (C) 0.4
     (D) 0.5

19. 25% of 10% of 200 is

     (A) 250
     (B) 100
     (C)   50
     (D)   5

20. The ratio of yellow paint to red paint to white paint
     needed to make a perfect mixture of orange paint is
     3 to 2 to 1. If 36 gallons of orange paint are needed
     to paint a cottage, how many gallons of red paint
     will be needed?

     (A)   2
     (B)   6
     (C) 12
     (D) 15

Directions: For Questions 21-35, note the given information, if any, and then compare the quantity in Column A to the quantity in Column B. On the answer sheet, fill in

- (A) if the quantity in Column A is greater
- (B) if the quantity in Column B is greater
- (C) if the two quantities are equal
- (D) if the relationship cannot be determined from the information given

Column A	Column B

21.   25% of 50   50% of 25

In a group of 150 books, 60 percent are fiction.

22.   Half the number of fiction books   The difference between the number of fiction books and the number of nonfiction books

---

Dawn has a drawer filled with socks. The ratio of brown socks to blue socks is 2:3.

23. $\dfrac{2}{3}$ The fractional part of the socks in Dawn's drawer that are brown

---

24. x^2 x^3

	Column A	Column B

25. The average of the three smallest positive even integers | The average of the three smallest positive integers

---

$$(x + 2)(x - 2) = 0$$

26. x 2

---

27. $\sqrt{36} + \sqrt{16}$ $\sqrt{52}$

---

28. 3^{12} 9^6

The volume of a solid cube is 27.

29. The height of the cube   3

$$\frac{x + 2}{y + 2} = \frac{x}{y}$$

30. x $y + 2$

	Column A	Column B

31.

	The sum of the integers from 1 to 100, inclusive	The sum of the even integers from 1 to 200, inclusive

---

$$\frac{x}{4} = 1.5$$

32.

	x	5

$$x > 0$$

33.

	x	x^2

A hiker completed a hike, walking at an average rate of 4 miles per hour. Had she averaged 5 miles per hour, the trip would have been completed two hours earlier than it was.

34.

	The number of hours in which the hike was completed	10

---

x is a positive integer.
y is the result of $100x$.

35.

	The sum of the digits in x	The sum of the digits in y

SECTION 3

READING COMPREHENSION

Time: 40 minutes

40 Questions

<u>Directions</u>: Each passage below is followed by questions based on its content. Answer the questions following a passage on the basis of what is <u>stated</u> or <u>implied</u> in that passage.

<u>Questions 1-5</u>

New Orleans was the site of the last major battle during the War of 1812, a lengthy conflict between British and American troops. The Battle of New
Line Orleans in January 1815 was one of the greatest
(5) victories in American military history. However, the great success of this battle did not actually bring about the end of the war. Surprisingly, the Treaty of Ghent, which declared the end of the war, had already been signed by both sides a month earlier.
(10) How can that be? There are two major reasons. The first is that New Orleans was relatively isolated and communication in the growing United States was not as simple as it is today. Thus, it is possible that the British commanders and the American
(15) general, Andrew Jackson, did not realize a treaty had been signed before they started their battle. A second reason is that there is a difference between a signed treaty and a ratified treaty. Even if all soldiers fighting in and around New Orleans had known of
(20) the treaty, it had not yet been ratified by the U.S. Senate. Thus, though the Treaty of Ghent took place in December, prior to the Battle of New Orleans, the war did not officially end until February 1815, when President James Madison ratified the treaty.
(25) Had the combatants in New Orleans known of the treaty, perhaps they could have avoided a tough battle, especially for the British. In the battle, a force of about 4,000 American troops decisively defeated an enemy of nearly twice its size. At stake

(30) for the soldiers was control of the waterways
of the Mississippi, and the fighting was fierce. A
combination of tactical mistakes and bad weather
doomed the British attack, costing them nearly 2,000
soldiers injured or killed. The Americans lost fewer
(35) than 200. But was the terrible battle all for nothing?
Some historians suggest that victory that day was
crucial for the American military in order to enforce
and help ratify quickly the peace treaty. Potentially,
with an American loss in New Orleans, the British
(40) could have found hope to continue the conflict.

1. The passage suggests that all of the following oc-
    curred near the end of the War of 1812 EXCEPT
    (A) The Treaty of Ghent was signed.
    (B) Communication with the battle line
        commanders was slow.
    (C) Andrew Jackson ignored the orders of
        President Madison.
    (D) Weather conditions hurt the efforts of the
        British soldiers.

2. The primary purpose of the passage is to
    (A) celebrate the tactical military maneuvers of
        Andrew Jackson
    (B) blame the British for fighting an
        unnecessary war
    (C) convince readers that peace treaties are
        often worthless
    (D) provide greater details about the end of a
        historical conflict

3. Which of the following is implied by the passage?
    (A) President Madison did not realize the Battle
        of New Orleans was possible.
    (B) The British may have had a chance
        for victory with better conditions and
        preparation.
    (C) The British troops knew of the treaty but
        attacked anyway.
    (D) Andrew Jackson did not know the
        difference between a signed treaty and a
        ratified treaty.

4. According to the passage, New Orleans was a strategic battle site because
   - (A) the American forces would be trapped in the swamplands if they lost
   - (B) the British were attempting to defeat a more numerous force
   - (C) it was the only location where American forces were better supplied than the British forces
   - (D) the Mississippi River was nearby and control of it was important

5. After which of the following was the War of 1812 officially at an end?
   - (A) The Battle of New Orleans
   - (B) British retreat from the Mississippi
   - (C) The president's ratification of the Treaty of Ghent
   - (D) Both armies signing the Treaty of Ghent

Questions 6-10

According to game maker Hasbro, approximately 750 million people have played the well-known game *Monopoly* since it was invented in the 1930s.

(*ne*) Charles Darrow is typically credited as the inventor
(5) of the world's most famous board game. However, he likely derived his version of *Monopoly* from one of several other games similarly involving realty buying and selling that were already in existence prior to the 1930s when he got his patent for the game.

(*0*) A probable reason that Darrow's *Monopoly* became the hugely successful game that still exists today is that he took a diligent approach to producing it. Other similar games existed, but some of them had no board or regulation pieces. With help from his wife and son
(5) who adorned the sets with detail, Darrow personally created the pieces and boards that became the first *Monopoly* game sets. His extra work in creating the entire environment that players needed gave his game something extra that other variations did not have.

(*0*) Darrow had marginal success selling his games in various parts of the country. Several Philadelphia area stores were the first to carry his game and sell it in large quantities. Despite this, Darrow had difficulty selling his game to the major game manufacturer
(5) of the time, Parker Brothers. He was told that his game was too complex and had fundamental errors in its design that would limit its appeal. Ultimately, the continued sales he managed on his own forced Parker Brothers to reassess the worth of his game.

(*)*) Eventually, the company agreed to produce the game and shortly thereafter it became the bestselling game in the country.

That success turned Charles Darrow into a millionaire, which is the ultimate irony. Darrow
(5) initially began work on *Monopoly* to help support himself and his family following the financial troubles tied to the stock market crash of 1929. Thus, Charles Darrow became a millionaire by producing a game that allows "regular" people to feel
(*)*) like they are buying and selling homes and real estate like millionaires.

6. The best title for this passage would be
    (A) "The Early History of Charles Darrow's Game"
    (B) "How Hasbro Introduced *Monopoly* to the World"
    (C) "A Comparison of Several Early Real Estate Board Games"
    (D) "Two Views of Charles Darrow's Life"

7. It is suggested by the passage that
    (A) Philadelphia was the only major city where he could sell his game
    (B) Darrow decided to make his game less complex after initially meeting with Parker Brothers
    (C) Darrow had no other skills to use after the stock market crash of 1929
    (D) Parker Brothers probably doubted that a complex game could sell well

8. Based on the passage, "irony" most nearly means
    (A) unexpected result
    (B) financial gain
    (C) marketing plan
    (D) satisfying revenge

9. With which of the following would the author be LEAST likely to agree?
    (A) Charles Darrow is not the first person to conceive of a board-based real estate game.
    (B) Charles Darrow preferred to achieve his goals without the help of others.
    (C) Charles Darrow chose to continue to sell his game despite criticisms.
    (D) Some of the things Darrow chose to do helped make his game sell better than other games.

10. Which of the following was NOT mentioned by the author as contributing to the ultimate success of *Monopoly*?
    (A) The addition of specific pieces and a playing board in each set
    (B) Darrow's efforts to initially sell the game on his own
    (C) The adjustments Parker Brothers made to the game
    (D) The enjoyment people get in pretending to be millionaires

<u>Questions 11-14</u>

Every year, hundreds of hopeful students arrive in Washington, D.C. in order to compete in the National Spelling Bee. This competition has been held annually since 1925 and is sponsored by E.W. Scripps Company. The sponsors provide both a trophy and a monetary award to the champion speller. In the competition, students under 16 years of age take turns attempting to properly spell words as provided by the moderator. The champion is the sole remaining student who does not make a mistake.

Most American students are familiar with the concept of a spelling bee because it is practiced in many schools throughout the country. The National Spelling Bee, however, is a much bigger setting and showcases only the best speller from all parts of the nation. Students who appear at the National Spelling Bee have already won competitions at local and state levels. Winning the competition nowadays requires the ability to perform under intense pressure against very talented students in front of a large audience. A student who wins the event in the twenty-first century will experience a much different challenge than the first winner, Frank Neuhauser, did in 1925 when he defeated only nine other competitors.

Clearly, the 80 years of the National Spelling Bee's existence attests to the importance of spelling in the English language. However, struggles with spelling English words goes back much more than 80 years. The captivating thing about spelling correctly in English is that it is in many ways without rules. English language has a powerful capacity to absorb new words from other languages and in doing so make them "English" words. As a result of this ability to borrow from other languages, the sheer number of words in English is much higher than any other language. Thus, spelling in many other languages involves fewer words, fewer rules, and fewer odd exceptions to those rules. It turns out that a spelling bee in most other languages would be a waste of time. Why is that? Well, without the myriad exceptions to common vocabulary, there would be very few words that everyone didn't already know.

11. The author of the passage intends to
    (A) review the history and current form of the National Spelling Bee
    (B) contrast the English language with other languages
    (C) compare the presentation of the current National Spelling Bee with the structure in the past
    (D) investigate the role that vocabulary plays in our lives

12. According to the passage, what is a major difference between the first National Spelling Bee and today's competition?
    (A) The word s used today are significantly harder.
    (B) Spellers in the past did not expect the competition to grow so large.
    (C) The competition no longer focuses on only English words.
    (D) There are more competitors.

13. In line 40, the word "myriad" most nearly means
    (A) dangerous
    (B) numerous
    (C) confusing
    (D) linguistic

14. Which of the following can be inferred from the passage?
    (A) A competitor at The National Spelling Bee has already won at least one smaller spelling bee.
    (B) Frank Neuhauser would not do well in today's competition.
    (C) The competition has grown too large.
    (D) E.W. Scripps Company desires to eliminate poor spelling in America.

Questions 15-23

The idea of black holes was developed by Karl Schwarzchild in 1916. Since then, many different scientists have added to the theory of black holes in space. A black hole is usually defined as a very dense celestial body from which nothing, not even light, can escape. But how do black holes start?

A black hole begins as a star. A star burns hydrogen, and this process, called fusion, releases energy. The energy released outward works against the star's own gravity pulling inward and prevents the star from collapsing. After millions of years of burning hydrogen, the star eventually runs out of fuel. At this point, the star's own gravity and weight cause it to start contracting.

If the star is small and not very heavy when it runs out of fuel, it will shrink just a little and become a white dwarf. White dwarf stars do not emit much energy, so they are usually not visible without a telescope.

If the star is bigger and heavier, it will collapse very quickly in an implosion. If the matter that remains is not much heavier than our sun, it will eventually become a very dense neutron star. However, if the matter that remains is more than 1.7 times the mass of our sun, there will not be enough outward pressure to resist the force of gravity, and the collapse will continue. The result is a black hole.

The black hole will have a boundary around it called the horizon. Light and matter can pass over this boundary to enter, but they cannot pass back out again—this is why the hole appears black. The gravity and density of the black hole prevent anything from escaping.

Scientists are still adding to the black hole theory. They think they may have found black holes in several different galaxies, and as they learn more about them, scientists will be able to understand more about how black holes are formed and what happens as the holes change.

15. The passage can best be characterized as
    (A) a convincing argument about the existence of black holes
    (B) a scientific account of the disappearance of white dwarfs
    (C) an informal approach to astronomic study
    (D) an instructive explanation of the formation of black holes

16. According to the passage, which of the following is an effect of the process of fusion?
    (A) The star does not immediately collapse.
    (B) The star generates hydrogen.
    (C) The white dwarf fails to produce light.
    (D) The star survives millions of years longer than average.

17. In line 17, "emit" most nearly means
    (A) contract
    (B) release
    (C) receive
    (D) weigh

18. According to the passage, which of the following causes a collapsing star to become a neutron star?
    (A) Mass less than 1.7 times that of our sun
    (B) Remaining fuel that can be used in fusion
    (C) Mass greater than 1.7 times that of our sun
    (D) Slow, brief shrinkage process

Questions 24-28

Carrie Nation gained notoriety as a hatchet-wielding woman during the early part of the twentieth century. She was married to an alcoholic
line and spent many years trying to reform him. When
(5) that seemed impossible, she left him and married David Nation. Some time after their marriage, Carrie and David Nation moved to Kansas. The sale of alcohol was illegal in Kansas, yet there were many establishments that sold alcoholic drinks. Carrie
10) organized the Women's Christian Temperance Union, which vehemently, and sometimes violently, fought the saloons. She believed that because saloons were illegal, she was within her rights to destroy them, so she wrecked saloons with her hatchet. Carrie
15) was arrested thirty times in many cities around the country. Some say her eccentric behavior was inherited from her mentally ill mother. Whatever the cause, Carrie Nation was a well-known personality in the early 1900s and her efforts most probably helped
20) the cause of temperance, which led to the national prohibition of alcohol in 1920.

24. The word "cause" as used in line 18 most closely means
   (A) goal
   (B) reason
   (C) excuse
   (D) rebellion

25. The main purpose of the passage is to
   (A) explain the causes that led to the national prohibition of alcohol in 1920
   (B) examine the reasons that Carrie Nation was so eccentric
   (C) present an overview of the life and actions of a famous woman
   (D) report on the Women's Christian Temperance Union

26. Which of the following does the passage imply was a reason for Carrie Nation's attitude toward temperance?
    (A) Her mother's mental illness
    (B) Her inability to have children
    (C) Her first husband's alcoholism
    (D) Her move to Kansas

27. Which of the following best expresses the author's attitude toward Carrie Nation?
    (A) Admiration
    (B) Disgust
    (C) Neutrality
    (D) Indifference

28. According to the author, what was the most probable legacy of Carrie Nation's actions?
    (A) The national prohibition of alcohol
    (B) The destruction of saloons by women around the country
    (C) The legislation prohibiting the destruction of saloons
    (D) The inquiry into the genetic link to mental illness

<u>Questions 29-36</u>

America's national parks hold amazing sights for those who visit them. Some of the most spectacular sights can be seen at Arches National Park in Utah.

ine When I was ten years old, I went to Arches for the
(5) first time. Even as I first entered the park, I could see the dramatic landscape. It was unlike anything I had seen in my hometown. Orange-red rock rose from the light desert sand to create rock formations that looked like sculpture.

10) Visitors today see the same rock formations that I saw, although those formations are changing ever so slowly. There are tall standing towers and spires of reddish stone that stick straight up into the sky. There are also formations that look like bridges and arches.
15) These are the structures that the park is named after. The amazing thing is that all of these formations are entirely natural.

Wind, water, and sand have eroded the rock over millions of years. The rock is made of many different
20) elements, so only the softer parts of the rocks have been rubbed away. The more resistant parts remain, creating these unusual shapes. Sometimes, gravity helps too, as chunks of rock fall to the ground, leaving behind a thin ribbon of stone that arches
25) across the sky.

Visitors to the park can get out of their cars and hike across the sand and rock. On that initial visit, I learned that visitors can walk on any of the rock formations that have not been named. I got a map
30) that told me where I was and which formations had names. I saw formations named "Delicate Arch" and "Landscape Arch."

I walked along the trails for three hours with my family. We all wore sturdy shoes and we each carried
35) a gallon of water. It was a clear day, and the orangey-red rocks rose into the blue sky, presenting their startling shapes to us everywhere we turned. Even the rocks that did not have names were like works of art. To this day, my visit to Arches National Park remains
40) a vivid memory.

29. The author's attitude toward Arches National Park is most probably one of
    (A) mild distaste
    (B) scientific curiosity
    (C) bored suspicion
    (D) admiring interest

30. In line 12, "spires" are most likely
    (A) very big buildings made of rock
    (B) short, wide rock formations
    (C) tall, slender rock formations
    (D) people who change slowly

31. Which of the following is NOT mentioned as something that has helped create the rock formations?
    (A) Gravity
    (B) Visitors
    (C) Wind
    (D) Water

32. "The more resistant parts" (line 21) refers to
    (A) the sections of rock that have not eroded
    (B) the sand that wears away the rock
    (C) the rock that falls to the ground
    (D) the areas in the park that are tough to hike

33. Which of the following best summarizes the primary purpose of lines 18-21 of the passage?
    (A) To provide examples of the striking beauty of the rocks
    (B) To introduce the reader to the geology of one particular park
    (C) To illustrate how the rock formations developed
    (D) To explain the author's fascination with the landscape

34. The author describes "a thin ribbon of stone" (line 24) in order to emphasize
    (A) that the rock has the texture of fabric
    (B) how orange the rock is
    (C) that the rock formation is naturally made
    (D) how delicate the rock formations look

35. According to the passage, which of the following is an activity in which visitors can engage at Arches National Park?
    (A) Hiking across the desert sand trails
    (B) Driving over the desert sand trails
    (C) Walking on named rock formations
    (D) Giving names to the park's geological features

36. Which of the following best summarizes the passage as a whole?
    (A) Visitors to Arches National Park cannot walk on the named formations.
    (B) A visit to Arches National Park offers natural wonders.
    (C) A family trip can be very exciting.
    (D) Most of the rock at Arches National Park is orange-red.

He is one of the greatest living scientists of
this age. In fact, he is perhaps one of the greatest
scientists of any age. Yet, he owes much of his
Line success not to mathematics or physics or any other
  (5) science, but to a disease. He is Stephen Hawking.

Born in 1942, three hundred years after the death
of Galileo, Stephen Hawking had an unimpressive
start to his scholarly pursuits. At his revered English
primary school, St. Albans, he was considered by
 (10) his teachers a good, but not exceptional, student. It
was not evident at the time that he would become
internationally acclaimed as a leader in several
scientific fields. He continued this moderately
successful academic trend at University College
 (15) in Oxford. Again, his professors thought him to be
intelligent, but not extraordinary in his efforts. Both
his cleverness and lack of diligence were noticed by
some of his instructors.

After graduating from Oxford, he continued
 (20) to Cambridge, another excellent school. Clearly,
Hawking was moving forward into a good
science career. However, it was at this time that
he encountered a life-changing challenge. He was
diagnosed with a disease that affects and damages the
 (25) nervous system. That meant that he was eventually
going to lose control of his muscles and spend his life
in a wheelchair. Surprisingly though, Hawking credits
this event with making his outlook on life strong
again. He claims that until then, he was often bored
 (30) by life. For a man with such a powerful mind, that
makes sense. He was talented, but he saw little use
for his talent and felt no pressure to work hard. His
diagnosis and impending physical problems forced
him to start living life to the fullest.

 (35) Most of Stephen Hawking's contributions to
science have come after learning of his disease.
His work in the field of physics has influenced
the greatest scientists alive. If the technology ever
becomes possible, he plans a trip into space with the
 (40) help of influential friends. Though he now moves

only with a special wheelchair and speaks only with
the help of a computerized speech enhancer, he still
has the ability to contribute to the world. He credits
his disease with forcing him to face the limited time
available in one lifetime. Stephen Hawking has made
a crippling disease the source of one of the greatest
scientific careers the world has known. Through his
misfortune, he learned to reach his greatest potential.

45)

37. The best title for this passage might be
    (A) "Stephen Hawking's Scientific
        Discoveries"
    (B) "Great Scientists of the 20th Century"
    (C) "The Early Life of Stephen Hawking"
    (D) "Stephen Hawking's Greatest Influence:
        His Disease"

38. In line 17, "diligence" most nearly means
    (A) parental guidance
    (B) scientific aptitude
    (C) hard work
    (D) scholarly advice

39. The passage suggests which of the following
    about Stephen Hawking?
    (A) He feels that he would achieve even greater
        success in science without a crippling
        disease.
    (B) He feels that his disease actually forces him
        to focus his energies and talents in ways
        that he hasn't previously.
    (C) He will continue to pursue a cure for
        his disease and use his understanding of
        biology to reach that goal.
    (D) He chose a science career specifically
        because he knew he would need medical
        help his whole life.

40. Which of the following describes Stephen
    Hawking's attitude toward his disease?
    (A) nonchalant
    (B) irate
    (C) giddy
    (D) motivated

SECTION 4

MATHEMATICS ACHIEVEMENT

Time: 40 minutes

45 Questions

Each question is followed by four suggested answers. Read each question and then decide which one of the four suggested answers is best.

Find the row of spaces on your answer sheet that has the same number as the question. In this row, mark the space having the same letter as the answer you have chosen.

Example: Sample Answer

$(5 + 3) - 2 =$ ● Ⓑ Ⓒ Ⓓ

(A)   6
(B)   8
(C)   10
(D)   13

The correct answer to this question is lettered A, so space A is marked.

---

1. Which of the following pairs of numbers are the two different prime factors of 36 ?

(A) 2 and 3
(B) 3 and 4
(C) 3 and 12
(D) 4 and 9

2. For what nonzero value of x will the expression

$\dfrac{x - 3}{4x}$ be equal to 0 ?

(A) −3
(B) −2
(C) 1
(D) 3

3. Two positive whole numbers are in a ratio of 3 to 4. If the smaller of the two numbers is 9, what is the average of the two numbers?

(A) 4
(B) 10
(C) 10.5
(D) 12

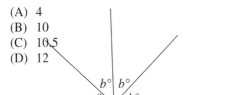

4. The four angles in the figure above share a common vertex on a straight line. What is the value of b when a equals 42 ?

(A) 38 degrees
(B) 40 degrees
(C) 42 degrees
(D) 46 degrees

5. What is 85% of 50 ?

(A) 150.75
(B) 135
(C) 42.5
(D) 39

6. A set of three positive integers has a sum of 11 and a product of 36. If the smallest of the three numbers is 2, what is the largest?

(A) 2
(B) 4
(C) 6
(D) 9

7. What is two-thirds of one-half?

(A) $\dfrac{1}{3}$

(B) $\dfrac{7}{6}$

(C) $\dfrac{1}{2}$

(D) $\dfrac{2}{3}$

8. If the distance around an oval-shaped track is 400 meters, how many laps does a runner have to run to cover a distance of 4 kilometers?
(1 kilometer = 1,000 meters)

(A)   4
(B)   10
(C)   15
(D) 1,000

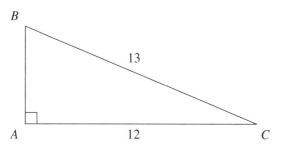

9. In triangle *ABC* shown above, the length of side *AB* is

(A) 5
(B) 7
(C) 11
(D) 14

10. If $f = 2$, and $f^j = 2f$, what is the value of j ?

(A) 0
(B) 1
(C) 2
(D) 3

11. If $\sqrt{a} + \sqrt{b} + \sqrt{c} = 15$, and $a = 36$ and $b = 25$, what is the value of c ?

(A) 4
(B) 16
(C) 49
(D) 81

12. There are x students is Mrs. Sproul's class, 4 fewer than twice as many as are in Mrs. Puccio's class. If there are y students in Mrs. Puccio's class, then what is the value of y in terms of x ?

(A) $\dfrac{x}{2} + 2$

(B) $2x + 4$

(C) $2x - 4$

(D) $\dfrac{x}{2} - 4$

Questions 13-14 refer to the following definition.

For all real numbers x,

$\#x = x^2$ if x is negative;
$\#x = 2x$ if x is positive.

13. $\#(-6) - \#(6) =$

(A) −24
(B) 16
(C) 24
(D) 30

14. What is the value of #[#x – #y] when x = 3 and y = –4 ?

    (A) –10
    (B)   12
    (C)   32
    (D) 100

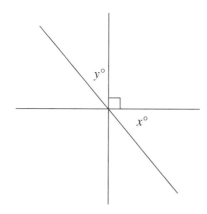

15. In the figure above, what is the value of x in terms of y ?

    (A) y
    (B) 90 – y
    (C) 90 + y
    (D) 180 – y

16. $\dfrac{4a^4b^6c^3}{2a^3b^5c^2}$ =

    (A) $\dfrac{2ac}{b}$

    (B) $\dfrac{ac}{b}$

    (C) $\dfrac{2b}{c}$

    (D) 2abc

17. In Mr. Johanessen's class, $\frac{1}{4}$ of the students failed the final exam. Of the remaining class, $\frac{1}{3}$ scored an A. What fraction of the whole class passed the test but scored below an A ?

(A) $\frac{5}{12}$

(B) $\frac{1}{4}$

(C) $\frac{7}{12}$

(D) $\frac{1}{2}$

18. When buying new clothes for school, Rena spends $20 more than Karen and $50 more than Lynn does. If Rena spends r dollars, then what is the cost of all three of their purchases in terms of r ?

(A) $r + 70$

(B) $\frac{r + 70}{3}$

(C) $3r - 70$

(D) $r + 210$

19. In a group of 100 children, there are 34 more girls than there are boys. How many boys are in the group?

(A) 33
(B) 37
(C) 67
(D) 68

20. If $6x - 7 = 17$, then $x + 6 =$

    (A) 6
    (B) 10
    (C) 14
    (D) 24

21. At Nicholas's Computer World, computers usually sold for $1,500 are now being sold for $1,200. What fraction of the original price is the new price?

    (A) $\dfrac{1}{10}$

    (B) $\dfrac{1}{5}$

    (C) $\dfrac{3}{4}$

    (D) $\dfrac{4}{5}$

22. If $\dfrac{3}{x} = \dfrac{y}{4}$, then

    (A) $xy = 12$

    (B) $3y = 4x$

    (C) $\dfrac{x}{y} = \dfrac{4}{3}$

    (D) $3x = 4y$

23. The ratio of boys to girls at Delaware Township School is 3 to 2. If there is a total of 600 students at the school, how many are girls?

    (A) 120
    (B) 240
    (C) 360
    (D) 400

24. 150% of 40 is

   (A) 30
   (B) 40
   (C) 50
   (D) 60

25. Jane studied for her math exam for 4 hours last night. If she studied $\frac{3}{4}$ as long for her English exam, how many hours did she study all together?

   (A) 3

   (B) $4\frac{3}{4}$

   (C) 6

   (D) 7

26. $\dfrac{0.966}{0.42} =$

   (A)   0.23
   (B)   2.3
   (C)   23
   (D)   230

27. Nicole was able to type 35 words per minute. If she increased her speed by 20%, her new typing speed would be

   (A) 38 words per minute
   (B) 42 words per minute
   (C) 55 words per minute
   (D) 70 words per minute

28. The first term in a series of numbers is 50. Each subsequent term is one-half the term before it if the term is even, or one-half rounded up to the next whole number if the term is odd. What is the third term in this sequence?

    (A) 13
    (B) 24
    (C) 30
    (D) 40

29. If the average of 7 and x is equal to the average of 5, 9, and x, what is the value of x ?

    (A) 2
    (B) 5
    (C) 7
    (D) 9

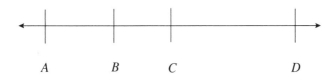

A   B   C   D

30. On the number line shown above, if segment BD has a length of 18, segment AB has a length of 5, and segment CD has a length of 12, then segment AC has a length of

    (A) 6
    (B) 11
    (C) 17
    (D) 23

31. The decimal representation of $2 + 40 + \dfrac{1}{100}$ is

    (A) 24.1
    (B) 24.01
    (C) 42.1
    (D) 42.01

32. What is the least possible integer divisible by 2, 3, 4, and 5 ?

(A) 30
(B) 40
(C) 60
(D) 90

33. If a car travels at x miles per hour, in terms of x and y, how long does it take it to travel y miles?

(A) $\dfrac{2x}{y}$

(B) xy

(C) $\dfrac{y}{x}$

(D) $\dfrac{x}{y}$

34. $\dfrac{4}{15} + \dfrac{3}{11} =$

(A) $\dfrac{12}{17}$

(B) $\dfrac{89}{165}$

(C) $\dfrac{44}{45}$

(D) $\dfrac{4}{55}$

35. James buys one halibut steak and two salmon steaks for $30.00. Dave buys two halibut steaks and four salmon steaks for $60.00. If halibut steaks cost x dollars each and salmon steaks cost y dollars each, what is the value of x ?

(A) $5.00
(B) $8.00
(C) $10.00
(D) It cannot be determined from the information given.

Question 36 refers to the following definition.

For all positive integer values of x,

$$(x) = \frac{1}{2}x \text{ if } x \text{ is even;}$$

$$(x) = 2x \text{ if } x \text{ is odd.}$$

36. $(1 + 5) =$

(A) 2
(B) 3
(C) 4
(D) 6

37. Which of the following equals $(4z + 1)$?

(A) $2z + \frac{1}{2}$

(B) $2z + 1$

(C) $4z + 2$

(D) $8z + 2$

38. There are eight buildings in Celeste's apartment complex. Each building is directly connected to each of the others with a tunnel. How many tunnels are there?

(A) 8
(B) 28
(C) 36
(D) 56

39. Zoo A has 3 monkeys. Zoo B has 8 monkeys. Zoo C has 16 monkeys. What is the average number of monkeys at the three zoos?

(A) 3
(B) 7
(C) 9
(D) 27

40. A steak costs $4 more than a hamburger, and a hamburger costs $4 more than a grilled cheese sandwich. If six grilled cheese sandwiches cost $2x$ dollars, how much will 4 steaks and 2 hamburgers cost?

(A) $2x + 40$
(B) $2x + 48$
(C) $6x + 34$
(D) $12x + 40$

41. If the base of an isosceles triangle is decreased by 40% and its height is increased by 10%, then what is the percent change in the area of the triangle?

(A) 17
(B) 30
(C) 34
(D) 40

42. $100xy$ is what percent of xy ?

(A)   10
(B)   100
(C)   1,000
(D) 10,000

43. If Matt's home is four miles from school and Laura's home is eight miles from school, then the distance from Matt's home to Laura's home is

(A) 4 miles
(B) 8 miles
(C) 12 miles
(D) It cannot be determined from the information given.

44. Two partners divide a profit of $2,000 so that the difference between the two amounts is half of their average. What is the ratio of the larger to the smaller amount?

(A) 6:1
(B) 5:3
(C) 4:1
(D) 2:1

45. What is the total value, in cents, of j coins worth 10 cents each and $j + 5$ coins worth 25 cents each?

(A) $35j + 125$
(B) $35j + 5$
(C) $10j + 130$
(D) $2j + 5$

Print your full name here

_____

ISEE

UPPER LEVEL

ESSAY TOPIC SHEET

Time - 30 minutes

Directions

You will have 30 minutes to plan and write an essay on the topic printed on the other side of this page. **Do not write on another topic. An essay on another topic is not acceptable.**

The essay is designed to give you an opportunity to show how well you can write. You should try to express your thoughts clearly. How well you write is much more important than how much you write, but you need to say enough for a reader to understand what you mean.

You will probably want to write more than a short paragraph. You should also be aware that a copy of your essay will be sent to each school that will be receiving your test results. You are to write only in the appropriate section of the answer sheet. Please write or print so that your writing may be read by someone who is not familiar with your handwriting.

You may make notes and plan your essay on the reverse side of the page. Allow enough time to copy the final form onto your answer sheet. You <u>must</u> copy the essay topic onto your lined answer sheet in the box provided.

Please remember to write only the final draft of the essay on the lined answer sheet and write it in blue or black pen. Again, you may use cursive writing or you may print.

REMINDER: Please write this essay question on the first few lines of your answer sheet.

Do you think the driving age should be raised to 21? Support your position with specific examples from personal experience, the experience of others, current events, history, or literature.

Notes

STUDENT NAME _____ ID NUMBER _____ GRADE APPLYING FOR _____

Please use a ballpoint pen to write the final draft of your composition on this sheet.

You must write your essay topic in this space.

Answer Key to ISEE Practice Tests

ISEE UL VERBAL 1

1. C
2. A
3. A
4. D
5. C
6. C
7. B
8. D
9. C
10. A
11. C
12. B
13. B
14. C
15. B
16. A
17. A
18. D
19. D
20. D
21. B
22. B
23. D
24. A
25. D
26. C
27. B
28. A
29. C
30. B
31. C
32. B
33. B
34. B
35. A
36. C
37. B
38. B
39. D
40. A

ISEE UL MATH 2

1. C
2. C
3. D
4. D
5. B
6. D
7. A
8. C
9. B
10. D
11. C
12. D
13. A
14. B
15. A
16. A
17. D
18. B
19. D
20. C
21. C
22. A
23. A
24. D
25. A
26. D
27. A
28. C
29. C
30. B
31. B
32. A
33. D
34. C
35. C

ISEE UL READING 3

1. C		21. C	
2. D		22. B	
3. B		23. C	
4. D		24. B	
5. C		25. C	
6. A		26. C	
7. D		27. C	
8. A		28. A	
9. B		29. D	
10. C		30. C	
11. A		31. B	
12. D		32. A	
13. B		33. C	
14. A		34. D	
15. D		35. A	
16. A		36. B	
17. B		37. D	
18. A		38. C	
19. C		39. B	
20. C		40. D	

ISEE UL MATH 4

1. A
2. D
3. C
4. D
5. C
6. C
7. A
8. B
9. A
10. C
11. B
12. A
13. C
14. D
15. B
16. D
17. D
18. C
19. A
20. B
21. D
22. A
23. B
24. D
25. D
26. B
27. B
28. A
29. C
30. B
31. D
32. C
33. C
34. B
35. D
36. B
37. D
38. B
39. C
40. A
41. C
42. D
43. D
44. B
45. A

Practice Test

Be sure each mark *completely* fills the answer space.

SECTION 1

1 Ⓐ Ⓑ Ⓒ Ⓓ	9 Ⓐ Ⓑ Ⓒ Ⓓ	17 Ⓐ Ⓑ Ⓒ Ⓓ	25 Ⓐ Ⓑ Ⓒ Ⓓ	33 Ⓐ Ⓑ Ⓒ Ⓓ
2 Ⓐ Ⓑ Ⓒ Ⓓ	10 Ⓐ Ⓑ Ⓒ Ⓓ	18 Ⓐ Ⓑ Ⓒ Ⓓ	26 Ⓐ Ⓑ Ⓒ Ⓓ	34 Ⓐ Ⓑ Ⓒ Ⓓ
3 Ⓐ Ⓑ Ⓒ Ⓓ	11 Ⓐ Ⓑ Ⓒ Ⓓ	19 Ⓐ Ⓑ Ⓒ Ⓓ	27 Ⓐ Ⓑ Ⓒ Ⓓ	35 Ⓐ Ⓑ Ⓒ Ⓓ
4 Ⓐ Ⓑ Ⓒ Ⓓ	12 Ⓐ Ⓑ Ⓒ Ⓓ	20 Ⓐ Ⓑ Ⓒ Ⓓ	28 Ⓐ Ⓑ Ⓒ Ⓓ	36 Ⓐ Ⓑ Ⓒ Ⓓ
5 Ⓐ Ⓑ Ⓒ Ⓓ	13 Ⓐ Ⓑ Ⓒ Ⓓ	21 Ⓐ Ⓑ Ⓒ Ⓓ	29 Ⓐ Ⓑ Ⓒ Ⓓ	37 Ⓐ Ⓑ Ⓒ Ⓓ
6 Ⓐ Ⓑ Ⓒ Ⓓ	14 Ⓐ Ⓑ Ⓒ Ⓓ	22 Ⓐ Ⓑ Ⓒ Ⓓ	30 Ⓐ Ⓑ Ⓒ Ⓓ	38 Ⓐ Ⓑ Ⓒ Ⓓ
7 Ⓐ Ⓑ Ⓒ Ⓓ	15 Ⓐ Ⓑ Ⓒ Ⓓ	23 Ⓐ Ⓑ Ⓒ Ⓓ	31 Ⓐ Ⓑ Ⓒ Ⓓ	39 Ⓐ Ⓑ Ⓒ Ⓓ
8 Ⓐ Ⓑ Ⓒ Ⓓ	16 Ⓐ Ⓑ Ⓒ Ⓓ	24 Ⓐ Ⓑ Ⓒ Ⓓ	32 Ⓐ Ⓑ Ⓒ Ⓓ	40 Ⓐ Ⓑ Ⓒ Ⓓ

SECTION 2

1 Ⓐ Ⓑ Ⓒ Ⓓ	9 Ⓐ Ⓑ Ⓒ Ⓓ	17 Ⓐ Ⓑ Ⓒ Ⓓ	25 Ⓐ Ⓑ Ⓒ Ⓓ	33 Ⓐ Ⓑ Ⓒ Ⓓ
2 Ⓐ Ⓑ Ⓒ Ⓓ	10 Ⓐ Ⓑ Ⓒ Ⓓ	18 Ⓐ Ⓑ Ⓒ Ⓓ	26 Ⓐ Ⓑ Ⓒ Ⓓ	34 Ⓐ Ⓑ Ⓒ Ⓓ
3 Ⓐ Ⓑ Ⓒ Ⓓ	11 Ⓐ Ⓑ Ⓒ Ⓓ	19 Ⓐ Ⓑ Ⓒ Ⓓ	27 Ⓐ Ⓑ Ⓒ Ⓓ	35 Ⓐ Ⓑ Ⓒ Ⓓ
4 Ⓐ Ⓑ Ⓒ Ⓓ	12 Ⓐ Ⓑ Ⓒ Ⓓ	20 Ⓐ Ⓑ Ⓒ Ⓓ	28 Ⓐ Ⓑ Ⓒ Ⓓ	
5 Ⓐ Ⓑ Ⓒ Ⓓ	13 Ⓐ Ⓑ Ⓒ Ⓓ	21 Ⓐ Ⓑ Ⓒ Ⓓ	29 Ⓐ Ⓑ Ⓒ Ⓓ	
6 Ⓐ Ⓑ Ⓒ Ⓓ	14 Ⓐ Ⓑ Ⓒ Ⓓ	22 Ⓐ Ⓑ Ⓒ Ⓓ	30 Ⓐ Ⓑ Ⓒ Ⓓ	
7 Ⓐ Ⓑ Ⓒ Ⓓ	15 Ⓐ Ⓑ Ⓒ Ⓓ	23 Ⓐ Ⓑ Ⓒ Ⓓ	31 Ⓐ Ⓑ Ⓒ Ⓓ	
8 Ⓐ Ⓑ Ⓒ Ⓓ	16 Ⓐ Ⓑ Ⓒ Ⓓ	24 Ⓐ Ⓑ Ⓒ Ⓓ	32 Ⓐ Ⓑ Ⓒ Ⓓ	

SECTION 3

1 Ⓐ Ⓑ Ⓒ Ⓓ	9 Ⓐ Ⓑ Ⓒ Ⓓ	17 Ⓐ Ⓑ Ⓒ Ⓓ	25 Ⓐ Ⓑ Ⓒ Ⓓ	33 Ⓐ Ⓑ Ⓒ Ⓓ
2 Ⓐ Ⓑ Ⓒ Ⓓ	10 Ⓐ Ⓑ Ⓒ Ⓓ	18 Ⓐ Ⓑ Ⓒ Ⓓ	26 Ⓐ Ⓑ Ⓒ Ⓓ	34 Ⓐ Ⓑ Ⓒ Ⓓ
3 Ⓐ Ⓑ Ⓒ Ⓓ	11 Ⓐ Ⓑ Ⓒ Ⓓ	19 Ⓐ Ⓑ Ⓒ Ⓓ	27 Ⓐ Ⓑ Ⓒ Ⓓ	35 Ⓐ Ⓑ Ⓒ Ⓓ
4 Ⓐ Ⓑ Ⓒ Ⓓ	12 Ⓐ Ⓑ Ⓒ Ⓓ	20 Ⓐ Ⓑ Ⓒ Ⓓ	28 Ⓐ Ⓑ Ⓒ Ⓓ	36 Ⓐ Ⓑ Ⓒ Ⓓ
5 Ⓐ Ⓑ Ⓒ Ⓓ	13 Ⓐ Ⓑ Ⓒ Ⓓ	21 Ⓐ Ⓑ Ⓒ Ⓓ	29 Ⓐ Ⓑ Ⓒ Ⓓ	37 Ⓐ Ⓑ Ⓒ Ⓓ
6 Ⓐ Ⓑ Ⓒ Ⓓ	14 Ⓐ Ⓑ Ⓒ Ⓓ	22 Ⓐ Ⓑ Ⓒ Ⓓ	30 Ⓐ Ⓑ Ⓒ Ⓓ	38 Ⓐ Ⓑ Ⓒ Ⓓ
7 Ⓐ Ⓑ Ⓒ Ⓓ	15 Ⓐ Ⓑ Ⓒ Ⓓ	23 Ⓐ Ⓑ Ⓒ Ⓓ	31 Ⓐ Ⓑ Ⓒ Ⓓ	39 Ⓐ Ⓑ Ⓒ Ⓓ
8 Ⓐ Ⓑ Ⓒ Ⓓ	16 Ⓐ Ⓑ Ⓒ Ⓓ	24 Ⓐ Ⓑ Ⓒ Ⓓ	32 Ⓐ Ⓑ Ⓒ Ⓓ	40 Ⓐ Ⓑ Ⓒ Ⓓ

SECTION 4

1 Ⓐ Ⓑ Ⓒ Ⓓ	11 Ⓐ Ⓑ Ⓒ Ⓓ	21 Ⓐ Ⓑ Ⓒ Ⓓ	31 Ⓐ Ⓑ Ⓒ Ⓓ	41 Ⓐ Ⓑ Ⓒ Ⓓ
2 Ⓐ Ⓑ Ⓒ Ⓓ	12 Ⓐ Ⓑ Ⓒ Ⓓ	22 Ⓐ Ⓑ Ⓒ Ⓓ	32 Ⓐ Ⓑ Ⓒ Ⓓ	42 Ⓐ Ⓑ Ⓒ Ⓓ
3 Ⓐ Ⓑ Ⓒ Ⓓ	13 Ⓐ Ⓑ Ⓒ Ⓓ	23 Ⓐ Ⓑ Ⓒ Ⓓ	33 Ⓐ Ⓑ Ⓒ Ⓓ	43 Ⓐ Ⓑ Ⓒ Ⓓ
4 Ⓐ Ⓑ Ⓒ Ⓓ	14 Ⓐ Ⓑ Ⓒ Ⓓ	24 Ⓐ Ⓑ Ⓒ Ⓓ	34 Ⓐ Ⓑ Ⓒ Ⓓ	44 Ⓐ Ⓑ Ⓒ Ⓓ
5 Ⓐ Ⓑ Ⓒ Ⓓ	15 Ⓐ Ⓑ Ⓒ Ⓓ	25 Ⓐ Ⓑ Ⓒ Ⓓ	35 Ⓐ Ⓑ Ⓒ Ⓓ	45 Ⓐ Ⓑ Ⓒ Ⓓ
6 Ⓐ Ⓑ Ⓒ Ⓓ	16 Ⓐ Ⓑ Ⓒ Ⓓ	26 Ⓐ Ⓑ Ⓒ Ⓓ	36 Ⓐ Ⓑ Ⓒ Ⓓ	
7 Ⓐ Ⓑ Ⓒ Ⓓ	17 Ⓐ Ⓑ Ⓒ Ⓓ	27 Ⓐ Ⓑ Ⓒ Ⓓ	37 Ⓐ Ⓑ Ⓒ Ⓓ	
8 Ⓐ Ⓑ Ⓒ Ⓓ	18 Ⓐ Ⓑ Ⓒ Ⓓ	28 Ⓐ Ⓑ Ⓒ Ⓓ	38 Ⓐ Ⓑ Ⓒ Ⓓ	
9 Ⓐ Ⓑ Ⓒ Ⓓ	19 Ⓐ Ⓑ Ⓒ Ⓓ	29 Ⓐ Ⓑ Ⓒ Ⓓ	39 Ⓐ Ⓑ Ⓒ Ⓓ	
10 Ⓐ Ⓑ Ⓒ Ⓓ	20 Ⓐ Ⓑ Ⓒ Ⓓ	30 Ⓐ Ⓑ Ⓒ Ⓓ	40 Ⓐ Ⓑ Ⓒ Ⓓ	

PART VIII—INDEX

Now's the time to consider the next step to higher education.

INDEPENDENT 529 PLAN RESOURCES GUIDE.

The importance of preparing for college now.

You want the best education for your child. Choosing the best high school in New York is a great first step. But there's more. Once you decide on high school, it's time to start thinking about a private college education.

This decision can be more challenging. With the rising cost of tuition, private colleges can be expensive. In fact, The College Board estimates that tuition costs have increased an average of 6% per year. So, families are increasingly concerned with the challenge of paying for tuition. And that's why planning for your child's college education may be one of the most significant financial decisions you ever make.

Tomorrow's tuition at *less* than today's price.

Fortunately, there is help with Independent 529 Plan...an innovative way to pay for private college tuition. Independent 529 Plan is the only private college-sponsored, national, prepaid 529 plan. It gives you an opportunity to save more for your child's private college education by allowing you to lock in tuition costs at *less* than today's price.[1]

Here's an example of how it works:
Let's suppose the college your child will eventually attend has a current tuition of $25,000 per year. If you prepay $25,000 today to cover one year of tuition, that amount will cover one year of tuition seven years from now — even though the projected cost at that time is $37,590 (assuming a 6% annual tuition rate increase). By prepaying, you could save $14,287, and that savings is federal tax-free.

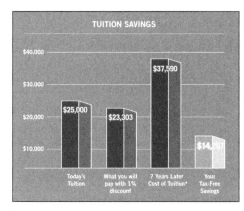

* This hypothetical illustration is based on an assumed annual 6% tuition inflation rate which may be more or less than actual tuition inflation. Minimum tuition discount rate is 0.5% less than current tuition.

Tuition inflation rates based on published studies by The College Board.

Independent 529 Plan is flexible...

Enroll and contribute at any time — You can buy the full cost of several years at once or start small by automatically contributing as little as $25 a month as long as a minimum of $500 is accumulated within two years.

Roll over funds from other 529 Plans[2] — You have the option to transfer funds from a 529 college savings plan to an Independent 529 Plan account for the same beneficiary once within a 12-month period without incurring federal income tax.

High contribution limits — Overall contribution limits cover the tuition and fees for five years at the most expensive college or university in the plan.

No eligibility requirements or income limits — There are no special eligibility requirements and no income limits for participation. If you are an adult U.S. resident who wants to help fund a private college education for children, grandchildren or anyone else, you are eligible.

National in scope — Many of the nation's top private colleges and universities already participate, with more joining all the time. Families that purchase tuition certificates today will be able to use them at any college that joins later. If a school should ever withdraw from the plan, that school would continue to honor all certificates purchased during and prior to the time of its participation.

Options for your purchase[2] — If your child decides not to go to a member college, you have options, including transfer and refund provisions.

Change the beneficiary at any time — You have the option to change the beneficiary to another "member of the family" within the federal 529 rules — even yourself!

Independent 529 Plan offers real value...

Get the most out of your purchase — By prepaying tuition now, you're buying tuition at today's rates and avoiding years of likely inflation. Plus, because each member college offers a special "tuition discount," you're actually buying future tuition at *less* than today's price.

Freedom from federal income taxes[3] — Although the value of your prepaid tuition will increase when tuition prices rise, it grows free from federal income tax.

Valuable estate and gift tax benefits[2] — Independent 529 Plan offers you significant estate and gift tax benefits that can reduce the taxable value of your estate.

- Contributions reduce the taxable value of your estate
- Contributions qualify for annual tax exclusions for each beneficiary
- Contributions qualify for annual gift tax exclusions for each beneficiary, if you are married
- Contributions in excess of the annual gift tax exclusion can be prorated over 5 years and treated as a gift in each of those years

To see how much you could save in tax exclusions with your contributions, please visit www.i529.org/princetonreview.

> A plan that's simple, provides peace of mind — and gives buyers equal access to federal student aid. What's not to like?
>
> Jane Bryant Quinn
> *Newsweek*, August 14, 2006

No program fees — With no start-up or maintenance fees of any kind, you can feel good about knowing 100% of your contributions will go towards tuition!

Alabama
Birmingham-Southern College
Faulkner University
Samford University
University of Mobile

Arkansas
Hendrix College
Lyon College

California
California Lutheran University
Chapman University
Claremont McKenna College
Harvey Mudd College
Mills College
Mount St. Mary's College
Occidental College
Pepperdine University
Pitzer College
Point Loma Nazarene University
Pomona College
Saint Mary's College of California
Stanford University
University of LaVerne
University of Redlands
University of San Diego
University of the Pacific
Westmont College
Whittier College

Colorado
Colorado College
Regis University

Connecticut
Fairfield University
Wesleyan University

District of Columbia
American University
Catholic University of America
George Washington University

Florida
Ave Maria University
Jacksonville University
Rollins College
Saint Leo University
University of Miami

Georgia
Agnes Scott College
Berry College
Clark Atlanta University
Emory University
LaGrange College
Mercer University
Oglethorpe University
Spelman College
Wesleyan College

Hawaii
Chaminade University of Honolulu

Idaho
Albertson College of Idaho
Northwest Nazarene University

Illinois
Augustana College
Bradley University
Elmhurst College
Illinois Institute of Technology
Illinois Wesleyan University
Knox College
Lake Forest College
Monmouth College
North Central College
Olivet Nazarene University
University of Chicago

Indiana
Butler University
DePauw University
Earlham College
Franklin College
Rose-Hulman Institute of Technology
Saint Mary's College
University of Evansville
University of Notre Dame
Valparaiso University
Wabash College

Iowa
Buena Vista University
Central College
Clarke College
Dordt College
Graceland University
Grinnell College
Loras College
Luther College
Northwestern College
Simpson College
Waldorf College
Wartburg College

Kentucky
Centre College
Transylvania University

Louisiana
Centenary College of Louisiana
Dillard University
Tulane University

Maryland
College of Notre Dame of Maryland
Goucher College
Johns Hopkins University
Loyola College in Maryland
McDaniel College
Mount Saint Mary's College

Massachusetts
Amherst College
Berklee College of Music
Boston University
Clark University
Gordon College
Hampshire College
MIT
Mount Holyoke College
Smith College
Springfield College
Wellesley College
Wheaton College

Michigan
Albion College
Hope College
Kalamazoo College

Minnesota
Carleton College
Gustavus Adolphus College
Hamline University
Macalester College
St. Olaf College

Missouri
Culver-Stockton College
Drury University
Hannibal-LaGrange College
Maryville University of Saint Louis
Rockhurst University
Saint Louis University
Stephens College
Washington University in St. Louis
Webster University
Westminster College

Nebraska
Creighton University
Doane College

New Hampshire
Franklin Pierce College

New Jersey
Centenary College
Drew University
Princeton University
Rider University
Stevens Institute of Technology

New Mexico
College of Santa Fe

New York
Bard College
Canisius College

Daemen College
Elmira College
Hartwick College
Hobart & William Smith Colleges
Ithaca College
Marist College
Medaille College
Nazareth College
Niagara University
Pace University
Rensselaer Polytechnic Institute
Roberts Wesleyan College
Rochester Institute of Technology
Skidmore College
Syracuse University
University of Rochester
Vassar College
Wells College

North Carolina
Catawba College
Greensboro College
Guilford College
Lenoir Rhyne College
Methodist College
Salem College
Wake Forest University

Ohio
Ashland University
Baldwin-Wallace College
Capital University
Case Western Reserve University
College of Wooster
Denison University
Hiram College
John Carroll University
Kenyon College
Mount Vernon Nazarene University
Muskingum College
Oberlin College
Ohio Wesleyan University
Tiffin University
University of Dayton
Wittenberg University

Oklahoma
Oklahoma Christian University
Southern Nazarene University
University of Tulsa

Oregon
George Fox University
Lewis & Clark College
Linfield College
Pacific University
Reed College
Willamette University

Pennsylvania
Allegheny College
Alvernia College
Arcadia University
Carnegie Mellon University
Chatham College
Dickinson College
Drexel University
Franklin & Marshall College
Gettysburg College
Grove City College
Immaculata University
Juniata College
Keystone College
La Salle University
Marywood University
Moravian College
Muhlenberg College
Saint Francis University
Susquehanna University
Thiel College
Ursinus College
Washington & Jefferson College
Waynesburg College
Westminster College
York College of Pennsylvania

South Carolina
Charleston Southern University
Claflin University
Columbia College
Converse College
Furman University
Presbyterian College
Wofford College

South Dakota
Augustana College

Tennessee
Belmont University
Carson-Newman College
Lambuth University
Rhodes College
Trevecca Nazarene University

University of the South
Vanderbilt University

Texas
Abilene Christian University
Austin College
Baylor University
Dallas Baptist University
Hardin-Simmons University
Lubbock Christian University
Rice University
St. Edward's University
St. Mary's University
Southern Methodist University
Southwestern University
Texas Christian University
Trinity University
University of Dallas
University of Mary Hardin-Baylor

Vermont
Middlebury College
Saint Michael's College

Virginia
Bridgewater College
Eastern Mennonite University
Hampden-Sydney College
Hollins University
Mary Baldwin College
Randolph-Macon Woman's College
Shenandoah University
Sweet Briar College
University of Richmond
Virginia Wesleyan College

Washington
Pacific Lutheran University
Seattle Pacific University
Whitworth College

West Virginia
West Virginia Wesleyan College
Wheeling Jesuit University

Wisconsin
Lakeland College
Lawrence University
Ripon College

Families that purchase tuition certificates today will be able to use their certificates at any college that joins later. If a college should ever withdraw from Independent 529 Plan, it would still be obligated to honor all certificates that were purchased prior to its withdrawal.

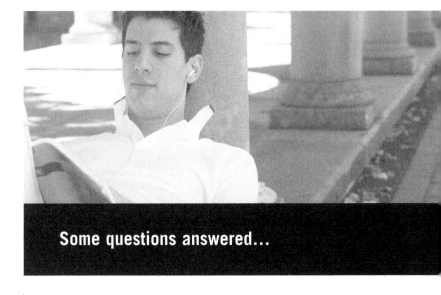

Some questions answered...

Q: Am I really buying future tuition?

A: Yes. You prepay tuition now to avoid years of likely tuition inflation when you redeem it later.

Q: How many colleges participate?

A: Currently there are over 250[1] member colleges, with more joining all the time.

Q: Are there any fees?

A: There are no start-up fees or maintenance fees, so 100% of your contributions go toward tuition.

Q: What if my child doesn't go to college or doesn't go to a member school?

A: You have options, including transfer and refund provisions.[2]

**FINANCIAL SERVICES
FOR THE GREATER GOOD™**

C38172

More expert advice from
The Princeton Review

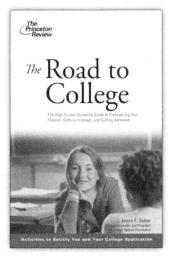

Cracking the SSAT/ISEE, 2008 Edition
978-0-375-76618-3
$19.00/$25.00 Can.

Thoroughly updated for 2008, *Cracking the SSAT and ISEE* provides the most comprehensive preparation possible, including 5 practice tests.

The Road to College
978-0-375-76617-6
$13.95/$17.95 Can.

How can a high school student build a resume that will get the attention of admissions committees and still enjoy his or her high school experience? *The Road to College* outlines a wide range of fun and meaningful activities that can positively impact a high school student's life, as well as his or her college applications.

For the next steps in your academic career, The Princeton Review also has a full range of test preparation books for high school AP and PSAT exams — find out more at PrincetonReview.com

Available everywhere books are sold or at PrincetonReview.com